Urbanism

The Academy of Urbanism was founded in 2006 with a mission to recognise, encourage and celebrate great places across the UK, Europe and beyond, and the people and organisations that create and sustain them. As part of this, the Academy runs an annual awards scheme. Each year the Academy gathers and shortlists nominations for the categories of Great Place, Street, Neighbourhood, Town and European City of the Year. An initial longlist of ten places is voted on by the 550 or so Academicians to create a shortlist of three. The shortlisted places are visited and written up by the Academy and the winner is chosen after a second vote.

The shortlisted places in the first two years of the awards, 2007 and 2008, were written up in the Academy's first two books: *Learning from Place* and *Urban Identity*. This book covers the 75 places shortlisted in the next five years up to and including the 2013 awards. Each of these places has been visited by a team of Academicians. They have spent time in the place, talked to politicians, officials and local people and sought to understand what it is that makes them special and how they have achieved what they have achieved. The assessment team produces a report and the Academy also commissions a poem, a drawing and a figure ground plan. Hundreds of people have been involved in this process, including many of the leading urbanists, planners and architects in the UK and Ireland. David Rudlin, Rob Thompson and Sarah Jarvis have drawn on this treasure trove of material to tell the story of these 75 places. In doing so, they have created the most comprehensive compendium of great urban places to have been published for many years.

urbanism

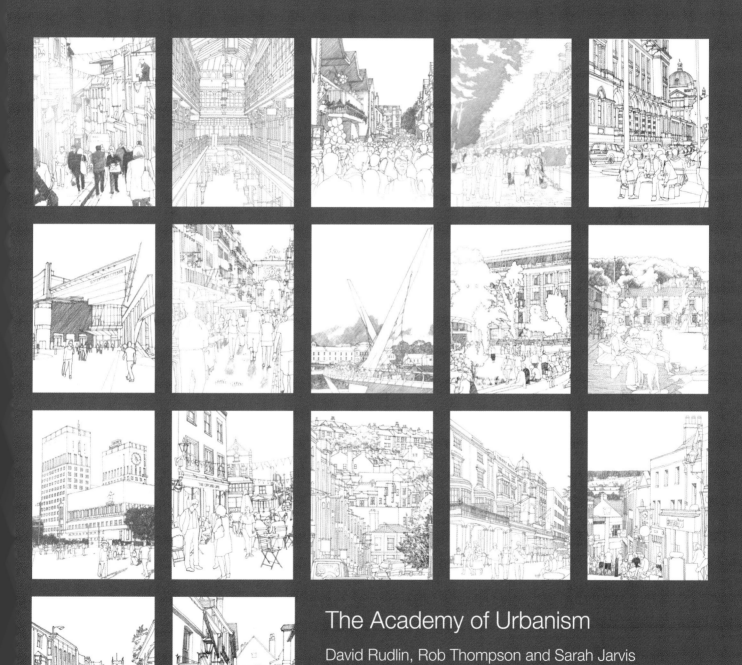

The Academy of Urbanism

David Rudlin, Rob Thompson and Sarah Jarvis

THE ACADEMY OF URBANISM

R Routledge
Taylor & Francis Group

First published 2016
by Routledge
2 Park Square, Milton Park, Abingdon, Oxon OX14 4RN

and by Routledge
711 Third Avenue, New York, NY 10017

Routledge is an imprint of the Taylor & Francis Group, an informa business

British Library Cataloguing-in-Publication Data
A catalogue record for this book is available from the British Library

Library of Congress Cataloging-in-Publication Data
Names: Academy of Urbanism (Organization)
Title: Urbanism / Academy of Urbanism.
Description: Abingdon, Oxon ; New York, NY : Routledge, 2016. | Includes index.
Identifiers: LCCN 2015046225| ISBN 9781138015623 (pbk.) | ISBN 9781315619422
(ebook)
Subjects: LCSH: City planning. | Cities and towns. | Urbanization. | Community development, Urban.
Classification: LCC HT166 .U7467 2016 | DDC 307.76--dc23
LC record available at http://lccn.loc.gov/2015046225

ISBN: 978-1-138-01562-3 (pbk)
ISBN: 978-1-315-61942-2 (ebk)

Typeset in Helvetica Neue LT Std by URBED

Printed in Great Britain by Bell and Bain Ltd, Glasgow

Publisher's Note
This book has been prepared from camera-ready copy provided by the authors.

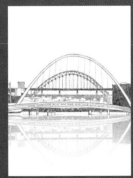

Contents

Clifton in Bristol was a runner-up
in the first year of the awards. This
book includes Bristol in the Cities
section as well as the St Pauls/
Montpelier neighbourhood.

Foreword

The Academy of Urbanism has been celebrating great places through our annual Urbanism Awards for ten years. Our archive of knowledge, ideas and opportunities for learning about urbanism, gleaned from our assessment visits, becomes more valuable with each year.

The best way of experiencing the qualities of urban places is to spend time there – enjoying their spaces, their activities and their people. Our assessors experience these qualities first-hand and transmit their impressions to the rest of the Academy in carefully and consistently prepared reports that allow and encourage fair comparison.

The Urbanism Awards are also an opportunity for places to re-evaluate their own perceptions, to see their attributes through the eyes of the independent assessors, and to celebrate the wider recognition that the Awards provides.

This, our third volume drawing on the evidence we have gathered, presents more of what we have learned more from places we have visited. In some cases, the lessons are in how to make the most of a place's distinctive physical character or the distinctive activities or attitudes of its citizens. In others, they are in the characteristics that great places tend to hold in common, such as leadership, stewardship and diversity.

As the Academy enters its second decade, we are extending the range of activities through which we learn from places, and establishing additional categories of membership. Our aim is to share our learning with everyone interested in how great places are created and sustained.

Our greater understanding of how communities can live together in diverse circumstances while sharing common civic values will help us to promote and sustain civilised and tolerant social attitudes. It should also reinvigorate our commitment to exposing and addressing the inequalities and unfairness that still pervade urban communities.

Urbanism provides 75 examples of great places – places from which we can learn new ways, or rediscover old ways, of living and working. The places we have visited are represented here in text, in the drawings of David Harrison and in the poetry of our poet in residence Ian McMillan, to capture and convey the essence of their character and success. There is no substitute, however, for first-hand experience. I hope that this book stimulates your determination to visit, or revisit, the places we have selected and experience for yourself the qualities of 'Space, Place, Life' we have recorded.

Steven Bee
Chairman The Academy of Urbanism 2016

Contributors and Acknowledgements

1. David Rudlin is a director of URBED, Honorary Professor at Manchester University and winner of the 2014 Wolfson Economics Prize. He started his career working on the redevelopment of Hulme in Manchester and has been at URBED since 1990. He is the author of the book *Sustainable Urban Neighbourhood* published by Routledge in 2009 which was described by Richard Rogers as 'the best analysis I have read of the crisis facing the contemporary city'. He is also joint chair of the Sheffield Design Panel, chair of BEAM in Wakefield and a in 2017 will become chair of the Academy of Urbanism.

2. Rob Thompson is an urbanist and planner with close to 25 years experience working on a range of urban design and masterplanning projects in local government and the private sector. Rob spent eleven years at Sheffield City Council, providing design guidance on major development and coordinated the city's Design Panel. He is interested in how emotional experience can influence and dictate the success of a place. He has a long-standing relationship with Sheffield School of Architecture where he has run a studio, sits on the Yorkshire and Humber Design Panel, and is an Academician of the Academy of Urbanism.

3. Sarah Jarvis is a writer about cities who has tried out several for size, living in Paris, New York and Dublin before settling in London. Since studying Geography at Cambridge University, Sarah has been exploring different ways to understand, communicate and actively influence how places work – from journalism and travel writing to academic research and consultancy. Sarah has an MPhil in Urban Planning from the Bartlett School UCL, and has worked on projects that range in scale from assessing urban renaissance across England to neighbourhood planning in Bankside. She also explores places visually – taking on commissions as an artist to examine the processes of change up close.

4. Ian McMillan has been the Academy of Urbanism's poet in residence since it started and has to date written 150 poems that are uncanny in their ability to capture the spirit of each place. He was born in 1956 in the village near Barnsley where he still lives. He is a solo performer and writer and in addition to the Academy has been poet in residence at Barnsley Football Club, Northern Spirit Trains and Humberside Police. He has written widely for the stage as well as BBC Radio, Yorkshire Television and BBC2's *Newsnight Review.* He also has weekly columns in the *Yorkshire Post* and the *Barnsley Chronicle*.

5. David Harrison or 'Harry the Pencil' as he is known, is a partner at John Thompson & Partners and an architect with wide experience of urban design and community planning. His projects include a number of significant mixed-use, waterside developments including the award-winning Charter Quay scheme at Kingston-upon-Thames and Putney Wharf, a high-density, mixed-use development that has brought a new vitality to a previously neglected waterfront area by the River Thames. Harry's paintings and drawings have regularly been displayed at the Royal Academy Summer Exhibition.

The Academy of Urbanism gathered for its Congress in Birmingham in 2015

In a very real sense, this book is the result of the work of many hundreds of people. The 550 or so members of the Academy along with the 180 Young Urbanists have all played a part by nominating places, shortlisting, attending the assessment visits, voting or just cheering in a partisan fashion at the annual awards dinner. Then there are the people in each of the 75 places that we describe who hosted visits, prepared presentations and background material and completed the Academy's self assessment reports – far too many of them to list here.

However, special mention goes to the Academicians who have taken on the role of lead assessor for the awards. This onerous but enjoyable task involves organising and leading the assessment visits and preparing the Academy's reports on each of the places which provided the starting point for this book. They include:

Chris Balch, Tim Challans, Nick Childs, Prof. Brian Evans, Dr Nicholas Falk, Kerri Farnsworth, Michele Grant, Richard Guise, Geoff Haslam, Philip Jackson, John Lord, David Lumb, Frank McDonald, Willie Miller, David Prichard, David Rudlin, David Taylor, Peter Studdert, Paul Warner, Lindsey Whitelaw, Nick Wright and Bob Young.

In addition to this we must acknowledge the role of the Academy's staff including Linda Gledstone, Stephen Gallagher, Jas Atwal, Bright Pryde-Saha, Zarreen Hadadi, Delano Bart-Stewart and Katy Hawkins. Stephen in particular has co-ordinated the work on the book, including proofreading. An important role has also been played by the Academy's board of directors including Andrew Burrell, Prof. Kevin Murray, Henk Bouwman, Janet Sutherland, John Thompson (Honorary President), David Rudlin, Steven Bee (Chairman), Pam Alexander OBE, Tony Reddy, Biljana Savic, Tim Stonor and Bob Young.

All of the drawings in this book are by David
Harrison, the Academy of Urbanism's artist in
residence for its first seven years. This drawing
is of Lincoln, which was shortlisted in the Town
category in the first year of the awards.

Introduction
Urbanism: The ingredient of great places

I n 1969 Desmond Morris wrote a book called *The Human Zoo* as a follow-up to his best-seller *The Naked Ape.* Those of us of a certain age will remember his television series showing that human behaviour is closely related to that of other primates. *The Human Zoo* widened his theories to look at how humans live together in cities. His central premise was that the human animal evolved to live in hunter-gatherer groups of around 60 people. This extended family group would need around 20 square miles to support its needs. Today the same area could accommodate a city of six million people. This, he argues, is not natural and it is hardly surprising that some people in cities act a little strangely. Indeed, Morris equates this strange behaviour to the compulsive traits exhibited by many animals when they are confined in zoos: mental health disorders, sexual perversion, violence etc. Hence in Morris' eyes the modern city is the human zoo.

However his conclusion is not entirely negative. Morris suggests that the remarkable aspect of city living is that most of us don't exhibit this compulsive behaviour. We have moved from living with 59 neighbours to 5,999,999 in the blink of an evolutionary eye and have coped extremely well. As he says: 'The least experienced zoo director would never contemplate cramming and cramping a group of animals to the extent that man has crammed and cramped himself into his modern cities and towns. By all the rules the human zoo should be a screaming madhouse… cynics may argue that this is indeed the case, but plainly it is not... aberrant behaviour is startling, not for its existence but for its rarity'. Indeed he goes on to argue that the secret to human success as a species is that we actually thrive in these conditions: 'Just as colonies of nesting seabirds are reproductively aroused by massing in dense breeding communities, so the human animal is intellectually aroused by massing in dense urban communities. They are breeding colonies of human ideas.'

The process by which this happens is called urbanism. Urbanism is the study of how humans live together and interact in cities, or indeed any form of human settlement. These human interactions happen in many and varied ways – from the interchange of ideas and knowledge, the flow of commerce and trade, the interactions of community and civil society, the problems of crime and disorder, the movement of goods and traffic, the provision of shelter and accommodation, and the workings of religion and creativity to the less tangible feelings of pride and belonging or anomie and loneliness. Urbanism is not just about urban design, architecture and planning, although it is relevant to all of these professions. Urbanism is the 'science' that underlies these professions, just as the science of horticulture underlies the professions of landscape architecture or gardening. A gardener without a clear understanding of horticulture would be a very poor gardener – so what of the urban design, architecture and planning professional who don't have a clear understanding of urbanism?

This was the impetus behind the formation of the Academy of Urbanism, whose tenth anniversary coincides with this book's publication. During George Ferguson's year as President of the Royal

Institute of British Architects (RIBA), he started a discussion about how the architecture profession needed to widen its concerns to better understand its impact on cities. George was later elected as mayor of Bristol and we will return to his very practical attempts to put these ideas into practice on page 16. Back in 2005 a working group was set up within the RIBA, chaired by John Thompson, but it soon became clear that the issues went much wider than the architecture profession. The working group therefore detached itself from the institute and became the Academy of Urbanism in 2006. Its aims were to celebrate and understand good urban places, which it encapsulated in the rallying cry 'Space, Place, Life'. Initially the Academy was to have 100 Academicians, elected by their peers as leaders in their profession. This erudite group would meet and debate urbanism, recognise good places through an awards scheme, publish books (such as this one), run an annual congress etc. However, it soon became clear that membership could not be confined to 100 and today there are around 550 Academicians plus over 180 Young Urbanists. The methodology of the Academy, however, remains the same: to explore the process of urbanism and place-making by learning from real places.

Urbanisn is at once very simple and fiendishly complicated. Most people can recognise good urbanism when they see it: whether walking down Las Ramblas on holiday in Barcelona; shopping on Regent Street in London or for that matter meandering through the arcades of Cardiff; wandering around the Ropewalks district of Liverpool or the Stockbridge neighbourhood of Edinburgh; or enjoying the marketplace in Richmond or the harbour in Tobermory. These are places that are lively and welcoming, attractive and safe, full of thriving businesses and contented people. Working out *why* these places are so good is the complicated bit. Understanding how to preserve and further enhance these places is more complicated still and creating those same characteristics in new developments is so complex that it almost always defeats us.

The reason that this is all so difficult is that urbanism involves the interaction of a large number of variables. Once this happens, levels of complexity multiply exponentially and it becomes very difficult to understand cause and effect. The tragedy of the urban professions is that they have failed to recognise even that this complexity exists. As many people have written, the urban professions operate in silos, each seeking to optimise the world from their particular perspective but failing to understand the impact of their actions on others. Highway engineers want to make traffic flow without killing people, environmental health professionals want to keep people healthy, police architectural liaison officers want to reduce crime, housing specialists want to improve the condition of the housing stock etc. All are, in themselves, perfectly sound, laudable and appropriate aims that no one would seriously disagree with. But none of these professions have a good understanding of the side effects of their actions. So who should be making these connections? Town planners might seem the obvious choice but they too have become mired in their rule books of parking ratios and privacy distances and are arguably the worst offenders. The planning profession has succeeded in smoothing the rough edges off urban areas, making them safer and removing conflicts, but in doing so they have often removed their urbanism, squashing the vitality and diversity that makes a great place. What about architects, who were, after all, the first to recognise the need for an Academy of Urbanism? In some respects architects are the most dangerous professionals of all because they are taught that architectural design is a creative process based on pushing boundaries and challenging received wisdom. It is a philosophy that can create an extraordinary museum or concert hall but is risky when applied to the masterplanning of a neighbourhood. Architecture as a creative act is profoundly dismissive of complexity when dealing at the scale of the neighbourhood or even the city.

The science of complex systems has developed significantly in recent years and there is a large academic field that is working to apply complexity theory to cities. This shows how the interaction of even a small number of variables can create incredibly complex systems. If these systems include a feedback loop by which successful forms are replicated, then over time patterns will start to emerge and the system will self-organise. This is something that Kelvin Campbell is focusing on through his Massive Small initiative. The simplistic rendition of the theory suggests that just as termite colonies have evolved through this process, so have humans settlements. The city is a human termite mound and, far from being designed, it has self-organised so that its complex systems have emerged spontaneously. The academic conferences exploring these issues are, however, quite disappointing;

while they have made some progress in modelling and understanding this complexity, little progress has been made on how this can help with the process of city planning.

Which brings us back to our gardening analogy. There are, of course, academic departments and research institutes studying the science of horticulture and the best gardeners need a working knowledge of this science. But it is not where they get the majority of their knowledge. A garden may not be quite as complicated as a city (although some gardeners would disagree) but gardeners know that you deal with this complexity with knowledge passed on from previous generations, with wisdom, good judgement and a feel for the processes that are at work. It is a very human, intuitive process that taps into our ability to understand something without necessarily knowing all of the details.

This is why the Academy of Urbanism works: because essentially it is doing the same thing. There are those within the Academy who argue that we should be collecting data on the places that we celebrate. We should be mining this data to understand why this particular neighbourhood or town works so well and why this other place is struggling. While this can't do any harm, it is a bit like researching the comparative beauty of two gardens. You will learn something from studying the soil, the prevailing wind, the susceptibility to pests and the skill with which the gardener has dealt with these, but you would be better trusting your judgement and, better still, talking to the gardener. In any case the Academy doesn't have the capacity to collect data on successful places and is happy to leave this to our partners in academia. What we do have is 550 Academicians who, like old gardeners, know what they are about. The Academy includes some of the leading urbanists in the country along with many specialists in all aspects of urbanism. This collective experience is the main resource available to us.

One of the ways that this experience is mined is through the Academy's awards. Every year the Academy collects nominations for its award scheme in five categories: Cities, Towns, Neighbourhoods, Streets and Places. A large, argumentative meeting in April narrows these nominations down to a longlist of ten and there follow two votes, the first to create a shortlist of three in May and the second to choose the winners, which are announced in November. The awards are given to places rather than organisations and there is no mechanism by which organisations can submit entries for an award. A team of Academicians visits each of the shortlisted places, spending normally a day walking around the place, talking to officials and local people. The Academy calls this process 'learning from place' and while it will never be able to come to terms with the full complexity of a place, it is more than enough to understand its story. This understanding is written up in an assessment report that is published on the Academy's website to help Academicians cast their final vote.

In its first ten years the Academy shortlisted and visited 150 places in this way. In doing so, it accumulated a treasure trove not so much of data, but of insight. Bringing this together for a wider audience is the aim of this book. The first two years of the awards have already been published by Routledge in the books *Learning from Place* and *Urban Identity*. This book covers the 75 places visited in the following five years of the awards scheme, from 2009 to 2013. Since that time there have been another three sets of awards and the hope is that the years 2014–2018 will appear in *Urbanism 2*.

This book uses as its starting point the visits conducted and the write-ups produced by Academicians at the time, combined with the drawings and maps that were created for each place and, of course the poem by Ian McMillan. For each of the places we have gone back to the original sources and sometimes the people involved to uncover the story of the place. In some cases the main plot lines happened 2,000 years ago and the key players were Roman. In other places there is a much more recent story of regeneration and design. The book is not intended to be read from cover to cover and we hope that you will dip in and explore. We have not tried to write a good practice guide or indeed a travel guide but just to understand the backstories of all these great places. In these stories lies the wisdom of the ages about how the complex and fascinating process of urbanism works. It is an art as much as a science and is a very human process of trial and error, insight and stupidity. Each of these places has been created by urban gardeners (some wise, some less so) and we hope that this book passes on a little of their collected wisdom.

Cities

We start this book with 15 great cities. All have been shortlisted for an Academy of Urbanism award in the only category that includes European places outside the UK and Ireland. These 15 cities join the six cities featured in the first two years of the awards and those that have been shortlisted since 2013 (which will be featured in the next book). While the early shortlisted cities were mostly capitals, including London, Berlin, Edinburgh, Amsterdam and Dublin, the 15 in this book include just three, Helsinki, Lisbon and Budapest (at least the Buda part – Pest is a provincial city in spirit). The others are upstart second cities and provincial centres and have a particular energy and drive that comes with being slightly uncertain of their position in the world. Most of them have an industrial past, and 12 of the 15 are significant ports. They are cities of commerce and industry rather than government and administration, places with large working-class and immigrant populations that make them vibrant, riotous and at times, in the darker alleys and back streets, a little seedy. They are a good cohort from which we can survey the health of the European city.

A city is just an overgrown town – at least so you would think. The early history of many of the cities in this book is similar to that of the towns that will be covered in the Towns section. They grew up around castles and ports and became fortified settlements providing a safe haven for commerce and community life. The oldest, Lisbon, is Phoenician in origin, while many of the others are Roman (from Budapest in the east to Newcastle at the end of Hadrian's Wall in the north). Then in the Middle Ages they divide between the Viking cities of Scandinavia, founded on sea trade (and raiding); the cities of central Europe protected behind their walls from said Viking raids; and the Mediterranean cities with their Moorish influences. The history of Europe is written in this web of cities and their political influence.

In the history of each of these cities there is a moment when they stopped being a town. Once this happened, they turned into a new type of place with a different dynamic. As we say in the introduction to the Towns section, many of the towns in this book are of a size that means that they have just one secondary school. The people in the town, at least those of a similar age, therefore know each other, or at least know of each other. Cities are different because they are full of strangers. When cities get to a certain size, people living there can walk through their streets and not meet anyone that they know. This is partly a function of size and partly the result of migration. Cities only become cities by attracting large numbers of people (strangers) from elsewhere. They therefore become melting pots (to use the cliché) and this combination of size and diversity makes them very different to towns. As the OECD has shown, cities are more productive than smaller places because they provide access to a larger pool of skilled workers, easy access to large markets, and rich networks of suppliers, customers, collaborators and competitors. These forces of agglomeration drive the growth of cities' economies and make them very different places to towns. This is not just true of the economy. It can be also seen in the arts, where the availability of cultural venues, large diverse audiences and communities of like-minded people with specialist interests feed off each other. A city of strangers is a much easier place to test boundaries and generally be outrageous than a town where everyone knows your parents!

All of the cities on the following pages have experienced a period of strong, sometimes explosive, growth at some point in their history when these forces of agglomeration took hold. Antwerp was at one point one of the ten largest cities in the world and Bristol was one of the three largest cities outside London in 14th-century England. However, the period that saw the largest growth of cities was the Industrial Revolution, when migrants to cities were pushed off the land or fleeing famine. The following pages include many cities that grew rapidly in the 19th century as they developed into industrial centres. Those on mainland Europe like Lyon, Hamburg, Antwerp and Valencia were already important cities that industrialised. In the UK, at the epicentre of the Industrial Revolution, the process was slightly different as modest towns like Manchester, Glasgow and Liverpool emerged from virtually nowhere to become huge cities. Once this growth has occurred, the business of cities becomes being a city. Places might have grown initially for reasons of defence or trade – or, in the case of Freiburg, because of rich seams of silver ore in the nearby hills – but they survive and prosper long after that original reason for their existence has disappeared. Their size and connections become their main asset, attracting more people and business in a virtuous circle of growth that quickly leaves nearby towns trailing in their wake.

It always feels, at the time, as if these cycles of growth will last forever, which of course they don't. Without exception, every city in this book has also experienced periods of severe decline. Having been the richest city in Europe, Antwerp lost two thirds of its population between the mid 16th century and 1800 as a result of war and the blockading of its port. Freiburg was almost wiped out when it found itself in the middle of the Thirty Years War in the early 1600s, its population falling to just 2,000. In 1755 Lisbon was destroyed by a huge earthquake killing 40,000 of its people, while Oslo was destroyed by fire so many time (14 in total) that the King ordered that it be rebuilt on a new site in 1647.

Wartime destruction, of course, is also a more recent phenomenon. British cities were badly damaged by bombing raids in the early years of the Second World War, clearing the way for many of the disastrous planning decisions of the post-war years. The destruction was, however, nothing compared to the damage wrought on German cities towards the end of the war by Allied Bomber Command, igniting firestorms that destroyed Freiburg and Hamburg. The difference is that German cities were more inclined to rebuild the city that had been destroyed (particularly Freiburg, which reconstructed an exact facsimile of its former medieval centre). In the UK, by contrast, planners imported the ideas of the Bauhaus and CIAM to build the modern city out of the ashes of destruction. The Germans must have seemed very backward at the time, but it is the modernism that scarred places like Newcastle and Bristol that has done the more lasting damage. What is striking about these episodes of destruction, be they the result of war or natural disaster, is the speed with which cities bounce back. Less than two decades after Hamburg's complete destruction in the Second World War it was the most exciting city in Europe, where the Beatles and many other British bands went to cut their teeth in its basement clubs. Within such short periods, entire cities can be rebuilt – provided, that is, that they retain the dynamism of their economies.

However, every city in this book has also faced the longer-term, more insidious threat of urban decline. Most of the cities experienced a loss of population in the second half of the 20th century. Indeed, research conducted for the Directorate-General for Environment for the European Commission suggests that 40% of Europe's cities of more than 200,000 people continue to lose population. None of the cities in this book has experienced population loss on the scale experienced by Detroit, although Manchester, Liverpool and Glasgow had lucky escapes. However, all of these cities suffered some level of depopulation in the latter part of the 20th-century, from Bordeaux to Antwerp, Valencia to Budapest. This was partly a story of dispersal as urban populations became more affluent and moved out to suburbs beyond the city's administrative area. However, cities, as we have said, are dynamic systems – all cities lose people all of the time through this process of suburbanisation. It is just that healthy cities attract new immigrants at a slightly greater rate than the outflow. It takes only a small drop in inward migration or a modest acceleration in the rate of dispersal to turn city growth into decline. Once this happens, it takes only a few years for the core business of the city – the fact that it is a city – to be undermined. This can lead to a cycle of decline every bit as rapid, and seemingly inevitable, as the virtuous cycle of city growth.

The cities in this book have found ways of breaking out of this cycle. Without exception, these cities have growing populations and all of them are convinced that this growth is the result of their astute urban policies. They have undertaken regeneration, revived their city centres, built iconic cultural institutions, changed their image, reduced crime, tackled congestion, built new urban housing and business quarters, installed trams and underground systems and promoted events and festivals. Put all this together and you have a formula for an urban renaissance that is sweeping across Europe. We would not, of course, wish to diminish the importance of any of these strategies, and can see that civic leadership can make a huge difference to a city's fortunes. However, it is also evident that the tide has turned and that the urban policy-makers in these cities are pushing at an open door. The years of deindustrialisation and urban decline are finally coming to an end and cities across Europe are once more starting to grow. They are shedding their poor images and their reputations for pollution, danger and poverty and becoming places that attract the new cultural and intellectual elites. Because of this they are driving economic growth and cultural development and taking their place once more at the centre of European civilisation. This seemed to be a distant dream as little as 20 years ago. But if you take the long view, as we do in this book, it is a return to business as usual. Cities have been at the heart of Europe's economy and cultural life for many centuries and, after a minor blip over the last 50 years, it is only right that they should continue be so.

Antwerp
Winner 2013

There's a diamond district here, inviting and shining
And that image of a jewel goes a long way to defining
This city by the water, this place that fashion built:
It's just the place to visit if you need a lace/suede kilt!

Well... Fashion's really fleeting keeping Antwerp on its toes
If things are always changing then Antwerp surely knows
How to keep one step ahead, how to freshen and remould
Ideas like setting diamonds in bands of solid gold.

Antwerp is a potent mix of history and thought,
Artistic centre, sporting field, noisy working port;
But if you want an image that can tie the city down
Think about a jewel in northern Europe's crown!

The early 1500s were a good time for the burghers of Antwerp. Positioned at the centre of a trading system for sugar and spice and all things nice (specifically silver and textiles), as well as a banking system that supported governments – including the court of Henry VIII in London – the city was the richest in the world. It had a population of 105,000 at a time when there were only ten cities in the world of this size and only one other (Paris) to the north of the Alps. By the mid 16th century it is estimated that 40% of world trade passed through the port of Antwerp.

Today the port remains central to the economy of Antwerp. Its 25 kilometres of quays along the River Scheldt between the city and the sea make it the second largest port in Europe after Rotterdam and account for half of the city's GDP, which, in turn, makes up 17% of Belgium's GDP. Today the city is famous for its diamond trade, and has a rapidly growing and diverse population of more than half a million (1.2 million in the wider metropolitan area) speaking 170 different languages.

However, the historical line between the city's glorious past and its prosperous present has not been easy. The good times of the early 1500s came to a sudden end with the Sack of Antwerp, otherwise known as the Spanish Fury, in 1576. Spanish soldiers, envious of its riches, destroyed the city and looted its wealth, killing some 7,000 people and razing 800 buildings. This heralded a long period of decline and conflict. In the 17th century the river was barred to trade and the port of Antwerp closed so that by 1800 its population had fallen to just 40,000.

The more recent history of Antwerp has also seen long periods of decline. From the 1950s to the 1990s, like many British cities, it suffered a period of depopulation. The Belgian attitude that 'the countryside is best' combined with growing car ownership and a weak system of building permits allowed the city to sprawl. Its population fell as low as 260,000, decimating the city's tax base and heralding a long period of city centre and inner-city decline, while its suburbs sprawled and its roads were choked with traffic. Its route back from the brink of collapse mirrors that of many of the UK cities in this book.

This recovery was the focus for much of the Academy of Urbanism's visit to Antwerp in September 2012. The city was rightly proud of its Strategic Spatial Structure Plan, adopted in 2006. This is a comprehensive, graphic plan for the city's revival which we shall return to in a moment. However, it was clear that the plan was only part of

Large high-profile projects, they decided, were not the way forward. They needed to invest for the long term, allow the city to regenerate at its own pace and grow recovery from the bottom up

the story of the city's regeneration. There had been earlier plans in 1983 and 1994 which had said very similar things but had not led to widespread change. In the 1990s there had been an international design competition called 'Stad aan de Stroom' ('City on the Stream') for the redevelopment of the Zuiderdokken and the Scheldt Quay – the abandoned port just to the north of the city. Despite a great deal of hype, this too had come to nothing.

The city had learned a number of lessons from these failures. The first was that the public sector had to back up their plans with significant resources. The second and perhaps the most important lesson was encompassed in the term 'slow urbanism'. Large high-profile projects were not the way forward, they needed instead to invest for the long-term, allow the city to regenerate at its own pace and grow recovery from the bottom up. Fortunately, these realisations in the late 1990s coincided with the devolution of

Above: The Museum aan de Stroom is the centrepiece of the Het Eilandje regeneration scheme for Antwerp's oldest port. The museum covers 'Metropolis, Power, Life and Death' – Antwerp's long history as a major international port.

Left: The city has seen the gradual urbanisation of its quaysides through Project Eilandje and Scheldt Quays.

Opposite: The Vespa Housing Programme: small infill schemes tacked by the programme.

regional government and funding to the municipality in 2000 and a period of political stability.

This was the real start of the city's recovery. One of the most important early projects was Spoor Nord, an abandoned railway station that was landscaped to create a new city park. A major regeneration scheme was undertaken in the Station Quarter which had become very run down. This was anchored by the city's decision to locate the new library in the area, generating confidence to attract private investment. A further regeneration initiative has taken place in the Sailor's Quarter – traditional haunt of sailors on shore leave and characterised by the sort of things that sailors like. The approach has been to crack down on crime in the area, improve the environment and to promote the development of gap sites but to otherwise accept the sex trade in the area as part of its traditional role.

The momentum of regeneration has built and finally progress is being made on the redevelopment of the city's quays. These have been masterplanned but are being developed incrementally by a range of developers rather than the previous approach of international competitions – symbolic of the city's faith in slow urbanism.

One of the most inspiring examples of the slow urbanism approach is the Vespa Housing Programme. This is a revolving fund that has been buying up vacant sites and derelict buildings in the city for the last ten years. The sites are subject to an architectural competition and are then developed and sold with the proceeds being reinvested in

further property. Not only is this a tool to deal with the micro problem sites that are otherwise very difficult to tackle, it has also given the city a stock of more than 300 interesting new buildings, attracted creative people back into the city centre and promoted a network of small architectural practices.

The Strategic Spatial Structure Plan was the culmination of these initiatives, rather than the reason they have happened. The plan set out seven strategic themes. The first four relate to the water, ecology, the port and the railways. The fifth is called the 'Porous City' and concerns the densification of built-up areas to support public uses. The sixth emphasises the polycentricity of local centres and the links between them. The seventh, the 'Mega City', is about the role of the city in one of the most densely populated parts of Europe. These themes are developed into specific policies such as the 'Hard Spine' to reurbanise the city's vacant waterfronts, the 'Soft Spine' to create a network of ecological spaces and the 'Green Singel', which is seeking to overcome the barrier of the ring road by creating a ring of urban parks.

Together the plan represents a coherent physical vision for the city that links strategic themes to detailed spatial policy in a way that is both logical and inspiring. Furthermore, the city has reorganised its internal structure to match that of the plan and backed it up with investment. However, while all this is true, the reality is that the plan has succeeded because it's time has come. The plan is pushing against the open door of the city's improving fortunes and therefore has the momentum to see its proposals implemented in a way that wasn't possible with previous plans.

Bordeaux
Shortlisted 2010

This city is a work of art, this city is a sonnet,
This city is a masterpiece, this city is a play
This city is a great idea with 'Bordeaux' chiselled on it
This city is a narrative with many things to say:
A tale of wine, of architecture, boulevards and cheese
Of sitting by the water or riding on the tram
Of strolling in the evening in the French-accented breeze
Of saying 'Bordeaux emphasises all the things I am
Or all the things I can become' because Bordeaux oozes promise
A promise of a past and future working to create
A present that is confident, exemplifies the premise
That planning twinned with action is what makes a city great.
It's a menu, it's a streetmap, it's education, it's a show
With more layers than an onion, I give to you...Bordeaux!

Above: Rue Sainte-Catherine, Bordeaux's main shopping street that runs straight as a die for 1.2km through the heart of the city.

'La perle d'Aquitaine', Bordeaux is the main city of south-west France. A busy colonial port and the centre of the world's wine trade, Bordeaux prospered to the extent that Haussmann used its graceful collection of grand boulevards, squares and parks as inspiration when he sought to remodel Paris. These ought to be the perfect ingredients of an attractive, liveable city; a place to while away the hours, a place for flâneurs. Sadly, by the end of the 20th century, nothing could be further from the truth.

As Bordeaux industrialised in the 19th and 20th centuries its historic street network struggled to cope with the increase in traffic and pollution. Boulevards were snarled up with traffic and medieval squares had been turned from meeting places into car parks where it was impossible even to sit outside, much less hold a conversation. The residents were choking and those who could moved out to the suburbs, leaving behind them neglected and declining neighbourhoods and an empty and uninviting historic centre. Perhaps fittingly for a city once ruled by Henry II of England, Bordeaux by the 1980s had fallen foul of a very British urban malaise. The fine architecture had become so completely coated in a layer of soot that the city had earned the nickname 'La Belle Endormie' or 'Sleeping Beauty'. Even the connection to the river – historically the city's lifeblood – had been cluttered and obscured by warehouses and an urban expressway that might have been good for traffic movement but did nothing for the image of the city. It was clear that something needed to be done. In 1995, when Alain Juppe became Mayor, an ambitious vision was developed that sought to arrest Bordeaux's decline and restore the city to its former glory by creating a sustainable city for the 21st century.

Bordeaux's boom started in 1653 – when it finally became fully part of France – and ran to the late 19th century. Like many Atlantic ports, its wealth was built on slavery and the sugar trade as well as the export of wine. The city was confined within its medieval walls until the mid 18th century. It was then that the city fathers set about providing a better connection to the river, and improving the view of the city for travellers arriving across the River Garonne. Louis XV's architect, Gabriel, was despatched from Paris in 1739 and designed the Place Royale (now Place de La Bourse) providing a striking, symmetrical crescent along the waterfront. The government of France relocated here during the Franco-Prussian Wars and again during the First World War.

> Bordeaux by the 1980s had fallen foul to a very British urban malaise

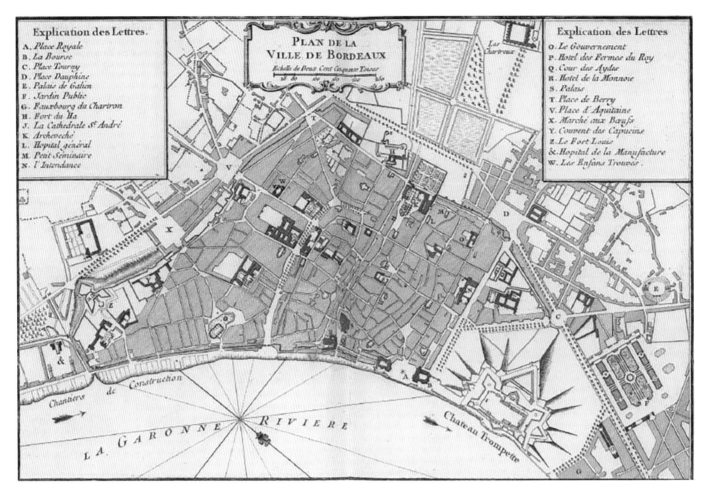

Explication des Lettres.
A. Place Royale
B. La Bourse
C. Place Tourny
D. Place Dauphine
E. Palais de Galien
F. Jardin Public
G. Fauxbourg du Chartron
H. Fort du Ha
J. La Cathédrale St André
K. Archeveché
L. Hopital général
M. Petit Séminaire
N. l'Intendance

PLAN DE LA
VILLE DE BORDEAUX

Explication des Lettres
O. Le Gouvernement
P. Hotel des Fermes du Roy
Q. Cour des Aydes
R. Hotel de la Monnoe
S. Palais
T. Place de Berry
V. Place d'Aquitaine
X. Marché aux Boufs
Y. Couvent des Capucins
Z. Le Fort Louis
&. Hopital de la Manufacture
W. Les Enfans Trouvés

Right: The plan of Bordeaux in 1754, just at the point when it was expanding beyond its old town and setting out its 'boulevards'.

Below: The tram and the taming of traffic has brought the streets back to life, while the cleaning of buildings like the Cathédrale Saint-André has revealed the beauty of the city's architecture.

The Place Royale set the standard for the expansion of the city. Along with the Quayside, three grand 'cours' (what Haussmann would later call boulevards) linked a series of urban set-pieces around the old town, creating a setting for a period of development that was remarkable in terms of its quality and coherence. The scale of the buildings and the uniform use of the city's honey-coloured limestone as well as a number of high-quality spaces with lavish fountains and statues combined to make Bordeaux the most beautiful city of the age. Although the sixth largest city in France, Bordeaux is second only to Paris in its number of protected buildings, with outstanding examples such as the Grand Theatre, the Cathedrale Saint-André and the Hotel de Ville.

From the Second World War onwards, however, there was a steady and sustained loss of population – 35% from the historic city and inner-city districts during this period. The rush to leave the city had reached epidemic proportions by the time Juppe took over office. The plan that he developed sought to get people to return to the historic core to

did more than anything else to symbolise the rebirth of the city.

The Quay project sought to re-establish the connection between the city centre and the river, removing the low concrete warehouses that lined the water's edge to create a high-quality public space/park as a setting for the quayside buildings. The centrepiece is the Miroir d'Eau, a mirror pool fountain that has inspired many imitators across the world. In Bordeaux, this sits on top of a cavernous underground car park. These initiatives have brought about a change in the relationship between residents and their city. A greater sense of pride has meant that previously neglected and unloved public spaces are now well used and cared for.

Finding a solution to the city's congestion was a vital part of these plans. This is often a difficult balance – too much stick and not enough carrot – but, as the car park under the mirror pool suggests, Bordeaux has tamed and hidden its traffic rather than banned it. It has also provided an alternative to the car in the form of a sleek, modern tram network. Opened in 2003, at a cost of €690 million, the tram

The Miroir d'Eau in front of the Bourse is the centrepiece of the regenerated Quayside.

was nothing if not ambitious – building 44 kilometres of track from scratch. However, it rode on the optimism of the time and has been a major success story, providing a viable alternative to the car (journeys that used to take an hour by car now take a fraction of the time), tackling inclusiveness and accessibility and acting as a catalyst for regeneration. Recognising its impact on the architectural heritage of the city and the need to minimise clutter, the tram employs a 'third rail' avoiding the need for overhead power lines. The system is a work in progress, a fourth line is planned and each of the tram's three initial lines has seen an incremental programme of extensions into neighbourhoods across the city.

spend time and socialise, and eventually hopefully to live. Traffic was removed from some streets and squares, opening up opportunities for street life to return. Spaces like Place du Parlement and Place de la Victoire were transformed from traffic roundabouts into lively squares resounding to the chatter and bustle of people sitting at the tables fanning around the cafes and restaurants lining the perimeter of the space throughout the day and evening.

A major programme of restoration and cleaning was introduced to tackle the condition of the historic building stock, which included generous grants to property owners in key locations. Revealing the beauty of the buildings under their layers of soot

This transformation has taken 20 years and has been so complete that the city of the 1980s is thankfully now a distant, slightly indistinct memory. Surely the city always glowed warmly in the evening sun, enticing visitors and locals to the tables lining its squares to sip a grande crème or tuck into steak tartare washed down with a carafe of something from just a few short miles up the road? Watching this scene it is easy to reflect on how Bordeaux is managing to reconnect with the spirit of centuries past, once more appreciating the importance of identity, Gabriel, Louis XV's architect, would have approved.

Bristol
Winner 2009

Above: The Clifton Gorge, through which the tidal River Avon flows to the sea.

This isn't easy. A poem is a machine of words and sounds
And Bristol's more than that. So much more.
Try getting Cabot Circus into a line: light reflecting on windows,
On the face of someone entering a shop with a smile. See:
Two lines! The Harbourside: I'll sit here for a moment and try
To write a line about how Bristol meets the water meets the sky
And then a line about how Clifton's streets somehow make you
Walk more slowly, taking in the view and more than the view,
The history, the sense of promise, the stroll down Whiteladies Road
Where you just can't decide where to eat except everywhere
And this poem's getting fuller and it feels like it might explode
With all the things I'm trying to squeeze into it. Okay then, admit it:
This isn't a poem, it's an open-top bus tour of a city
That's a poem all by itself. Bristol: epic work, constantly redrafting.

We should start by declaring an interest. Before George Ferguson was elected Bristol's first Mayor in November 2012, he was a leading member of the Academy of Urbanism. Indeed, George was one of the original champions of the Academy when he was President of the Royal Institute of British Architects in 2004. His concern was to widen the focus of the architecture profession away from iconic buildings towards good cities. The Academy has come across many stories of great city mayors; indeed the importance of stable and inspirational leadership is a common thread running through many of the cities in this book. Most city leaders are politicians who come to realise the importance of urbanism. Bristol, for a time, had an urbanist mayor who, while a member of no political party, came to realise the importance of politics.

Of all the great provincial cities in the UK, Bristol is probably the only place where this could happen. It is a city with a conscience, a mix of radical politics and middle-class affluence. The city of the graffiti artist Banksy, whose works may be anti-establishment but still sell for huge sums in international art galleries. The city of Tricky, Portishead and Massive Attack – and, if you don't know who they are, you won't understand how cool the Bristol music scene has been over the years and there is probably no point trying to explain drum & bass. A city with its own local currency, the Bristol Pound, that you can use to pay local taxes and in which George took his entire salary while mayor. A city full of activists and local initiatives, from the squats of Telepathic Heights to the self-build housing and community business groups, green energy initiatives and local food growing. It probably has the most committed and engaged community of any large city in the UK and for this reason was designated as European Green Capital in 2015. If there is anywhere where an urbanist mayor can make a difference, then it is Bristol.

Most city leaders are politicians who come to realise the importance of urbanism. Bristol, for a time, had an urbanist mayor who came to realise the importance of politics.

The modern liberal Bristol is perhaps a response to the city's much darker history. Bristol is one of the UK's great mercantile cities and because of this it was the centre of the slave trade. Its early history is similar to that of many of the towns and cities in this book – a Saxon fortified town, suppressed by a Norman castle just outside the city gates (now the green space known as Castle Park). The city was built at the confluence of the River Frome and the River Avon, where the Bristol Bridge provided the first inland crossing point – the name Bristol simply means 'the place of the bridge'.

By the 12th century it had become a major port and by the 14th century Bristol, York and Norwich were the three largest cities in England outside London. Like Lisbon (Page 44), Bristol became a centre for exploration, sending out ships to China, Africa and the New World, culminating in John Cabot's voyage to the Americas in 1497. The proceeds of these voyages and the newly discovered products (particularly tobacco) made the merchants of Bristol very rich indeed. Mercantile cities like Bristol and its great rival Liverpool are different to the great industrial cities that came later. Mercantile cities, which also include London, were powerful and accumulated huge wealth. There far more merchants that there were mill owners in the later textile cities and they exercised far greater power over the population. Bristol's age of discovery was funded by the Society of Merchant Venturers, which was founded in the 13th century and received its Royal Charter in 1552, giving it a monopoly on Bristol's trade. The society managed the port and pretty much ran the city. It funded the Clifton

Suspension Bridge as well as the Great Western Railway linking the city to London. It also, of course, ran the slave triangle by which ships from Bristol would set out for Africa, trading arms, alcohol and textiles for slaves to be taken to the West Indies, who in turn were traded for sugar and tobacco that was shipped back to Bristol. Many slaves were brought back to Bristol as servants and the city grew rich on the odious trade that flourished from 1700 until the Abolition of the Slave Trade Act of 1807. During that time, more than 2,100 slaving ventures sailed from Bristol, trading more than 500,000 slaves. The Society of Merchant Venturers still exists in Bristol, although its activities are confined to charitable works. The city, meanwhile, remains slightly uneasy about this aspect of its history.

At its peak, slavery accounted for 60% of Bristol's trade. Abolition saw the city's fortunes decline, but it also coincided with the start of the Industrial Revolution. Throughout the 19th century Bristol's population grew from around 66,000 to 330,000 although this was eclipsed by the even greater growth of the northern industrial cities. Bristol was overtaken by Liverpool as the pre-eminent Atlantic port. Ironically Bristol's greatest engineering achievements were (largely unsuccessful) attempts to arrest this decline in its status. The first of these, the Floating Harbour designed by William Jessop, attempted to resolve one of the key problems with the port: its huge tidal range which limited the time when ships could enter the harbour (the expression 'all shipshape and Bristol fashion' comes from the calls made by the crew as a ship made its way along the sandy, treacherous river that was navigable only at the high point of its 14-metre tidal range). Jessop's floating harbour impounded the river so that ships floated and could move around when the tide was out. Despite being an engineering triumph, the Floating Harbour was a commercial flop because the higher port fees that had to be charged to fund the venture made the port even less viable. By the time it was competed, the docks had already started moving downriver to Avonmouth and Portishead. A sand company was the last commercial user of the Bristol Docks. When they closed in 1991 the city's quayside was turned over to apartments   and leisure uses.

Bristol made further attempts to regain its position with the opening of the Great Western Railway and its great station at Temple Quay. This, together with the *SS Great Britain*, was meant to provide direct passenger services between London and New York. The railway and the ship were the wonders of their age, designed by Bristol's greatest

Above: Bristol's Mayor and founder of The Academy of Urbanism, George Ferguson.

Opposite top: The Floating Harbour in the heart of the city

Opposite below: The *SS Great Britain,* which is now a visitor attraction.

son, Isambard Kingdom Brunell. However, both were to face financial problems. The *SS Great Britain*, the largest ship by far of its age, was so large that it couldn't get out of the harbour and was trapped there for a year. She was plagued by technical problems and eventually ran aground in Ireland, bankrupting her owners the Great Western Steamship Company, leaving the New York route to be claimed by Liverpool and Southampton.

It wasn't until the early 20th century that Bristol found its cutting edge once more. The Bristol Aeroplane Company, that created the iconic Bristol Plane as well as becoming a luxury car maker became part of British Aerospace. Bristol was heavily involved in the international consortium that built Concord and remains an important aviation centre, with Airbus and Rolls Royce based in the city. Its mercantile past has also left it a strong legacy of professional and financial services and as the 20th century progressed, Bristol once more overtook its northern rivals in terms of wealth if not size.

Today the Floating Harbour is once more at the heart of life in the city with the Bristol Harbour Festival taking place every July. Former harbourside warehouses have been converted into apartments, offices and cultural facilities such as the Arnolfini Gallery and the Watershed Media Centre. Meanwhile the harbour is lined with floating bars, restaurants and tourist attractions, including the SS Great Britain, which was eventually brought back from the Falkland Islands where it had ended up. The city has a straggling retail core with its shopping split between the upmarket Park Street around the university and the more mass-market Broadmead shopping centre to the east. The latter was developed in the 1950s on an area heavily bombed in the Second World War, and has since been extended with a modern covered shopping centre to become the city's main shopping destination. Until recently, the two retail areas were divided by an intrusive ring road that cut through the core of the city bisecting public spaces like Queen Square (see page 226). The removal of this road together with the development of vacant sites along the harbour has created a much more coherent, attractive city centre.

Whether Bristol can truly be considered a Green Capital compared to previous holders of the title like Copenhagen is a moot point. In terms of energy use, recycling rates, cycling and congestion, Bristol still has a long way to go – like every other British city. George may have lost out to a mainstream politician in the 2016 mayoral election but in terms of commitment and engagement from its grass-roots activists the city is still way ahead of the field. If any city can be transformed then Bristol is the place.

Budapest
Shortlisted 2011

Budapest was shortlisted in the same year as Helsinki and for the Academy assessment team that visited the two cities it was something of a culture shock. Walking through Budapest with its noise, traffic, crowded pavements, grime and graffiti was a jolt to the system after the civilised order of Helsinki, yet it was also very familiar – this could be Paris or Rome, a noisy, sometimes riotous European city. With a population of 1.7 million – Budapest, like its fellow shortlisted cities in 2011, Glasgow and Helsinki – is a large city in a small country. It is home to 17% of Hungary's population and accounts for 35% of the national GDP. It is a city that, after years of population loss following the fall of communism, is now growing rapidly, driving a strong economy. The city lies at a crossroads between eastern and western Europe and the Balkans. At the time of our visit this meant that it was full of young people from across the continent having a good time (since then its geographical position means that it has also become the centre of the Syrian refugee crisis). As Imre Ikvai-Szabo, the Deputy Mayor, told us, 'if Rome is a woman, and London a teenager, Budapest is still a kid'. None of us quite understood what he meant but it seemed to contain a truth about the exuberant city.

Budapest is of course not one city but two: the royal city of Buda perched on a series of hills overlooking the Danube and the fortified city of Pest on the flat eastern banks of the river. The city has ancient roots; it was once a Roman capital, a major centre in the Ottoman Empire and one of the two great cities of the Austro-Hungarian Empire. The cities of Buda and Pest merged in 1873, heralding a time of great prosperity and a period of growth that created the modern city and gave it many of its finest buildings. It had originally been predominantly a low-rise city with two-storey buildings on narrow streets. Its late-19th-century growth spurt saw the city rebuilt at five and six storeys on the same building plots, creating the canyon-like streets that characterise the city today. The city was also extended, based on a plan drawn up by the Capital Council of Public Works, chaired by Budapest's equivalent of Haussmann – Baron Podmaniczky. This extension has its fair share of grand boulevards and set-piece squares (the grandest being Heroe's Square). It is telling that the modern strategy for the renewal of the city is called the Podmaniczky Programme, because it shares the ambition and scope of its 19th-century predecessor.

After the Second World War Hungary spent just over 45 years as a Soviet-type 'people's republic' and was scarred by the 1956 revolution when the overthrow of the government prompted a Soviet invasion of the city in which 2,500 Hungarians were killed. Hungary was subsequently to play a key role in the collapse of the Soviet Union when it opened its borders to Austria in 1989, setting in train a sequence of events that led to the fall of the Berlin Wall.

'If Rome is a woman, and London a teenager, Budapest is still a kid'

City by the Danube, city of the mind
City that resists the easy flowing rhyme;
City of light and motion redefined.
City built on people's need to make a home
Where earth and air and water intertwine:
A city built on commerce and crossings of ideas
And a city where, from bridges one to nine
History feels essential as the hazy morning clears,
And the Budapest sun begins to shine.
But history's just a bridge to the present, and the sense
That Budapest is easing forward to a time
As exciting and shape-shifting and delightful and intense
As anything this city has experienced before:
The future feels like Budapest, so open up the door!

Below: CORNERfilm, a pop-up bar in an otherwise derelict block.

Right: The city's original two storey buildings (top) were replaced with grander larger structures at the end of the 19th century.

Bottom left: One of the very deep courtyard buildings that have traditionally housed the city's poor.

The scars of the communist era are particularly evident on the outskirts of Budapest, many parts of which are dominated by large, grey apartment blocks. These state-owned blocks were sold off to residents in the early 1990s for a third of their value in the hope that the surplus value would be used to fund improvements. This only partly worked because many families sold up and moved out of the city causing its population to fall from its peak of just over two million (this is because the families were replaced by smaller households; vacant flats are almost unknown). A condominium programme funded jointly by residents, the municipality and the districts (we explain below the complex government structure) is slowly improving these blocks, including energy efficiency measures.

The Soviet era left fewer scars on the central parts of the city other than allowing it to become run-down and dilapidated. This has been put right in the last 20 years that have seen enormous investment in the building stock. There is still much to be done but confidence has returned and while the city's population is yet to return to pre-1989 levels, it has stopped shrinking and started growing. The last decade has seen a new focus on city planning. The long-term Urban Development Concept in 2003 was followed in 2005 by the mid-term Podmaniczky Programme and Structure Plan and in 2008 by an Investment Strategy. A central part of the plan is the regeneration of the banks of the Danube, as they are no longer required for industry and docks. The city is turning back towards the river and there are ambitious schemes for development along the banks and on one of the large islands in the river. This they call the 'vertical' regeneration of the city. The 'horizontal' regeneration runs east–west along the new Metro 4 line that travels deep under the centre. This is yet to open but has cost €2.1 billion with 7.4 kilometres of track and ten stations. The city is also creating a series of public spaces around the old city walls and commissioning a major extension to its City Hall by the Dutch architect Erick Van Egeraat.

Budapest's administration is either a textbook example of localism or a hopelessly complex and unworkable system, depending on your viewpoint. There are 23 district councils covering the city, which run many aspects of its administration.

The city-wide municipality has a co-ordinating role, meaning that it tends to take the blame for things that go wrong without having the powers to make sure that they don't. We visited the 9th District to see a regeneration programme for an inner-city residential district that was exemplary. However, the variation in districts in terms of their character, demography and political control makes consistency and co-ordination difficult. This means that Budapest is planned through negotiation and partnership between the different layers of government. In a telling phrase, Richard Ongjerth, director of the Hungarian Urban Knowledge Centre, told us that in Budapest the public sector 'buries its money'. By this he meant that public money is spent on infrastructure, public transport, roads, public realm etc… Having made this investment in infrastructure city benefits from the growth of private-sector investment. Urban development is thus promoted by the city but not really controlled by it. In this respect Budapest may be a more relevant example for the UK context than the rather unattainable perfection that we saw in Helsinki and other more centrally planned cities.

Freiburg
Winner 2010

Have a look at Freiburg in many different ways;
High up in a cable car shifting slightly in the air
Walking through the old town with a hungry tourist's gaze
Wandering through a gallery, with time to stand and stare
Or sitting in a cafe with a glass of local wine.
From every different angle Freiburg is a city
That takes the time to sparkle, takes the time to shine
In a way that's somehow more profound than pretty.
There's nothing wrong with pretty but that's not the whole story
Of a place as multi-layered, multi-faceted as this
With history, culture, architecture and a dash of scenic glory
As expansive as a group hug or intimate as a kiss:
So much is hidden from your gaze; it's a mystery, it's an iceberg
With hidden depths and striking beauty from all angles: Freiburg!

Above and opposite: The Vauban neighbourhood in Freiburg.

Opposite top left: an aerial view of the city after wartime bombing.

Freiburg is the only winner of an Academy award to have its own Academy of Urbanism charter. After it won the 2010 City Award, the Academy organised a study tour to the city, out of which came the *Freiburg Charter* containing 12 principles for the creation of a sustainable city, developed with Freiburg's Head of Urban Planning Wulf Daseking. The *Charter* set out a vision for future city planning based upon neighbourhood and community, public transport, resource efficiency, green space, social harmony and cultural advancement, a strong economy and life-long learning. These, of course, are well-worn phrases found in every city vision and neighbourhood regeneration strategy; the motherhood and apple pie of urban planning – What marks out Freiburg is that for 30 years it has acted on these principles and in doing so has built one of Europe's greenest, most progressive cities. The lessons from Freiburg are not so much about what we should be aiming for, but how to go about hitting the target.

The independence of spirit and bloody-mindedness that has created Freiburg is written into the very name of the city, which literally means 'free

town'. Free, that is, from the local lord or king, a city of free citizens rather than serfs. This is a freedom that has been hard won since the city's foundation in 1120. At various points in its history the citizens of Freiburg have had to fight for their freedom and at one point, in 1368, to purchase it. This they could do because at the time it was one of the richest small cities in Europe, made affluent by the silver mines in the surrounding hills and at one point even minting its own coins. Part of this wealth poured into the construction of the city's great cathedral, the Münster of Freiburg, which was started in 1200 and completed in 1530. Being independent of spirit, the citizens rejected the Reformation and stuck to their Catholicism, the cathedral becoming the seat of an archbishop. The university was founded in 1457, making it one of the oldest in Germany, and has grown into an elite institution specialising in the natural sciences and humanities.

The main risk to the city over the centuries has been war. Located in the contested territory where the borders of Germany, France and Switzerland meet, Freiburg has been occupied many times. Over its history its 'free' citizens have been ruled by the French, the Spanish and the Swedish as well as various parts of the German Confederacy and of course the

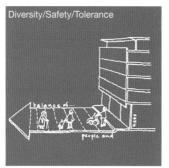

Diversity/Safety/Tolerance

City of Neighbourhoods

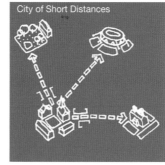

City of Short Distances

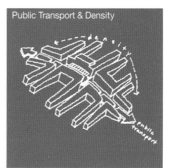

Public Transport & Density

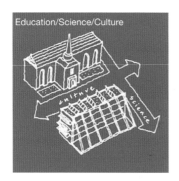

Education/Science/Culture

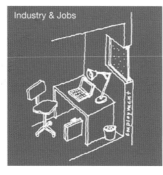

Industry & Jobs

Nature & Environment

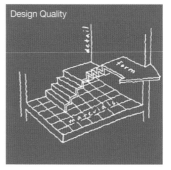

Design Quality

Long-term Vision

Communication & Participation

Reliability, Obligation, Fairness

Co-operation & Partnership

Austrians. During the Thirty Years War in the early 1600s the city was fought over constantly and saw its population collapse from more that 12,000 to less than 2,000. However, it was the Second World War that did the most damage to the city. Bizarrely, this started in 1940 when a Luftwaffe squadron mistook Freiburg for a French city and dropped 69 bombs so unexpectedly that no air raid siren was sounded, killing 57 people. However, this was nothing compared to the bombing raid by the British on 27th November 1944. Despite Freiburg having no obvious military targets, 441 Lancaster bombers dropped 14,000 high-explosive and incendiary bombs, igniting a firestorm that destroyed 80% of the city but miraculously left the cathedral largely intact.

After the war, cities across Europe took different approaches to reconstruction. In Britain cities like Coventry built entirely new modernist city centres. In Germany, most cities took the opportunity to rationalise their urban cores, putting in street grids and accommodating the car. Freiburg, however, was very old-fashioned and its planning director Joseph Schlippe decided to reconstruct on the old medieval footprint plot by plot. How the planners of Coventry laughed! While they were being feted by the likes of Le Corbusier, Freiburg was rebuilding the muddled, inefficient city that everyone else had been trying so hard to erase until the wartime bombers did the job for them. This approach was not even popular with the voters of Freiburg, who eventually sacked Schlippe for being too conservative. But he survived long enough to create the walkable, historic city that is now the envy of all those cities that were more 'ambitious' after the war.

This was the foundation of Freiburg's late-20th-century flowering into an eco-city. The conservatism of a city that rebuilt its historic core stone by stone, also caused it not to do away with its tram system in the early 1970s. It has also retained its system of Bächle – rills that run with water through the city's streets, originally as a water supply to fight fires but now as a way of keeping the city cool in summer. They are symbolic of the way in which this intellectual city has evolved its conservatism into a strong conservation movement following the oil crisis of the 1970s and a campaign locally to oppose a proposed nuclear power station. Today 35% of its electorate vote for the Green Party and with this backing its long-term mayor set about transforming the city with its chief planner, Wulf Daseking.

This transformation has affected all parts of Freiburg. It is, however, the city's two urban extensions that have attracted most attention: Rieselfeld and Vauban, both of which were initiated in the early 1990s. Rieselfeld, in German, means 'sewage farm', which is what the site used to be, while Vauban was the former French military base. Rieselfeld was the first to be planned and has been built as a medium-rise, relatively high-density residential neighbourhood and is perhaps the less successful of the two, lacking variety and local facilities. Vauban was able to learn the lessons from this and also grew from more radical beginnings. In the early years the French barracks were squatted by hippies and after a court battle they were given the right to stay in four of the 20 barracks. A campaigning group, Forum Vauban, was established to argue that the remaining 35 hectares should be developed as an entirely car-free neighbourhood. The council acquired the land and eventually went into partnership with the Forum to develop the concept for the neighbourhood. It is not quite car-free but residents wanting a car have to pay €18,000 for a parking space in one of the solar garages on the edge of the development. Both neighbourhoods were built at the end of tram lines that were extended into the neighbourhoods at the very beginning of the development and both are laced with generous cycleways and footpaths. They were largely built via a Baugruppen system by which groups of residents buy a plot, engage an architect and build their own apartments. This has been successful in creating a strong sense of community and belonging, although this might sometimes flip over into a slightly authoritarian eco-policing, if some of the articles written about the neighbourhoods are to be believed (in one case, a car parked within Vauban was stoned by residents).

These neighbourhoods may not be perfect, but they are there. While the rest of Europe has advocated and debated eco-urban design, Freiburg has got on and done it. It may have made mistakes but at least it has built. This is why the Academy of Urbanism developed the *Freiburg Charter* to capture the lessons and encourage others. The *Charter* is full of important principles, such as diversity, safety and tolerance, the compact city of short distances in which 'the aspects of everyday life can be laid out and accessed within walking distance by all members of society', the importance of open space, quality design and collaboration with local people. There is nothing in the *Charter* that other cities have not been trying to do for years. But, in the hands of the free citizens of Freiburg, these principles have transformed the city and created an eco-model that we all need to at least try and emulate.

Above: One of the Bächle that run with water through the city's streets.

Opposite above: An aerial view of Rieselfeld, which covers 70 hectares and includes 4,200 homes.

Opposite: The 12 principles of the *Freiburg Charter*.

Glasgow
Winner 2011

My Dad was a Scot; to him Glasgow was Utopia,
And Heaven and Nirvana, and all points in between
And he'd be proud to find the city's still a cornucopia
Of water, stone, laughter, and endless, endless green.
Let's give this place a name: A Seat of Reinvention,
A City with a Mission, A Gallery on the Clyde,
A city where the promise matches the intention:
The promise is renewal, the intention's local pride
And Glasgow as a city goes far beyond these shores;
It's so large and so ambitious you can see Glasgow from space
As it mixes art and commerce and it opens up the doors
To business and to culture with a grin upon its face.
My dad was right. This place is special.
So raise a glass and let's go
And shout a toast at the top of our voices:
I give you Glasgow!

A number of the presentations that we saw when the Academy assessment team visited Glasgow included an infamous front cover from the *Observer Magazine* from 1977 with the headline 'Home Rotten Home: What it's like to live in the worst corner of Britain', by which, of course, they meant Glasgow. This was the city's nadir and in hindsight also its turning point. It is difficult to believe that this is the same city described in 2009 by Condé Nast as 'a fantastic world class city', by the OECD as 'the New Berlin' or even more improbably by *Vogue* as 'the chicest city in the world'.

However, once you spend some time in the city, walking around the city centre – its stylish shops, new financial district and creative Merchant Quarter – and travel around the environs of Kelvingrove, the redeveloped Clyde Waterfront and the new urban quarter of Crown Street, the hyperbole is not so far fetched. In the words of *Time* magazine, 'brimming with style and culture, Scotland's second cit y is a revelation'. Glasgow is a city transformed and it is almost impossible to imagine it as it was when it had an unemployment rate of 60% and was described in the *Observer* piece as a 'Hellish mix of drink, poverty and violence'. Well, almost impossible. On visiting the city's East End and hearing about districts like Carlton, where male life expectancy is just 53.9 years (compared to 67.4 years in Iraq, as the *Sun* newspaper

Right: Lunchtime workers in Royal Exchange Square.

Below: The view along St. George Street in Glasgow.

No other city has recovered so well having fallen so low

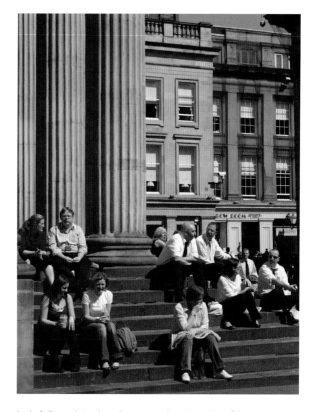

helpfully pointed out), you realise that the Glasgow of old has not been entirely banished despite huge efforts and investment by the council and other agencies.

Glasgow's transformation may not be complete but the extent of its renaissance is astonishing. No other city has recovered so well having fallen so low and it holds lessons for the reinvention of industrial cities across the Western world. Glasgow's origins, however, are not as an industrial city. It started as a religious centre founded on the apparently rather dubious myth and relics of St. Mungo. The cathedral is the oldest in Scotland and Glasgow University is the fourth oldest in the UK (after Oxford, Cambridge and St Andrews).

Glasgow developed as a trading centre on the Clyde and prospered on the back of slaves in the cotton and tobacco trades, much like Bristol. Such was its wealth and growth rate in the early 19th century that a new town was built. This extension was gridded, like a North American city, regardless of topography. In one of the presentations on the Academy assessment team's visit, it was described as 'Chicago on the Clyde – the most easterly American city'. There was in fact an interchange of ideas between Glasgow and the United States. Glasgow architects helped to shape the architectural character of cities like Chicago and then reimported the American influence to Scotland. So successful was Glasgow's new town that the city centre shifted westwards so that today Trongate and High Street,

Opposite: Sauchiehall Street, one of Glasgow's main shopping streets.

Below: Festival crowds gather in the regenerated former ship yards

the rather desperate slogan 'Glasgow's Miles Better' with a smiling picture of *Mr Happy*, that unaccountably had a huge impact. A little later the city opened the new Burrell Collection to great acclaim and in 1988 staged a Garden Festival. However, the really big breakthrough was its designation as European City of Culture in 1990. This was used by the city to capitalise on its early successes to entirely relaunch itself.

The two decades since then have seen the physical transformation of much of the city. The city centre has been regenerated and is now the most successful retail centre outside London. The Merchant City has been revived as a cultural quarter and the universities are expanding and being restructured to create a new learning quarter, while the city centre has expanded towards the river with the new International Financial Services District. To the west the former shipyards on the Clyde now house the Scottish Exhibition and Conference Centre (known locally as the Armadillo) together with the new Digital Media Village as well as the HQ buildings for the BBC and Scottish Media Group. To the east the Clyde Gateway project is being managed by an urban regeneration company that used the 2014 Commonwealth Games to kick-start a £2 billion regeneration programme beginning with a Games Village of 700 units and four new venues. Across the city 21,000 social housing units are being redeveloped and neighbourhoods like Crown Street (the former Gorbals) are being used as models to regenerate other neighbourhoods around the city.

The results are impressive. In the decade to 2007 the city's economy grew by 20%, creating 63,000 jobs and attracting 45,000 new residents. The city's confidence is reflected in its carefully managed image: 'Scotland with Style'. The momentum of its recovery carried it through the recession and the worst days of public-sector cutbacks. In 2009 there was a £3.95 billion investment programme underway partly because of the Commonwealth Games.

Today Glasgow really does have style and confidence. In the UK we are not always very good at recognising that we have our own great cities to rival Milan, Barcelona, Copenhagen and Chicago. Glasgow still has some work to do before it can match these cities in every respect, but considering where it was in the 1980s it is remarkable that it can be spoken about as being in the same league.

which were once the heart of the city centre, now mark its eastern boundary.

By the beginning of the 20th century Glasgow's population had grown to more than a million and the city was designing and building half of all the iron-built, sea-going ships on the world's oceans. It was one of the pre-eminent industrial cities of Empire specialising in heavy engineering – one of the 'shock' cities of the age, doubling and trebling in size as it sucked in people from the Highlands and Ireland. At its peak Glasgow was a city of great contrasts. It contained some of Europe's most notorious slums and yet was able to stage the Empire Exhibition in 1938 that attracted 13 million visitors. It was also able to commission world-class architecture like George Gilbert Scott's Glasgow University Building and Charles Rennie Mackintosh's School of Art.

It was from these heady heights that Glasgow fell. In the latter half of the 20th century the industrial base collapsed and the population halved – partly through well-intentioned but ultimately misguided slum clearance. Glasgow became the 'home rotten home' described by the *Observer*. Its route back from the brink has been an object lesson in city regeneration. Its fortunes turned in the 1980s with the establishment of the Tourist Board, who tried to rebrand the city with

Gothenburg
Shortlisted 2012

You will need: cutlery and a bib.
You will embrace: the light on the water.
You will hear: that roar as that goal is scored.
You will walk: through woods and stand for a moment,
Listening.

You will need: to steady yourself stepping onto the boat.
You will embrace: shopping like you embrace a friend.
You will hear: songs that stay with you for ever, or longer.
You will walk: down streets that dazzle with colours,
Refracting.

You will need: time, so make some and take it with you.
You will embrace: midnight, and beyond, still dancing.
You will hear: birds singing in Swedish. No, really: listen.
You will walk: and walk, and walk, and still this city's
surprises
Are waiting...

Below: The Kuggen building is part of the Chalmers University of Technology and was designed by Wingårdh arkitektkontor.

S econd cities can be slightly pushy. Remember Glasgow's 'Miles Better' campaign – a not so subtle suggestion that Edinburgh was by comparison rather straight-faced. Sweden's second city Gothenburg also likes to make out it is a more laid-back, welcoming sort of place than Stockholm. But in truth Gothenburg doesn't really compete with the capital city (which is 500 kilometres away and faces towards the Baltic). Gothenburg rules the west coast as capital of the Västra Götaland region and its story is intertwined with that of its near neighbours in Denmark and Norway. Stockholm's power comes from being the seat of national government while Gothenburg grew as a world centre of shipbuilding and an international port looking west across the Atlantic to the New World that would prove such a magnet to thousands of Swedish émigrés.

Today the mighty Eriksberg crane, symbol of Gothenburg's shipbuilding might, is surrounded by dockside apartments, hotels, offices and university buildings. With the collapse of the shipbuilding industry in the 1970s, the city embarked on a major programme of economic and social regeneration, to reposition and diversify Gothenburg and its region. A new industry was identified – innovation and research – and a methodical process of regeneration began in the port districts along the River Göta. Several decades on, it is widely seen as an exemplar of waterfront regeneration.

Encouraging people to even think of the docks as a place where they would want to work, let alone live, however,

There is an efficiency in the way that the Scandinavians develop their cities that seems to be entirely beyond British planners

was not easy. Although it is not far from the city centre, opening up what had been a closed maritime district where few people went and even fewer lived was a major challenge. Gothenburg City Council was determined to avoid the mistakes seen in the redevelopment of London's Docklands and determined instead to pursue a sustainable development model, balancing economic, environmental and social objectives. The key has been what is known as 'triple helix collaboration', with the public sector actively working in collaboration with industry – including major Swedish corporations such as Volvo and Skanska – and academia, particularly the Chalmers University of Technology as well as the University of Gothenburg.

Working together, they created a series of specialist science parks or 'innovation arenas': Lindholmen Science Park specializes in mobile internet, intelligent vehicles and transport systems, media and design; Sahlgrenska is an incubator largely for new medicine and life science businesses; and Johanneberg specialises in urban development, energy, materials and nanotechnology. New businesses moving into the parks become partners in the development with both responsibilities and a stake in how the area develops. The aim is that 5,000 people will be working in new high-quality jobs in industry, academia and the public sector within ten years.

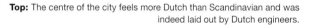

Below: Lilla Bommen is currently Gothenburg's tallest building and is known as the Lipstick. It was designed by Ralph Erskine in 1990 as the headquarters of the construction company Skanska.

Top: The centre of the city feels more Dutch than Scandinavian and was indeed laid out by Dutch engineers.

Above: The exhibition of the RiverCity plans for Gothenburg's former docks.

Below: Map of Gothenburg in 1888 by Ludvig Simon.

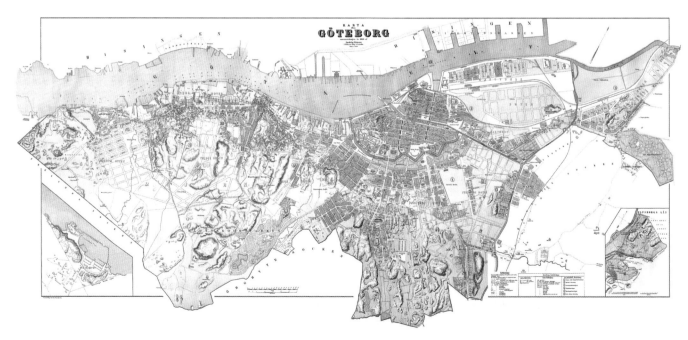

Just as happened in the early 20th century with shipbuilding, these new industries have brought a rise in the population. The city has the largest student population in Sweden and has experienced significant levels of immigration. Unusually for a Scandinavian country, this has led to social segregation, something that the city council recognises as one of its greatest challenges. Twenty years ago they developed Health Impact Assessments to assess the potential effects of planning decisions. More recent consultation has focused on dialogue with different groups, including making sure that the needs of children and young people are reflected in the city's plans and decision-making.

The city also feels a deep-seated responsibility to live sustainably. Walking and cycling are actively promoted with fully segregated cycle paths throughout the city. Gothenburg has been investing heavily in new public transport, funded, in part, by road pricing charges on private vehicles entering the city. Major improvements include a new cross-city rail link to complement the existing tram, bus and passenger ferry networks serving communities on both banks of the Göta. Increasingly, vehicles are being powered by renewable sources of fuel and pioneering work is being undertaken in the use of locally-produced biogas. Energy consumption is also being tackled in buildings through strict building standards and minimising the use of carbon in energy production, and much of the city is connected to municipally owned combined heat and power plants.

Above: The Academy assessment team.

So far, so Scandinavian. However, to understand what is distinctive about Gothenburg, you need to explore the streets and established neighbourhoods of the centre. As you do this, you realise that it feels like a Dutch rather than a Scandinavian city. It was founded at the start of the 17th century at the behest of the Swedish king, who needed a port with access to the Atlantic trade routes. Dutch engineers were engaged to drain the marshy land along the coast and such was their influence that for its early years the language and laws of the city were Dutch rather than Swedish. The historic neighbourhood of Haga, surrounded by a defensive ring of canals, has survived, with its wooden houses and cobbled street, making it a perfect candidate for reinvention as a boho district of tiny cafes and shops.

Beyond this lie relaxed, comfortable neighbour-

hoods such as the long streets off Linnégatån leading to the vast green lawns of Slottskogen, a landscaped urban park, busy with softball players on long summer evenings. Green space and flowers are a feature throughout the city. As for many other Swedish towns and cities, the conference trade (strictly adhering to its seasonal timetable, straight after the summer holidays when the schools go back) is another valuable source of business. New hotels are being built across the city, or carved out of existing buildings, like the 500-room Clarion Hotel next to the railway station in the former Post Office. Not surprisingly for a place with such a strong sense of place, Gothenburg is a growing tourist destination, although visitors have been coming to the historic amusement park Liseberg since 1923, mostly to ride on Balder, its famous wooden rollercoaster. A more recent attraction, both in the city and along the string of small islands of the Bohuslän coast to the north, is food – seafood in particular. In 2012 Gothenburg was named Food Capital of Sweden, and its tally of Michelin stars is steadily increasing. Apparently, the local fish grow slowly because of the icy waters and develop a superior flavour – something that could be an analogy for Gothenburg as a whole. One of the most famous restaurants is Sjömagasinet, in the former East India Company's dockside warehouse at Klippan. The wooden interior is a lavish reminder of the city's maritime heritage, furnished with chandeliers, oars and the occasional suspended model sailing ship.

All of this in a relatively small city of not many more than half a million people (twice that in the wider metropolitan area). This, however, is set to grow as the docks relocate westwards, opening up five square kilometres of land for development. RiverCity, as the project, is called will double the size of the city's core population. The masterplan, based on compact city principles, will knit the new and old cities together through public transport and water links. It is still early days but this is a project that dwarfs all of the other Scandinavian exemplar projects in Stockholm and Malmo that have been so influential across Europe. If RiverCity does what it plans to do, it will become one of the most significant urban regeneration projects in Europe.

This Scandinavian model can be chastening for those of us working in urban regeneration in the UK. There is an efficiency in the way that the Scandinavians develop their cities that seems to be entirely beyond British planners. This is partly based on the ability to control and direct a much larger proportion of locally raised taxation and partly to do with strong local leadership and planning powers. However, more than anything else it comes from having got things right in the past and enjoying the confidence of the public and politicians that the future will be just as successful.

Hamburg
Shortlisted 2013

Above: The port remains at the heart of Hamburg's economy.

Opposite right: The Elbe Philharmonic Hall under construction.

Table for two, or more. Table for four.
Table for everybody: that's Hamburg,
Your spoon shines in the German sun
As you plunge it in to your Aalsuppe

Or soup of everything, which is of course
A definition and distillation of Hamburg,
City where each day has barely begun
before the ideas start flowing, the questions:

Which gallery to visit, which theatre to go to,
Which square, which cafe? The essence of Hamburg
Is somewhere between pavement and sky,
The Harbour Promenade and this website provider,

Ancient and modern and inbetween flow to
The heart of the place, the centre of Hamburg
Which is here at this table, where ideas fly
In an Aalsuppe of thinking, where we're all insiders

In a Hamburg that's built with chutzpah and care,
I've booked your table in Hamburg. I'll see you there.

A large, incongruous shape looms over the city of Hamburg. Nicknamed by local people the Elphi, it seemed like a good idea at the time. It is one of those concepts that is easy enough to render in the architect's CGIs, and was greeted with great enthusiasm back in the mid 2000s, the days of the 'starchitect' and the belief that iconic buildings could revive whole cities. But now, ten years later, five years after the original opening date and at more than three times the original €241 million budget, the city is not so sure. The building is the Elbe Philharmonic Hall designed by the architects Herzog & de Meuron and perched on the roof of an old warehouse, Haispeicher A. It will be the tallest inhabited structure in the city, containing a hotel and apartments alongside the concert hall and is the centrepiece of the massive HafenCity regeneration area.

Maybe the looming presence of the Elphi is a reference to the castle built by the Emperor Charlemagne on a rocky outcrop amid the marshland of the lower Jutland Peninsular – which is how Hamburg got its name, 'Ham' meaning 'watermeadow' and 'Burg' meaning 'castle'. The castle that stood at the confluence of three rivers, the largest being the Elbe, was built to protect the Holy Roman Empire from the Vikings. It wasn't tremendously successful in this respect – the castle and the town being sacked and burned on numerous occasions.

It was in 1189 that Hamburg's fortunes changed when another Emperor, Frederick I, made it an Imperial Free City – a city state, answerable only to the Emperor. Indeed, for centuries Hamburg was a sovereign country and after the unification of Germany in 1871 it became one of the 16 states that make up the Federal Republic of Germany. Back in 1189 Imperial Free City status gave Hamburg exemption from taxes on trade and it quickly grew into the main port serving northern Europe. Over the next five centuries it played a central role in the Hanseatic League, a trading network of free cities stretching from Russia to London, that controlled the northern seas. The League may have started by co-operating to protect its ships and build lighthouses, but by the 14th century it was raising armies and challenging whole nation states, fighting wars against both Denmark and Holland. Eventually, the influence of the League waned in the 16th century and Hamburg's dominance was challenged by its great rival Rotterdam.

The trade flowing through Hamburg and its international port shaped the city. In the 1960s, when a certain pop group from Liverpool took up a residency in Hamburg's red light district, it had developed a reputation as a place with a seedy underbelly. As George Harrison of the Beatles said, 'the whole place was full of transvestites, prostitutes and gangsters'. It was exciting and

Left and below left: The Academy assessment team visiting the HafenCity InfoCenter at Kesselhaus.

Below and right: Views of the completed waterfront.

dangerous and in the early 1960s it represented freedom for many British young people. In fact its history was not unlike the Beatles' home town of Liverpool, an international port that had grown massively in the 19th century but had fallen on hard times. Both cities generated great wealth while also housing large working-class and immigrant communities. Immigrants today account for nearly 15% of Hamburg's population and are to be found in the diversity of the inner-city districts such as St Georg and St Pauli (where the Beatles played), which surround the more corporate city centre.

What is extraordinary is that both these inner-city districts along with the city centre had been destroyed only 17 years before the Beatles arrived. RAF bombing raids as part of Operation Gomorrah in 1943 created a firestorm that ripped through the centre of Hamburg, leaving 42,600 civilians dead. Subsequently, the city became part of the British Zone of occupation while much of its hinterland was absorbed into East Germany, a mere 30 miles away. The city's economy suffered as a result. Like the northern cities of the UK, Hamburg's gritty vitality at the time came as much from its post-industrial decline as it did from its wealth.

However, this is the second largest city in Germany with a catchment population of five million (the city population is 1.8 million). Its decline was never going to be as great as that of the cities of the UK or indeed those of East Germany. Its revival following the reunification of Germany has made it one of the richest cities in the world with a GDP per capita of €50,000, an 88% employment rate and 120,000 businesses. Its port has grown rapidly as markets in eastern Europe have opened up, and Hamburg now handles 134 million tonnes of trade

a year. To provide finance for shipping, the city developed a strong banking sector and is home to the Berenberg Bank, Germany's oldest bank. Alongside this it has retained a heavy industrial base including the shipbuilders Blohm & Voss and the one of the Airbus factories employing 13,000 people. The city's other great economic sector is the media, which employs over 70,000 and includes a number of television and radio stations, a large publishing industry and the national newspapers *De Spiegel* and *Die Zeit*.

Which brings us back to HafenCity. Many of the cities in this book have seen their older ports abandoned as new ports are built nearer the sea to handle larger vessels. This is happening in Oslo, Antwerp, Helsinki and indeed Manchester and Liverpool, but nowhere has this taken place on the scale of Hamburg. HafenCity is an area of 2.2 square kilometres full of canals, river channels and basins that is being redeveloped to accommodate 12,000 residents and 40,000 jobs. Work started in 2003 and the Dalmannkai/Sandtorkai neighbourhoods are now largely complete, along with the new U4 metro line and two new stations. The scheme has created a whole new business district for the city and has already become a centre for e-commerce.

HafenCity is characterised by solid seven-storey buildings of understated rather than iconic architectural quality. All very Hamburg, except, that is, for the Elbe Philharmonic Hall, which is very solid and Hamburg up to the seventh floor of the original warehouse but is then topped with 20 storeys of glass and steel. If it works, it will be the crowning glory of HafenCity and become the postcard image of Hamburg. If it doesn't, it is going to be an embarrassment that is very difficult to ignore!

Helsinki

Shortlisted for 2011

An elemental city, this: Fire and air,
Earth and water. Fire of a sunset
Over the rooftops, layer on layer
Of red on redder. Perfect subject
For a poem like this, a celebration
Of an elemental city: Water shining
In a necklace of islands, an incantation
In a sea-based language, a watery lining
On the sleeve of a city's fashionable coat,
City built on ancient earth, Helsinki soil;
And the air of excitement grabs at your throat
And simmers and bubbles and comes to the boil
In a city that's certainly most elementary:
Fiery and watery, airy and earthy...Helsinki!

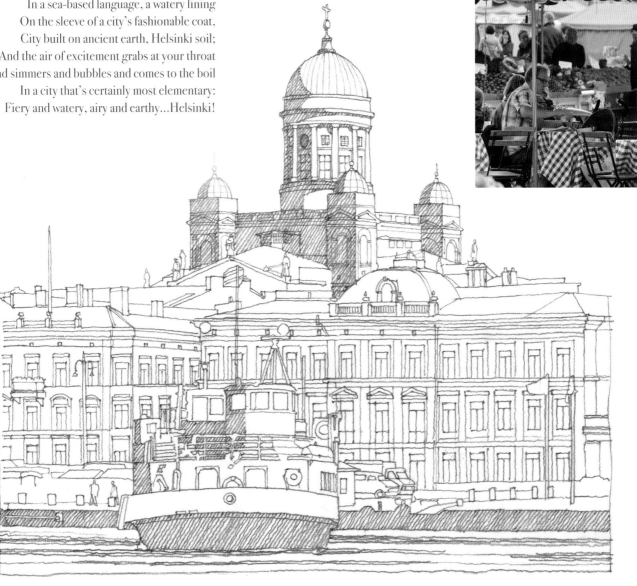

Vuosaari on the eastern edge of the conurbation, where it is co-located with the airport and well placed for trade with Russia. Within the city there are plans to grow the population by 100,000 over the next 20 years and about half of this will be achieved through the redevelopment of the city's old waterfront. Because of its star-like shape, Helsinki has an extraordinary 200 kilometres of waterfront and, now that the main port has moved out of the centre, much of this is available for development. Most of the remaining population growth will take place on infill sites with only a small amount being achieved through new urban extensions. However, even the latter will be served by the city's extensive public transport system, including plans for a metro extension to the west and a new ring railway line. Like many of the Scandinavian cities in this book, Helsinki exhibits a level of organisation and efficiency that can be bewildering to a British planner. This runs from the national scale where, we were told, Finland is more like a club than a country, to the municipality and through to neighbourhood planning.

Finland is a very new country, having been a province of Sweden until a pact between Napoleon and Alexander I saw it become a Russian Grand Dutchy in 1809. It was at this time that the rocky peninsular where Helsinki now stands was chosen as the location of the new capital, which was planned by the German-born architect Carl Ludvig Engel. Because of this, Helsinki does not have an old town; it is laid out as a logical grid with a very organised feel. This short history is reflected in the structure of the city, which is made up of large plots without the subdivisions that you find in really old places. As a result, the grain of the city can be rather coarse. The connection between an organised society and the organised city is encapsulated by the Senaatintori (Senate Square), which has the cathedral on one side and the Government Palace, city hall and university on the three other sides.

Finland became independent in 1917 in the turmoil of the Russian Revolution and the country suffered its own civil war in the years that followed. It was on the front line in the Second World War but when the war ended it played a canny game and avoided being absorbed into the Soviet Union. Helsinki is a city on the edge of Europe geographically and historically. Its history has seen it tugged between the East and the West and this is reflected in its character. Indeed, throughout the Cold War it was used by American film-makers when they

Academicians visiting Helsinki as part of the awards assessment visit could not help harbouring certain feelings of jealousy towards its city planners. Here is a city that can make plans and see them built. A city where two thirds of the land and virtually all of the development land is owned by the city council. Where planners can draw a grid of streets that the city builds. Where they can write rules for development that are implemented because the sites are leased (not sold) to developers. Through the ownership of schools, social services, the public transport system and even the energy company, the city can ensure that the tram is extended into new neighbourhoods, that there is provision of services and that the energy consumption is minimised.

And Helsinki is a city with big plans. The city region, which consists of four municipalities, is reshaping itself into a city able to compete on a world stage. The vision started with an international architectural competition and sought to exploit Helsinki's role as a bridge between Europe and Russia. A fast rail link is being built to St. Petersburg and Helsinki has recently relocated its port to

You can see why British planners might be jealous. But with the envy came a slight unease

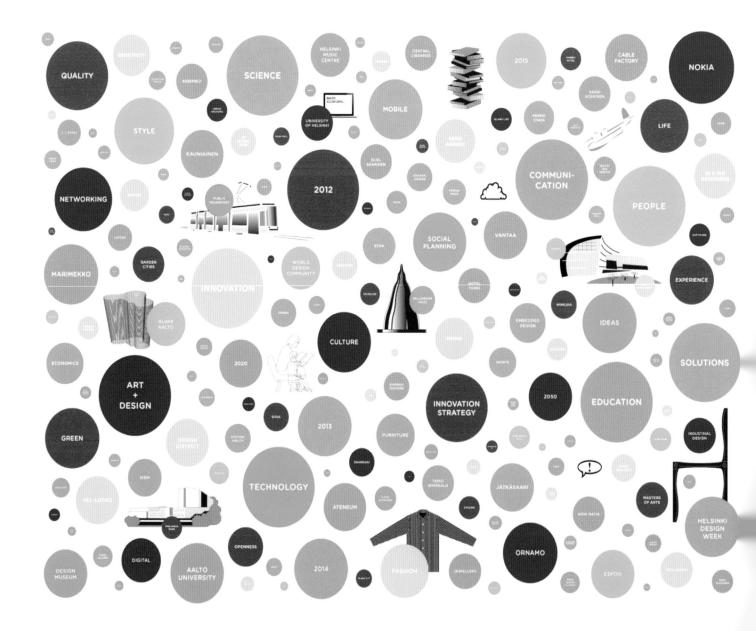

wanted to film Russia and by Russian film-makers when they wanted to film America.

Finland did, however, become reliant on trade with the Soviet Union and its economy came close to collapse after the fall of the Berlin Wall in 1989. The speed with which it managed to recover from this and the way it promoted knowledge and innovation to achieve this is still seen as a model for economic development. Its recovery was helped in no small measure when Nokia, already Finland's largest company with interests in logging and engineering developed the first mobile phone. This development began when the Finnish army asked the company to modify a system that Nokia were already using to communicate with distant logging operations. Once the wider implications were understood, Nokia and Finland found themselves in at the very beginning of the mobile revolution and have become global players as a result.

Today Helsinki's strategy is to promote economic growth through education, quality of life, innovation and internationalisation through the EU and links with Russia and the Far East. The policy is based on a triple helix of the public and private sectors and the universities. Indeed, 43% of adults in Helsinki have a university degree and its seven universities have 90,000 students. There is a strong focus on creativity with the new Aalto University, which brings together three colleges and focuses on art and design. The Academy assessment team visited the Cable Factory, a huge building where Nokia once made transatlantic telephone cables, which is now home to some 250 creative companies and, of course, is also owned by

the city. In 2012, the year of the city's bicentennial, Helsinki was World Design Capital, following in the steps of Turin and Seoul.

To have the chance to plan on such a scale! You can see why British planners might be jealous. But with the envy came a slight unease. The new neighbourhoods we visited were beautifully planned and designed but perhaps lacked a little soul. To be honest, the same was true of the city centre, which was subdued compared to many other European capitals. Finns are a reserved people and the climate for much of the year is such that life goes on indoors. There was also a slight unease when we discussed engagement. We met HELKA – the Helsinki Confederation of Community Associations – also funded by the city. They described an active network of community associations who, through the Finnish system, are responsible for the management of their housing blocks in both the public and private sectors. However, despite the presence of a public planning shop (Laituri), there seemed to be little public debate over the plans for the city. Finland is the country with the lowest level of corruption – according to the OECD – and there is a level of trust that means that the public assume that the authorities will act in their best interests. This is something that disappeared in the UK some time in the 1950s. As a result, Helsinki is the most civilised of places and always scores well on tables ranking the world's most liveable cities. It is clean and safe, well organised, beautifully designed and full of highly educated people – and only occassionally a little dull.

Opposite above: The masterplan prepared by the city for the Western Harbour.

Opposite below: A representation of the design community in Helsinki developed for its year as World Design Capital.

Below: The redevelopment of the former Arabia pottery works to create a new urban extension including the Aalto University School of Arts, Design and Architecture.

Lisbon
Winner 2012

Seven hills, they say, seven viewpoints
From which to see this place grow and
change.

First hill: the Hill of History, of people
Building a city from stone, sea and air.

Second hill: the Hill of Singing; hear it
In the cadence of speaking, the word-dance.

Third hill: the Hill of Art; Capturing light
In a frame, movement in a sculpture.

Fourth hill: the Hill of Commerce; these shops
Are theatres, galleries, participatory sports.

Fifth hill: the Hill of Newness; Gulbenkian
thinking
And street art remaking itself every night.

Sixth Hill: The Hill of Continuity: sit at this cafe
And everyone who has ever sat here sits with
you.

Seventh Hill: The Hill of the Future: brighter
Than the reflecting sun on these walls, much
brighter.

Fado, a melancholic, mournful music, encapsulates the spirit of Lisbon. Passionate and haunting in equal measure, it tugs at your heartstrings, speaking of loss or what the Portuguese call 'saudade' or longing for what might have been. It speaks of Lisbon's rich and often tragic history, a story of untold wealth and wretched disasters in Europe's oldest and most westerly city.

Older than Rome, Lisbon was founded by the Phoenicians around 1200 BC. They were one of the first great Mediterranean civilisations known, amongst many other things, for inventing the alphabet, which they used to give Lisbon its name, which simply means 'safe harbour'. It may be on the western edge of Europe, but for the millennia when the only way to travel between the Mediterranean and the rest of Europe was by sea, the western coast of Europe from Ireland to Africa, was the world's main trade route. The first safe port outside the Strait of Gibraltar was therefore set to became the centre of the universe. Never was this more true than between the 15th and 17th centuries when explorers like Vasco da Gama opened trade routes to India and the Orient, importing spices to Europe. Soon after, sailors from Lisbon discovered Brazil, making it part of a growing empire with Lisbon at its centre, the richest city in the world.

Such riches can, of course, attract trouble, and Lisbon is a city that has been fought over for centuries. In

Rousseau incorporated Lisbon into his argument against cities in favour of a more natural way of life

1108 it was invaded by Norwegians, a fact that seems to make little sense until you realise that they were one of many waves of crusaders heading for the Holy Lands and Lisbon at the time was a Moorish (Muslim) city. By 1255 it had become the capital of the Portuguese Territory and soon after its university was established.

The most momentous event in its history happened on All Saints Day, 1 November 1755. Three monstrous earthquakes, closely followed by a fire and a tsunami, left close to 40,000 people dead and much of the city obliterated. The tsunami destroyed cities all around the Atlantic, and the earthquake was to change Europe in the Age of Enlightenment. Some saw it as a judgement on the city but struggled to explain why Alfama – a former Muslim neighbourhood, turned red light district – had survived. Voltaire used it to argue against the idea that there is a benevolent god, while Rousseau incorporated Lisbon into his argument against cities in favour of a more natural way of life.

A month after the disaster Manuel da Maia, supervised by the Marquês de Pombal, presented the king with five options for reconstruction. The first

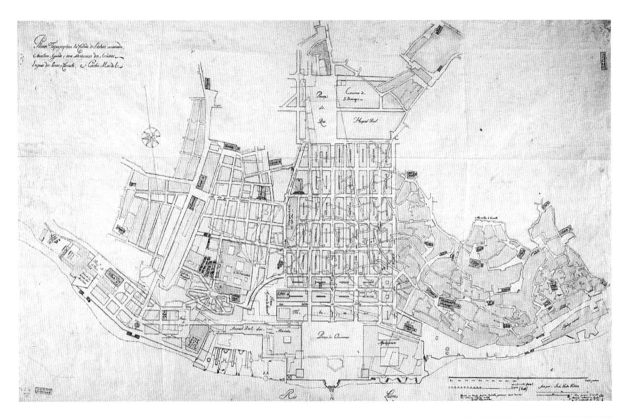

Top: The masterplan for the rebuilding of Lisbon after the 1755 earthquake by Eugénio dos Santos and Carlos Mardel.

Above: One of the miradouro, or lookout points, that top the city's hills.

Right: Much of the life of the city takes place on the street.

relocated the city to a new site and the second rebuilt it as it had existed. Two further options reconfigured the plan and widened streets while the last option cleared the site and started afresh with a new grid of wide squares and avenues. The king opted for this last plan and within a year the rebuilding had commenced. The area – known as the Baixa Pombalina, after the Marquês – included the world's first earthquake-proof buildings based on prefabricated frames attached to wooden stakes driven deep into the unstable ground which, became known as the Pombaline style.

Lisbon's recent history has been no less traumatic with the 20th century seeing two coups d'état. The first in 1926 heralded a period of persecution and dictatorship as Antonio Salazar – first as Finance Minister and then Prime Minister – led an economic revival but at a terrible cost, through censorship, force and terror. The second in 1974 brought the regime to an end in a bloodless coup that was known as the Revolution of the Carnations.

Lisbon has emerged from its long history as a captivating city; chilled-out with a faded, fin-de-siècle charm. Its grid of streets provides teasing glimpses over the River Tagus, which imbues the city with a distinctive light, an effect magnified by the reflections from the azulejos, the ornately tiled houses that can still be found in Alfama. On each of the city's hills miradouro, or lookout points, provide a breather after the steep climb with the reward of grandstand views across the rooftops. Very old (and very new) trams rattle improbably through the tight streets, either side of which locals perch meditatively, watching the world go by or simply ignoring it. It's that sort of city.

In recent years Lisbon, along with the rest of Portugal, has suffered greatly through the global recession. The city's mayor, Antonio Costa, has needed to be creative in finding ways to enhance the city while retaining its distinct character. The strategy is based on a 'city of neighbourhoods' including a unique form of localism. Perhaps as a reaction to the country's authoritarian past, this involves a new structure of government, decentralising powers, responsibilities, service delivery and staff to parish level. These new structures include 'participative budgeting': devolving 5% of the city's capital budget to local groups, who are able to put forward and vote on city improvement projects. This is proving an effective mechanism for delivering locally driven improvements across the city and stimulating a higher level of participation and engagement.

The aim is to deliver 'a city for the future, a city for its people', the Lisbon Master Plan provides the 'top-down' spatial framework for this localism. It sets out seven strategic goals for the future development

of the city, which include reversing population loss, reducing congestion, connecting the city back to the river, encouraging green networks and enhancing the city's public realm. The population loss has seen more than 600,000 move out to the suburbs, commuting by car and causing chronic congestion and pollution. The response has been investment in trams, improved pedestrian networks and ambitious plans for a 161km network of cycleways. New green links are also being created, such as the ecological network linking the city's main parks to the Monsanto forest park, which acts as a green lung for the city.

The development of the port in the 19th century effectively separated the city from the water's edge, and as recently as 1994 the waterfront was designated as a port, despite the fact that much of it was no longer operational. The World Expo in 1998 broke the mould with the creation of Parque das Nações, a new residential neighbourhood together with a business district and oceanarium. The Champalimaud Centre, a state-of-the-art facility for science, medicine and technology, opened in the riverside area of Pedrouços in 2010, incorporating high-quality public spaces to encourage public use.

Much of Lisbon's life takes place on the street – in its squares, streets and spaces spilling out from the bars and restaurants – and the public realm is a key feature of Lisbon. The streets are carpeted in patterned black and white cobbles, known as the 'calçada portuguesa', which are a defining feature of the city. These historic patterned streets are being extended through an incremental approach to pedestrianisation engaging the parish councils and community groups through their devolved budgets. This is proving an effective way of achieving 'more with less' at a time of severe economic and financial stress.

Lisbon is not just a city for living in, it is a city that feels 'lived in'. The city has prospered despite its economic woes through the bottom-up involvement of the community and neighbourhoods. This mix of strife and hope can still be heard as the strains of fado permeate the city's streets.

Left: The calçada portuguesa, black and white paving that is characteristic of Lisbon.

Lyon

Shortlisted 2013

Convergence of two rivers:
They shine in mid-morning light
And reflect all the convergences of Lyon,
All the meetings, all the transformations.

World Heritage site and modern city,
Birthplace of film and a centre of silk,
And a tablecloth's unfurled in a restaurant
For the convergence of eater and lunch.

There's old town and new thinking,
And last time I was in Lyon I had a dream
Of a silk tablecloth held up in the clear air,
And someone was projecting a film on it,

A film of a great city, a meeting of rivers,
A convergence of ideas reflected in water.

Lyon's story is written on its walls. Back in the 1970s the city was 'industrial, polluted and sad' according to Halim Bensaïd, founder member of CitéCréation, a group of mural artists who have completed at least 60 large-scale works in the city. They were encouraged by the mayor at the time, Michel Noir, who was looking for a quick fix to start the transformation of the city. Some of the murals are trompe-l'œils, (painted facades on blank walls) and others are extraordinary flights of fancy, but some of the most powerful are those that reveal the history and identity of Lyon and its people. A good example is the États-Unis district, a social housing project designed in the 1920s by the Lyon-based urban visionary Tony Garnier. This had become a no-go area, but a project to create a series of murals of Garnier's original utopian drawings on the gable ends of each block has been transformational.

Lyon has perhaps always seen itself as independent, creative and a little bit different. France's second largest city is today the capital of the Rhône-Alpes region but was once the capital of the Roman province of Gaul. It is a city that is both a World Heritage site and a place of industry and trade. Its story, like those of many of the cities in this book, is one of ancient roots, industrial growth, post-industrial decline, bad planning and finally reinvention and renaissance. Every city's decline seems to follow a similar path but their renaissance is unique to them.

Lyon's path into decline was indeed one followed by many European cities in the latter part of the 20th century. Loss of traditional industries and the decline of its manufacturing base led to heavy population loss. This was compounded by some terrible planning decisions and poor-quality architecture in the 1970s and 1980s along with heavy-handed road engineering, particularly around Perrache Railway Station. The result was a city with widespread poverty and social exclusion, poor health, pollution and congestion. Lyon's approach to these all too typical problems has been anything but, perhaps defined by its history as a crucible for ideas, imagination and risk-taking through the centuries.

Lyon is sited at the confluence of two major rivers, the Rhône and the Saône. It was the birthplace of two Roman Emperors and has been at the epicentre of European trade for two millennia. It stands at the intersection of trade routes from northern Europe, the Mediterranean and Italy and further to the east across the Alps. Lyon was the first stop for Italian silk merchants trading with France, so when King Louis XI decided that France should develop its own silk industry as an alternative to the expensive Italian silks, Lyon was the obvious location. By the beginning of the 16th century Lyon had become the capital of the European silk trade. Thousands of silk workers – known as 'canuts' – flocked to the city and by the middle of the 17th century there were over 14,000 looms. The industry continued to grow through the early years of the Industrial Revolution but was hit hard by the silkworm epidemics that began in the early part of the 19th century and that saw the industry all but wiped out by its end.

Those same trade routes also shaped the city's culinary identity. Lyon became a mixing pot for foods and spices from across Europe while the abundant landscape around the city provided a diverse and enviable range of produce. Lyon developed its own distinctive cuisine, typified today by Paul Bocuse, one of the world's greatest chefs. The city's gastronomic life is centred on its main covered market, the place to go for anything from marron glacés to quenelles. Lyon has so many restaurants that you could eat in a different place every evening for ten years.

During the Second World War Lyon was a stronghold of the French Resistance group Libération Sud, fighting against the Nazi occupation under the regime of Klaus Barbie, known as the 'butcher of Lyon', The underground publication *Libération* became the most widely read resistance newspaper during the war

Above: The États-Unis district, designed in the 1920s by Tony Garnier, with a mural of one of his drawings.

Lyon has so many restaurants that you could eat in a different place every evening for ten years

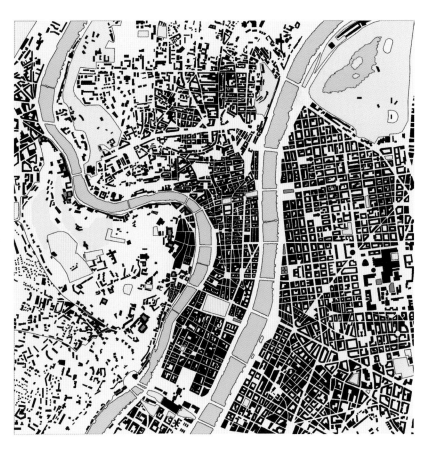

and inspired the national daily launched by Jean-Paul Sartre in 1973. A memorial to Jean Moulin, perhaps France's most revered Resistance fighter, has pride of place outside the town hall.

The years after the war, however, were not kind to the city and the regeneration efforts that started with the murals have grown into one of the most ambitious programmes anywhere in Europe. From the start the city decided that it was not just going to address its problems one by one but would look to the future to re-imagine what an attractive, liveable city should look like. This has been done through the Urban Agency, set up in the 1980s as part of a national strategy for regeneration across France. It has played a critical role in advising and providing leadership on city infrastructure and urbanism, public housing and cultural facilities. This is never easy in France, a country with a labyrinthine public sector. Agreeing plans in Lyon means seeking consensus across 37 separate public agencies, not to mention other communes and arondissements (including nine in Lyon itself). The city's achievement in building this consensus while retaining the clarity and ambition of its vision should not be underestimated.

One of the most ambitious projects is La Confluence, encompassing the regeneration of over 150 hectares of former docklands at the tip of La

Presqu'île, the island that sits between the city's two rivers. Beginning in 2003, and projected to continue until 2030, with a cost of €3 billion, the scheme aims to showcase the city of tomorrow. Led by a public–private company, SEM Lyon Confluence, the project combines the refurbishment of former docklands warehouses and the creation of new mixed-use neighbourhoods with new public spaces and landmark buildings. The former include the Place Nautique and Saône Park. The latter includes the extraordinary Musée des Confluences by the Austrian architects Coop Himmelb(l)au with collections covering natural science and anthropology. As with the Elbe Philharmonic Hall in Hamburg, the museum was an attempt to lead regeneration through iconic architecture that has run hugely over budget.

The masterplan for the peninsula is based on the importance of daylight to health and energy consumption. This has a lineage stretching back to

Tony Garnier, who set out his utopian vision for Une Cité Industrielle in 1904 with houses designed to maximise sun and wind so that they would be energy self-sufficient. In La Confluence, regulations ensure that even on the shortest day – 21 December – each home will have at least two hours of sunlight. This is part of a wider package of measures that has made the development France's first World Wildlife Fund Sustainable Neighbourhood and is part of plans to help Lyon peg its CO_2 emissions to the year 2000 levels by 2020.

More recently the focus has been to improve connections around Perrache Railway Station. Works have sought to repair the urban fabric by improving pedestrian connections, reducing levels and creating places to stop and linger, including a piazza at the front of the station. The embankments along the Saône, once dominated by major roads, have been developed as a linear park, providing natural habitats as well as footpaths to provide a pleasant link between the northern and southern halves of Lyon's central peninsula. Lyon's congestion issues have been tackled through a raft of transport improvements. The city now has a well-integrated, efficient public transport network of trams and trains including a direct high-speed airport link through the 'RhôneExpress'. It was also the first city in Europe to introduce a public bike hire schemes which is supported by clear, generous cycle routes and good signage.

Air pollution and quality of life is also being addressed through a major greening strategy. This includes the enhancement of existing parks and the creation of new parks and green spaces of all shapes and sizes. The latter range from the 80ha Parc de Gerland (complete with its botanical garden) and the reclaimed linear spaces along the city's two rivers, to smaller 'infill' spaces such as the proposed Parc Sergent Blandan and temporary community gardens in more densely-developed areas, which fulfil both a physical and a social function. City-wide policies on building materials and the colours of building facades, together with a lighting strategy, has helped to reinforce a sense of place, enhancing Lyon's already rich built heritage as well as making for a more pedestrian friendly experience.

All of these improvements create a setting for the life of the town. The city promotes an extensive programme of arts events and festivals drawing visitors throughout the year and culminating in the 'Fête des Lumières' held every December. This dates back to the Middle Ages but the modern festival uses light shows and lasers rather than candles. It is as good a symbol as any of the way that lyon uses its past to shape a dynamic future for itself.

Manchester
Shortlisted 2009

You hear this place before you see it; the noise and the buzz
Of a city brimming with self-belief,
A music that comes from laughter and football
And walking a certain way down Piccadilly.
Like this: the arms, the confidence.

You see this place before you hear it; as your plane touches down
Past the Manchester lights that glow with the knowledge
That this is a city that believes in itself
And a certain way of talking on the last tram home.
Like this: quip first, gag second, punchline after.

You live in this place like you live in your own skin:
It takes you over, you're a streetplan, a future entwined
With a past so they both show their best face
To a world that just has to bow to the inevitable:
Like this: we're here, just accept it, we're Manchester, Manchester!

It was 11.17am on a warm Saturday morning in June 1996 when the largest bomb to explode in England in peacetime went off, outside Marks & Spencer's in Manchester. The IRA had given a warning 90 minutes before and the authorities had cleared the area but 220 people were still injured and a large part of the city centre was destroyed. Not perhaps the prettiest part of the city centre. There was, it is true, extensive damage to the Victorian Corn Exchange and the Royal Exchange Theatre – which sits like a lunar landing pod inside what was once reputed to be the biggest room in the world – was knocked off its foundations. But otherwise the buildings that bore the brunt of the blast were concrete and not well liked, including the Arndale Centre and its hated magnolia-tiled facade. Early Monday morning the council swung into action, first with a clean-up, then with a masterplanning competition and then, within a few short years, a whole new city centre quarter. It was almost, so the joke went, as if the bomb had been commissioned as a demolition job. This was far from being the start of Manchester's renaissance, which had been going on for some years, but the city's reaction to the bomb illustrated to the world how far it had come, how effective it could be.

It was in 1835 that a French visitor to Manchester, Alexis de Tocqueville, wrote of the city: 'From this foul drain pure gold flows forth. Here it is that humanity achieves for itself both perfection and brutalisation, that civilisation produces its wonders, and that civilised man becomes again almost a savage.' Manchester was the shock city of its age, the first out-of-control mega city. We marvel today at the slums and barrios of the developing world's rapidly expanding cities but imagine when nothing like that had ever been seen before. In the early 19th century London and Paris were already huge cities but Manchester seemed to appear from nowhere – the world's first industrial city. Friedrich Engels, whose family owned a mill in Manchester, documented the results in his book *The Condition of the Working Class in England,* published in Leipzig in 1845, (but not in England until 1891). His friend Karl Marx, who was living in London at the time, was a regular visitor and the two worked together on the *Communist Manifesto* in Chetham's Library in Manchester.

In her book *The Economy of Cities*, Jane Jacobs has a chapter entitled 'Manchester Bad, Birmingham Good'. Writing at the end of the 1960s, she argued that Birmingham, the city of a thousand trades, with its tradition of lock and gun manufacture and jewellery-making was ideally placed for the modern age. It was a city full of small-scale entrepreneurs who understood innovation and therefore made the city the best location for the expanding car industry. Manchester, by contrast, was a city dominated by massive mills with large monolithic workforces. Excellent as incubators of political activism, supporters of football clubs and creators of working-class music and culture; hopeless as innovators and entrepreneurs. And, for the next 20 years, she was right. Manchester's industry went into steep decline as it lost its textile trade along with half of its population. By the mid 1980s the world's first industrial city had become the world's first collapsed city – the Detroit of its day. Not that Mancunians ever accepted this.

The irony is that it was the large monolithic workforces, soon to be the large monolithic unemployed (mixed with a huge student population) that confounded Jane Jacob's predictions. From the depths of Manchester's collapse came a music culture that would dominate the world through Madchester's Second Summer of Love in 1988. Manchester's

The city's reaction to the bomb illustrated to the world how far it had come, how effective it could be

Opposite: A reflection of the Hilton Tower (there is only one of them), designed by Simpson Haugh Architects and the tallest building in the city.

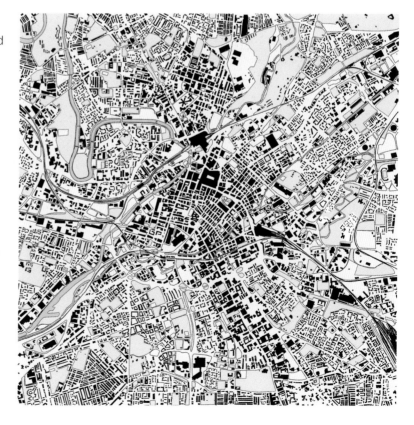

working-class culture, mixed with footballing success gave the city a swagger and attitude (think of George Best) that was captured in the city's music, from the Fall to the Smiths, the Happy Mondays to Oasis by way of the Stone Roses. This attitude was personified by the svengali of Manchester's music scene, Mr. Anthony H. Wilson (as he liked to be called), local TV personality, founder of the Factory and Hacienda clubs and owner of Factory Records, home to Joy Division and New Order. The city's arrogance, was captured perfectly on the T-Shirt with the slogan 'On the sixth day God created MANchester'. It also characterised the city's developers, from the late Carol Ainscow at Artisan to

Ask and of course Urban Splash. In a world obsessed with street culture, knowledge industry and creativity, it was Manchester's mix of working-class culture and academia, rather than Birmingham's artisan entrepreneurs, that won the day.

Between the censuses of 2001 and 2011 Manchester's population grew by almost 20%, which is astonishing for a city that had lost population for the previous four decades. It was in 1986 that the first city centre apartment was created in the converted Granby House. So uncertain was the market at the time that the heavily subsidised flats were sold for just £16,000 and very quickly appeared on the resale market for twice that. Other schemes were promoted nearby and within a few years the area became part of the Central Manchester Development Corporation. Unlike some of its peers, Manchester took the pragmatic decision to work with the Corporation that had been imposed by a government hostile to the council's politics. Over eight years it would transform the area from Castlefield in the west to Piccadilly in the east.

It was about this time that the city decided to bid for the 1996 Olympics (it bid again for the 2000 Games). However, when the city's leaders visited Barcelona (host of the 1992 Games), they were taken aback. Manchester had considered itself the equal of Barcelona but in terms of urbanity it wasn't in the same league. On returning to Manchester, they decided that the redevelopment of the Hulme district – a notorious housing estate next to the city centre – was an opportunity to create a more urban city. Heaven and earth were moved to adopt an urban design guide for Hulme in the face of fierce opposition. The guide covered issues like density, a mix of uses, permeable streets and building line and was not

particularly radical – within a few years the same issues would be contained in government guidance. But in Hulme it was opposed by the highway engineers, the housing associations, the police and many others. It was forced through with the backing of the council leadership, who went even further by saying that the Hulme Guide would apply to the whole of the city until such time as a Manchester Design Guide could be produced.

This fraught period in Hulme shaped the way that Manchester has developed ever since. The *Manchester Guide to Development* was published in 1997, by which time the IRA bomb had rocked the city. First in the redevelopment of the bomb-damaged area, which was to be called the Millennium Quarter, then in the redevelopment of other parts of the city, the urban principles were applied. Having not won the Olympics, Manchester played host to the 2002 Commonwealth Games and in preparation for this attention turned to the East Manchester regeneration area, where the Games facilities were built along with plans for 12,000 new homes. Since that time there has been a procession of major redevelopment schemes in the city: the New Islington Millennium Village, the redevelopment of Spinningfields along the river as a new business quarter, the development of a tram network that now stretches for 70 kilometres the Knowledge Capital and Oxford Road Corridor initiatives with the universities and in neighbouring Salford the Media City development – northern base for the BBC and Granada Television. These major projects, along with many other significant schemes, have transformed the city.

Behind this success lies political stability. Manchester's boundaries are so tightly drawn that the city doesn't include many of its suburbs. This makes it solidly Labour, so while all the other large English cities have changed political hands in recent years, Manchester has been in the same political hands with Sir Richard Leese being council leader since 1996 and deputy before that and Sir Howard Bernstein being chief executive since 1998 and deputy before then. This longevity and stability has allowed for the long-term planning that cities need.

Manchester's renaissance cannot be overstated; having been the world's first industrial city, it was also the first to implode in the post-industrial age and the first to show that rebirth is possible. Like Glasgow, it still doesn't quite match up to Barcelona or Milan, but it will get there and it won't be long. Its recent success has given it back its swagger. No, that's not true; its swagger never went away, it was what sustained the city in its darkest days and lies at the root of its recovery.

Above: Sir Richard Leese, who has led the city council since 1996.

Opposite top: The reopened Stretford Road running through the redeveloped Hulme.

Opposite centre: A view down Cross Street in the Victorian heart of the city.

Opposite bottom: Shop fronts in the Northern Quarter (see page 140).

Opposite bottom right: The Gay Village in Manchester during Pride Weekend www.clickclickbloom.co.uk.

NewcastleGateshead
Shortlisted 2009

Above: *The Angel of the North* by Anthony Gormley, commissioned by Gateshead Council, is perhaps the most well-known sculpture in the UK.

That Northern Angel welcomes you with open arms and smiles:
He's not wearing a shirt because this region's never cold.
He's standing halfway to the sky, can see for miles and miles
Just how this place renews itself by blending new and old;
From the Baltic to St James' Park, the Metro to the Sage
You can feel regeneration's pulse and hear renewal's heart.
The gorgeous Angel's calling in a brand new golden age
Driven by music, dance and story, fuelled by song and art.
A river splits these cities and yet gives them definition:
Take me walking by the Tyne and let me hear the future sing
In a strong north-eastern accent full of joy and erudition
That's taken heart from yesterday and knows tomorrow brings
A redefining of the centre, acknowledgement that today
Newcastle, Gateshead and the north's revival's here to stay!

Bridges are the key to understanding NewcastleGateshead, the hybrid city that straddles the gorge of the River Tyne, tied together by seven bridges that tell the story of its growth. As in London and Westminster, Buda and Pest or Manchester and Salford, Newcastle and Gateshead are two halves of a single city that have been separated by history and the draughtsmen of administrative boundaries. Newcastle was a Norman stronghold built by a southern king to subjugate the north. Gateshead was the lands of the Bishop of Durham, closely guarded from the coveting gaze of the burghers of the upstart city that wanted its coal. Both sides of the river industrialised based upon that coal, which was shipped down the coast to warm the backsides of London; it was said in the winter of 1642 that London froze because Parliamentary forces blockaded the Royalist Tyne. The ships that carried the coal were built locally, developing into the shipbuilding industry, while the ballast of sand and ore that came back in the ships gave rise to the glass and iron industries that would build the bridges and locomotives (designed by George and Robert Stephenson) that would drive the Industrial Revolution. This can all be read in the bridges spanning between Newcastle and Gateshead.

Today NewcastleGateshead is at the heart of a city of around 750,000 people along the banks of the Tyne. It is a city that has reinvented itself following the decline of its heavy industrial base and it is now a major centre for offices and retailing, and its nightlife was ranked by TripAdvisor as the third best in Europe behind London and Berlin.

The original name for the settlement was Pons Aelius, 'Pons' meaning 'bridge' and 'Aelius' being the family name of the Emperor Hadrian. The Romans built a bridge over the Tyne where the northern end of Ermine Street that ran south to civilisation (see Steep Hill, Lincoln page 194) met the eastern end of Hadrian's Wall. The wall actually ended a few miles to the east in the Newcastle suburb of Wallsend. The derivation of the name 'Gateshead' means 'the head of the Roman road'. However, despite having the bridge and a fort, the settlement on either side of the river was little more than a village. It remained as such during the great Kingdom of Northumbria and the flowering of civilisation emanating from nearby Lindisfarne. The 'new castle' was built by the Normans on the rocky outcrop that had been used by the Romans. They had been having a great deal of trouble with the north, suffering a number of defeats and setbacks and facing invasion by the Danes and the Scots. They would take their revenge through the 'Harrying of the North' 1068–70, the nearest that England has seen to genocide, in which 100,000 people died. Newcastle was one of the strongholds from which this atrocity was perpetrated. It was a place of fear built to subjugate the local people and it was further fortified in 1172 when the stone keep that still stands was constructed.

It was the Normans that built the second bridge over the Tyne and in the centuries that followed merchants were attracted by the bridge and to the protection offered by the fort so that a town started to grow. By 1265 walls had been built around the town and it became an important border stronghold in the wars with the Scots that would continue for the next four centuries.

NewcastleGateshead may not be quite as poetic as Budapest but the joint billing has allowed both to thrive

Above and left: The bridges of Newcastle create some of the most dramatic urban scenery in the UK.

Opposite above: An early engraving of the High Level Bridge, designed by Robert Stephenson.

Opposite below right: The Millennium Bridge by Wilkinson Eyre with the Baltic Gallery in the background.

Indeed, it is said that the name 'Geordie' applied to the people of Newcastle comes from the city's role in repelling the Jacobite Rebellions against George I in the 1700s. Long before this, Newcastle had grown into a city of some 10,000 people and was a major centre for trade in wool and coal, a centre of religion and a seat of learning. Its bridge, having been rebuilt on a number of occasions, was now lined with houses, three towers and a chapel.

A disastrous flood in 1771 swept this bridge away and it was replaced with a stone bridge. However, the real problem was the steep winding streets squeezed between huddled buildings that led from either end of the bridge. The solution came in 1849 when the High Level Bridge, designed by Robert Stephenson, was opened. This was an engineering marvel, a bow-string girder bridge more than 26 metres above the high watermark that carried both the road and the new railway line high over the gorge. A few years later the low level bridge was replaced by the Swing Bridge, opened in 1876. This was funded by William Armstrong, who owned the Elswick arms factory. Using technology that he had developed to pivot large cannon, the bridge was the largest swing bridge in the world and allowed ships to reach the western part of the river (and his factory) for the first time. He would soon expand his business so that rather than just arming ships he started building them and would become one of the main shipbuilders on the Tyne.

The Tyne Bridge, designed by Mott, Hay & Anderson Engineers (now Mott MacDonald) has become the iconic bridge across the Tyne. It was opened in 1925 when the city was perhaps at the height of its powers. It had grown into a northern industrial powerhouse based upon heavy engineering, shipbuilding, glass and ceramics. It had also grown to dominate its surroundings, including the more impoverished Gateshead. By the 1960s, under its charismatic council leader T. Dan Smith, the city set out to transform itself into the 'Brasilia of the North'. The planning department became the most important

part of the council and set about clearing the city's slums, building extraordinary multi-level road systems and clearing 'outdated' parts of the city centre (see Grey Street page 174). Gateshead joined in with enthusiasm, sacrificing its town centre to elevated road schemes and the *Get Carter Car Park*, otherwise known as the Trinity Square scheme, a Brutalist shopping centre and multi-storey car park on the most prominent site in the town, with a restaurant on its top floor that was never occupied. The vacant unit was however used in a scene from the icon 1960s film 'Get Carter' staring Michael Caine.

Meanwhile, down in the gorge the riverside wharves had fallen into disuse and dereliction. This brings us to the final bridge in the NewcastleGateshead story. The Millennium Bridge, opened in 2001 and designed by Wilkinson Eyre Architects, completed the drama of the bridges of the Tyne. It was built as part of the NewcastleGateshead Quayside regeneration that has taken place over the last two decades. The Quayside won the Great Place award in the Academy of Urbanism's second year and is written up in the Academy Book *Urban Identity*. It has once more shifted the focus of the city to the riverside, which has become the cultural heart of the city. The key developments include the Sage Gateshead, a concert hall and music venue that opened in 2004 and is home to the Royal Northern Sinfonia. Further down the quayside is the Baltic Centre for Contemporary Art, opened in 2002 in a former flour mill. This has grown into one of the most important contemporary arts spaces in the UK and hosted the Turner Prize in 2011, when the exhibition attracted more visitors than it does in London. Both of these institutions are in Gateshead and have for the first time in 2,000 years of history given Gateshead claim to equal billing with its upstart neighbour. So henceforth Gateshead will no longer be subsumed as a district of its neighbouring city like Westminster or Salford but, like Buda and Pest, will become one place. NewcastleGateshead may not be quite as poetic as Budapest but the joint billing has allowed both to thrive.

Oslo
Shortlisted 2012

Take a deep breath, here in the city's shining centre;
Breathe deeply, deeper. Deeper.
They say that when you breathe you're breathing in
Tiny particles of history. Deeper.

So somewhere in the centre of this shining city
Your deep breath mingles with the breath of kings
And poets and the makers of the Sagas.
And the others who made this city a great one,

Built from the words of Ibsen, and the long proximity
Of water, built from Edvard Munch,
Built from the House of Literature
And the long proximity of sky. Deeper, breathe deeper

The air of a city that survives and prospers,
The air of a city like no other.

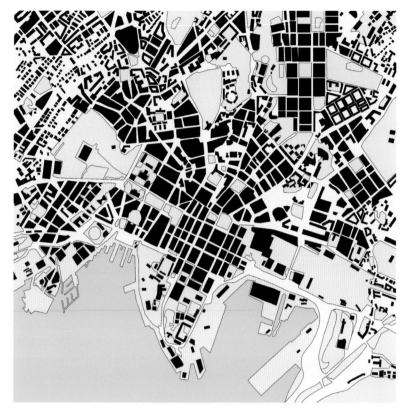

Which European city is the second most expensive in the world, after Tokyo? Which is the fastest growing, having seen its population rise by 2% a year for the last 15 years? The answer to both of these questions is to be found at the northern end of a long fjord from which the Norwegians have dominated the seas for 1,000 years. Today Oslo continues to dominate the seas, although this is no longer by means of the longboats that can be seen preserved in its Viking ship museum. Today the shipping registry Norske Veritas, based in the city, is responsible for 16.5% of the world's shipping and Oslo is home to some of the world's largest shipping companies and maritime insurers.

Arriving in Oslo by boat today, the fruits of this prosperity and growth are impossible to ignore. The first thing that you see is the Opera House, completed in 2008. This is a huge cultural facility, home to the Norwegian National Opera and Ballet and with three auditoriums, the largest seating 1,300. It was designed by Oslo's homegrown 'starchitects' Snøhetta following an international competition in 2003. Behind the Opera, lining up along the waterfront, stand a row of further 'iconic' buildings known as the Barcode Project. This too is the result of a competition for the development of the former docklands that previously stood isolated between the railway lines and the water. A project to tunnel the main road into the city opened up the area for development and another competition was organised in 2003, which was won by the local practice Dark Architecture, working with the Rotterdam Architects

The city that grew up on the land below the castle became known as Oslo – or 'meadow at the foot of the hill'

MVRDV. It is a project that has divided opinion locally. Developed by a partnership between the state, a private developer and the national railway company, it was designed to accommodate the rapid growth of the city while preserving the character of the old town and protecting the city's greenery. The buildings have been occupied by international companies including PricewaterhouseCoopers and Deloitte, along with 500 'champagne apartments' (to use the description of one of the scheme's critics) linked at ground-floor by a mall full of designer boutiques. In a survey by the local paper *Aftenposten*, 71% of the local population opposed the project and 30,000 people signed a petition opposing the scheme. It is seen by some as cutting the city off from its waterfront and casting long shadows from the low Nordic sun on the surrounding neighbourhoods. The scheme raises issues that are common to many of the cities described in this book: how to manage growth, how to balance conservation with 'iconic' architecture and how to recognise iconic architecture that is going to have a lasting value and not look an embarrassment in ten year's time.

Oslo has a pretty good track record in this respect. Its city hall is recognised as one of the finest modern buildings of the 20th century. Designed by Arnstein Arneberg and Magnus Poulsson, this too was the result of a competition, although in a less prosperous age it took many years to complete. The original competition was run in 1918 with building starting in 1931, only to be disrupted by the war, so that it wasn't completed until 1950. The building is best known today as the setting for the Nobel Peace Prize ceremony. Alfred Nobel was a Swedish industrialist and arms manufacturer who created the prizes that bear his name in his will after his death in 1896. He specified that the Peace Prize should be administered by Norway to be given to the person who has 'done the most or the best work for fraternity between nations, for the abolition or reduction of standing armies and for the holding and promotion of peace congresses'. The Nobel Committee is appointed by the Norwegian government and The Peace Prize is awarded on 10 December each year.

It is speculated that Nobel asked for the Peace Prize to be administered by Norway because of the country's track record in mediation and peace keeping (unlike the more warlike Sweden). Oslo's history has, however, not always been so peaceful. As we saw on page 45, Lisbon was conquered by a Norwegian army in 1108 who were en route to the Holy Lands as part of the Crusades. They did not, however, come from Oslo because, according to the Norse Sagas, it was only founded in 1049 by King Harald Hardrada. For those of you who remember your history, he was the Viking king who invaded England in 1066 to be defeated (and killed) by the English King Harold at the Battle of Stamford Bridge a few weeks before the English were themselves defeated by the invading Normans at the Battle of Hastings. Askerhus Castle above Oslo was built at about this time and the city that grew up on the land below the castle became known as Oslo – or 'meadow at the foot of the hill'.

The town grew rapidly and by 1300 had become the capital, even if it did have a problem with fire. Apparently, the city was destroyed by fire 14 times until at last in 1624 the king ordered that it be relocated and laid out on a more orderly plan. The city was renamed Christiania and grew to become a major commercial and artistic centre. The old town is still called Christiania and is laid out on its original grid. The name Oslo was not reinstated until 1925.

Today Oslo is a city of around a million people set within a metropolitan area of around 1.5 million. Its population growth is fuelled by strong inward migration and it has become a diverse multicultural city. Much of the migration has taken place in the eastern parts of the city. Many cities have a cultural divide between their east and west ends but in Oslo this is particularly pronounced. The eastern part of the city is working class, multi-cultural and left-leaning in its politics while the western end is middle class and conservative. The two halves of the city speak different dialects and rarely mix. There is, as one might expect, ongoing debate about the extent to which the people of the east are able to participate in the city's prosperity. There is concern about the cost of living, which is higher even than London or Paris, and the development pressures that result from this growth. However, this city of 40 islands and 343 lakes on the northern edge of Europe is clearly doing something right.

Valencia
Shortlisted 2010

A beach at sunset. A tall drink in a morning cafe. A song
That echoes in your mind long after that song has ended.
I'm just trying to define Valencia: solitude and throng,
Silence and music, elements transformed and blended
In the Spanish air, a Mediterranean way of thinking
Formed by the years and moulded like wind moulds a wall,
Changes a building subtly. Back in the cafe, I'm drinking
In the view and the sounds and synthesising it all
Into Valencia: leisure, culture, surefooted confidence
In the past and the future, in yesterday and today,
And walking down to the beach I find it all makes sense,
Valencia sense, Valencia understanding, and I have to say
As I pay and leave my table and wander down the street
Valencia is the kind of place that makes your life complete!

Great cities hate to be upstaged, so imagine how Valencia felt in 1992 when it was forced to watch other Spanish cities enjoy worldwide attention and garner both plaudits and tourists: Barcelona hosted the Summer Olympics and reminded the world of Gaudi with that backdrop to the diving; capital Madrid enjoyed the year-long festival that goes with the mantle of European Capital of Culture; and Seville hosted the World Expo and hogged the architectural magazines. It was a chastening experience for Valencia, Spain's third largest city. But sometimes with adversity comes determination. Stung into action under the leadership of long-term mayor Rita Barbera Nolla, the city embarked on an ambitious programme of transformation to put itself firmly back onto the world stage.

The strategy was a mix of major projects, events and investment in local neighbourhood facilities. The most visible symbol of the strategy was the development of the City of Arts and Sciences, a surreal series of buildings on a vacant site along the River Turia. Designed by local 'starchitect' Santiago

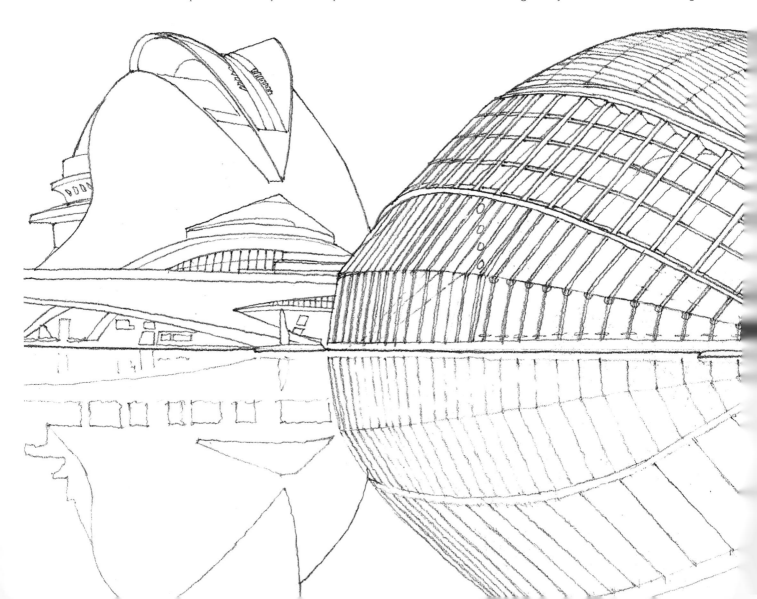

Calatrava, the complex includes an IMAX theatre, science museum, aquarium, opera house, exhibition area and gardens, creating a new series of attractions for the city as well as some iconic buildings for its postcards. Indeed, Calatrava's distinctive forms, sparkling in the strong Mediterranean light, have recast the image of Valencia.

Crises of identity are nothing new for Valencia. Established by the Romans in the 2nd century BC on the eastern coast of the Iberian Peninsula, the city has long fought for its language and culture in the face of successive occupations by Christians and Moors. As a busy port Valencia has been a meeting point of cultures and religions from across the Mediterranean. It was in 1238 that the Kingdom of Valencia was created when the Moors occupying the city were defeated by King James I of the neighbouring Kingdom of Aragon. He established the new kingdom with himself as king, creating a charter, a new government and a new language. However, he retained its diverse population, continuing a tradition of tolerance. Just as Christians had been allowed to practise their religion under the Moors, so the Muslims were allowed to continue under

Calatrava's distinctive forms, sparkling in the strong Mediterranean light, have recast the image of Valencia

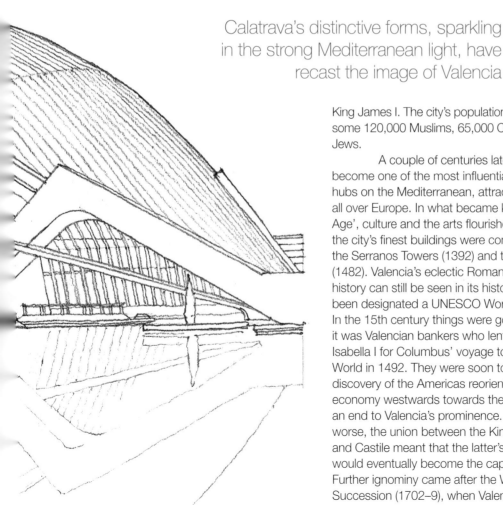

King James I. The city's population at the time included some 120,000 Muslims, 65,000 Christians and 2,000 Jews.

A couple of centuries later Valencia had become one of the most influential cities and trading hubs on the Mediterranean, attracting merchants from all over Europe. In what became known as its 'Golden Age', culture and the arts flourished, and many of the city's finest buildings were constructed, such as the Serranos Towers (1392) and the Silk Exchange (1482). Valencia's eclectic Roman, Moorish and Gothic history can still be seen in its historic core, which has been designated a UNESCO World Heritage Site. In the 15th century things were going so well, that it was Valencian bankers who lent funds to Queen Isabella I for Columbus' voyage to discover the New World in 1492. They were soon to regret this as the discovery of the Americas reoriented the European economy westwards towards the Atlantic, putting an end to Valencia's prominence. To make matters worse, the union between the Kingdoms of Aragon and Castile meant that the latter's capital, Madrid, would eventually become the capital of a united Spain. Further ignominy came after the War of Spanish Succession (1702–9), when Valencia was punished for

Opposite top: Valencia in 1870, showing the river before its course was diverted following the Great Flood of 1950.

Opposite below and left: Views of the city taken on the Academy assessment visit.

supporting Charles of Austria, leading to the abolition of the city's charter and a long period of arms' length occupation and rule from Madrid.

It wasn't until the second half of the 19th century that Valencia began to thrive once more with the revival of local traditions and the Valencian language. Its identity was threatened once again after the Civil War when the Franco regime prohibited the speaking or teaching of Valencian. However, with the restoration of democracy, the ancient Kingdom of Valencia became a new autonomous entity, the Valencian Community. Today the Valencian language must be taught in every school and the city's identity, which has endured such a turbulent history, comes to life every March with Las Fallas. This five-day-long celebration follows the creation and eventual destruction of gigantic ninot – papier mâché puppets that communities spend the entire year building only to see them go up in smoke in a cacophony of firecrackers at midnight on the last day of the festival. October sees yet more pyrotechnics celebrating James I's liberation of the city and founding the kingdom, a festival that also honours the patron saint of love and sees young lovers offer each other sweets or macarons wrapped in handkerchiefs.

A defining moment in Valencia's recent history happened in October 1957. The rains that year were heavy and the River Turia, usually a dusty stream, burst its banks, killing 81 people and causing widespread destruction and displacement of population. In the reconstruction that followed the river was diverted into a flood channel around the city, while the former river bed was transformed into a 9 kilometre linear park.

The disaster was a warning to a city that became an early pioneer of environmental planning. Attempts to limit its growth were not, however, particularly successful and Valencia is now part of a conurbation of two million people in a region where, despite occasional floods, water is very scarce. Sustainable development has become central to the city's agenda and one of the most effective measures

is the protection of landscape corridors that allow the cool sea air to permeate into the centre of the city and promote natural cooling. The city has also promoted local food production, as might be expected from the birthplace of paella, where eating and drinking is such a big part of local culture. The city's position on a fertile coastal plain provides Valencia with a bewildering supply of fresh produce that is displayed in local markets. To protect this food production, a series of natural parks and environmental protection areas have been designated, safeguarding the small-scale market gardens or 'huertas' that support these traditional farming and fishing communities. Initiatives have also been developed to reduce car use. The city has a comprehensive and integrated metro and tram system serving both the city centre and surrounding districts. Despite the heat, efforts to increased the use of the bicycle have been very successful with the introduction of an urban cycle scheme and a network of cycle routes that now totals 125 kilometres.

The bold strategy to transform the city that had its genesis in 1992 is paying off. The City of Arts and Sciences complex attracts around two million visitors a year and has become a backdrop for any number of television advertisements and fashion shoots. In 2007 Valencia became the first European city to host the Americas Cup yacht race. The recession may have checked progress but the underlying trend remains positive, an important recent step being the completion of the high-speed rail service, connecting Valencia to the rest of Spain.

Many cities have undertaken 'grand projets'. What has made Valencia under Mayor Nolla's leadership has been the way the city has balanced these architectural statements with local initiatives. The planning system has been used to provide social housing and neighbourhood community facilities, particularly in the provision of community sports and leisure facilities. Using local land law, Valencia has identified new development areas and prepared integrated management plans to require private landowners and developments to provide both social housing and community facilities. This includes using compulsory purchase powers to tackle the multiplicity of ownerships and a competitive process for selecting development partners.

Valencia is an inspiring story of city leadership, the link between destination and place-making, and the role of grand projets in urban planning and city regeneration. Rather than relying on a single approach, Valencia has sought to deliver a co-ordinated approach that improves the lives of its inhabitants, responds to the city's unique environmental pressures and delivers some memorable buildings that will leave a lasting legacy.

Towns

As an Academy we can sometimes fall into the trap of thinking that the truest form of urbanism is to be found in cities – the larger the city, the more intense the urbanism. The implication can be that towns have a slightly watered-down form of urbanism, less intense and less exciting. The 15 towns described in the following pages thoroughly disprove this point. They might not fizz with the street life, hustle and bustle and go-getting energy of the cities described in the first section of this book, but they are no less urban. They have a distinctive form of urbanity, one based on friends and neighbours rather than the anonymity of strangers. An urbanism in which people of all classes and incomes mix and relate to each other, as opposed to the social stratification of big cities. An urbanism that stems from continuity and tradition rather than vitality and constant change. It may seem a small thing, but there is a very special sense of community in a place with just one secondary school; where each generation went to school together. They may not know or like each other very much but they at least have a shared history regardless of their background. As part of the Academy of Urbanism assessment visits we have been to many towns where these special bonds still exist despite the pressure from incomers. The best towns are the smallest scale at which urbanism can exist, while also being the largest scale of settlement that operate as single communities. This is the magic of a good town and when it works it can create very special places that survive and thrive for centuries. Over that time, as the towns in this book illustrate, they have faced many challenges: from invading armies to traffic congestion, from the Black Death to edge-of-town supermarkets, from the Enclosure Acts to further invasions of retired people. The question is can towns weather the modern challenges as effectively as they did the historical ones?

The 15 towns in this book include 12 from England, three from Ireland and just Stirling from Scotland. Despite their geographical spread, it is striking when writing their stories how similar they are. A number date back to the Romans; in Chester and Chichester we have two of the most important settlements in Roman Britain and in Stirling we have one of their most northerly outposts. By the early Middle Ages most of the towns had been established, Westport and Falmouth being the exceptions. This was a time of war and our towns were mostly defensive places fortified by the Saxons as places of refuge from invaders (usually Vikings). Then in 1066 the Norman Conquest swept across the country and changed everything. Many of the towns have castles that were built by the Normans, not to defend the town but to subdue it. Their influence reached as far as Galway, where the whole town was fortified to subdue the surrounding lands. The Normans also built the great cathedrals and monasteries that can still be found in many of these towns and, while the Norman lords may initially have been resented, with the help of their castles they ushered in an era of peace in which many of our towns thrived. Then in 1536 Henry VIII set in motion the Dissolution of the Monasteries which had a catastrophic effect on many English towns. Some, like Chester and Shrewsbury, were given the chance to convert their monastery into a cathedral (an offer that Shrewsbury politely declined). Others, like Bury St Edmunds, gained their freedom from the rule of the abbot but also lost their economic role and never quite recovered.

The three Irish towns have a different history. Derry~Londonderry and Galway were, in different ways, colonial outposts, the former being Norman and the latter being founded as part of the 'Plantation' of Ireland by English and Scots Protestants. Meanwhile, Westport was built at the behest of an English landowner because the old town was spoiling his view.

For centuries the towns in this book were among the most important places in the British Isles. They were bigger, more powerful and more prosperous than many of the places that would later grow to become great cities. Towns were centres of administration, religion and commerce (all three of which were closely intertwined) and were the highest form of urbanism to be found outside the capital cities. This is why in the English language the word town, has very urban conurbations — as in 'downtown' 'painting the town red' or 'townhouse'. Then came the other great event that was to change towns: the Industrial Revolution. Initially, a number of our towns became industrial centres. Shrewsbury built the world's first iron-framed building as a flax mill and Stroud and Hebden Bridge became important textile centres. This was based on a ready supply of wool, fast-flowing watercourses for power and good connections (by packhorse, at least). However, all of these towns were left behind in the wake of the explosive growth of the industrial cities. Towns with well-established local governance often sought to resist industrialisation, unlike smaller places like Manchester. However, many of the towns were just in the wrong place, isolated from good transport connections or hemmed in by steep valleys, with little room to expand.

Since the Industrial Revolution the towns of the British Isles have changed beyond recognition. Those within the ambit of one of the great cities have been subsumed and industrialised and few of these now feature on lists of great towns. Most of the towns in this book were far enough away from the large cities to retain their identity and economic role. Yet, while this distance may have provided some protection, it also brought with it the risk of becoming a backwater. The towns that have thrived tended to be market towns that have for centuries served not just their own population but also a much wider agricultural (or maritime) catchment area. They have provided marketplaces, services, administration and social life for rural communities much larger than the population of the town. In this, they have created a new form of urbanism away from the big cities. In the long-running BBC radio soap opera *The Archers*, the residents of the village of Ambridge look to the nearby town of Borchester when they want to go shopping, go to the bank, meet in a wine bar or have an illicit affair. From the perspective of the village, the local market town retains a sense of escape and excitement even if it is dismissed as a provincial backwater from the perspective of the city. This is the niche carved out by many of the towns in this book, which has allowed them to thrive despite being surrounded by giants. It is, however, a niche that is increasingly under pressure.

Britain has a lot of towns. They are spread across the land each around a day's walk from the next. This was the natural state of things when farm labourers needed to be able to walk to market and back in a day. It meant that each town held a virtual monopoly on trade within this catchment area. This economic equation was first challenged by the Enclosure movement from the 1760s, which saw agricultural labourers pushed off their land, many of whom migrated to the large cities, reducing the catchment population around towns. Then from the 1840s with the railways, and in the 20th century with mass car ownership, it became possible to travel much further and back in a day. Suddenly, towns found themselves struggling to compete with much larger places. Some, like Scarborough, turned this to their advantage by attracting tourists. Others found their economic role undermined as the ring road that they had fought so hard to build ended up allowing people who once visited to bypass the town on their way to attractions elsewhere. In an age when 40% of young people go to university, towns have also seen an exodus of their brightest school-leavers, most never to return.

They find themselves competing in a global market in which cherished local employers become minor subsidiaries of international corporations and in which the turnover of their entire high street can be eclipsed by a single supermarket built on a roundabout on that bloody ring road.

But all is not lost. As the 15 towns described in the following pages demonstrate, there is new life in these old towns. Well, 14 towns demonstrate this – not everywhere can have a world-class university like Cambridge. The ways in which these towns have reinvented themselves varies but there are some common themes. In most cases the trick has been to attract new people and spending power from one of three sources: retirees, visitors and commuters.

The last of these has been seen as a threat by many towns who fear that they will become dormitory settlements in the commuter belt, pushing up house prices and squeezing out local people. This can be a problem, especially within the ambit of London. However, elsewhere commuters have reinvigorated the economy of places like Hebden Bridge, Richmond and Skipton (which features in the Streets section). Indeed, the towns of Lancashire and Yorkshire can often be divided into those with good rail connections to a large city, which are doing well, and those without, which are struggling. What these commuter towns are doing is importing wealth from the big cities to be spent in the local economy. This can have negative consequences such as rising house prices and chi-chi shops taking over the high street, but it can also be a force for good.

The visitor economy can have a similar effect. Clearly, there are places like Scarborough that have lived and died by their visitor economy for much of their history. However, many of the towns benefit from visitors. They come to visit the cathedrals and castles but they linger because of the attractions of the high street and the chance to eat in a good restaurant. It is, again, a means by which towns can import wealth to support their economy.

Then there are the people who come to make their home in towns beyond the commuter belt. Many of these will be retired and, in an ageing society, this group is a powerful force that towns can tap into. Retired people are attracted by the historic environments and a quieter way of life. However, they bring with them skills, experience and energy. Many can expect up to 20 years of active life post retirement and these active retired people have invigorated the communities of many towns by volunteering time, fundraising, serving on committees and being elected to town councils. One of the best examples is Ludlow, the winner of the Academy's first Great Town award in 2006. This was a declining backwater too remote for commuters but has been completely transformed by an influx of retired professionals.

However, not all incomers are commuters or retirees. Places like Falmouth, Stroud, Hebden Bridge and Totnes have attracted younger incomers, people seeking alternative lifestyles and wanting to live in like-minded communities. They have invested their savings in new businesses and put their children into local schools. This is not something seen in all of the towns, but it is significant because it is a reversal of a trend that has seen population, particularly young people, move away from towns.

The towns described in the following pages have each addressed these issues. They show the potential for reinvention as well as the problems that can arise. Incomers can so easily undermine that special form of community and urbanism that is found in the town rather than the city. There is always a risk that the new people unwittingly alter the very thing that attracted them about living in or visiting the town in the first place. Successful towns are those that manage to absorb these new people and benefit from the resources that they bring while remaining true to themselves. No one likes a pastiche of a town; authenticity is the thing, and a town that can fake that has got it made.

Bury St Edmunds

Shortlisted 2012

Great stories, they say, have a narrative arc
And yet they should fit in a nutshell;
Be accessible as the best public gardens,
As spacious as a cathedral:

You see what I did there? I cleverly put
Places from Bury in this little verse
To distil the essence of Bury St Edmunds
That shining coin in Suffolk's purse!

The Nutshell: smallest pub on the globe
The Arc: a 21st-century mall
Breathe in the air at the fine Abbey Gardens
The cathedral delights and enthralls.

You see what they did there? They cleverly
showed
Ancient and modern can both rub along
So let's raise our voices to Bury St Edmunds,
In a medieval plainchant and a popular song!

Bury St Edmunds, or Bury as it is known, is a town of 35,000. Today it is a prosperous place sitting midway between Ipswich and Cambridge, but still a difficult commute into London. It is an eclectic mix of ancient abbey town, Regency spa and modern industrial centre, brewing Greene King Beer and refining the sugar beet grown on the surrounding farmland.

Some say that the town got its name as a description of an actual event; it was where King Edmund of East Anglia was buried after his body was recovered following the battle against the 'Great Heathens' (the Vikings) in 879. However, as with Shrewsbury, the 'bury' is just the Saxon word for 'town'. Edmund was killed after refusing to renounce Christianity and in the century after his death a cult grew up around his martyrdom, leading to his canonisation (at one point becoming the patron saint of England). His burial place became an important shrine and the abbey was built around it, and the town built around that, growing to become one of the most important centres for pilgrimage in Christendom.

The abbey was rebuilt by King Canute in 1020 following his conversion to Christianity. He was a Viking who became king of England, Denmark and Norway – The legend of him commanding the waves was meant as a demonstration that a king's power is nothing compared to that of God. He offered his crown at the shrine of St Edmund to atone for the sins of his Viking forebears. The abbey and the town became rich, both as a centre of power and as a shrine attracting thousands of pilgrims with all the merchandising that went with it. William the

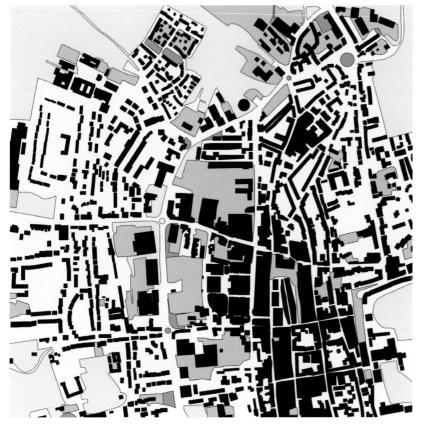

Conqueror appointed the French Abbot Baldwin – one of his personal physicians and a man of great influence – to oversee the monastery. He set about a further round of rebuilding and is also credited with planning large parts of the town. Indeed, the abbey and the town were indistinguishable; a visitor in 1538 wrote 'A man who saw the abbey would say it was a city, so many gates, so many towers and a most stately church'. The Dissolution of the Monasteries therefore had a profound effect. The townspeople finally gained their freedom from the abbot and set about appropriating the abbey buildings for their own use – church, hospital, school etc. Bury, however, would never regain its past glories. It was no longer a place of pilgrimage although in the Georgian period it bolstered its tourism trade as a spa town. The Regency architecture that survives today, such as the Theatre Royal and the Athenaeum, provides an interesting counterpoint to the 10th-century medieval street pattern devised by Abbot Baldwin, which combine to give the town its unique character.

Today, like many towns in the south-east England, Bury St Edmunds is struggling to balance the preservation of its heritage and the desires of

'A man who saw the abbey would say it was a city, so many gates, so many towers and a most stately church'

its population to keep things as they are with the pressures for growth. The council has worked with the Prince's Foundation to develop a vision for the town based on the idea of 'One town made up of many villages'. This encompasses both the town's existing neighbourhoods and the new housing that it needs to accommodate. The vision seeks to build 'tomorrow's heritage' by requiring the highest design quality for all new development. This is reflected in the improvements that have been made to the town centre, where there has been an emphasis on encouraging street life, with a simple yet effective combination of strategies: pavements have been widened and clutter removed; street markets have been encouraged and empty space above shops has been brought back into use as living accommodation. This has helped link the old town to a major new retail scheme built on the former cattle market. Now called the 'Arc', this open shopping mall is anchored by a new Debenhams and includes retailing and housing as well as a performance venue. The town may no longer attract pilgrims, but it remains somewhere worth visiting; a town that understands its rich history but that equally hasn't been afraid to try something different and reinvent itself.

Cambridge

Shortlisted 2010

Place of thinking and talking and writing
City of reading and punting and gazing
The day's stimulating, the night is exciting,
The morning is thoughtful, the evening's amazing!
Take me on the water down the River Cam,
Take me on a guided tour around the city streets;
Cambridge is for everyone, you don't need an exam
To make a visit to Cambridge complete!
Some cities, blessed like this one with history everywhere,
lazy and just celebrate the past
Cambridge mixes everything with chutzpah and with flair
And Cambridge's vista is vast!
growing, transforming, zeitgeisty and pretty
That jewel of the flatlands they call Cambridge city!

Handsome, historic Cambridge with its bridges and chapels, punts and professors: it might look like an East Anglian market town, minding its own business, but when that business is world-class research and innovation, it is clearly playing in a very different league. Linking both tradition and innovation is the university. On the one hand, it is the driving force behind the 'Cambridge Phenomenon', the town's explosive growth in the knowledge economy around the edge of the town. On the other hand is the conservatism and land ownership of the university's colleges that has ensured that the town centre remains unquestionably beautiful. But Cambridge is 'town' as well as 'gown', King's Hedges as well as King's Parade. It is a place with poorer neighbourhoods and suburbs as well as huge pressures for growth across an area that stretches much further than the Backs, the science parks or even the necklace of pretty villages round about. With average houses prices at around nine times average incomes, there is a danger of Cambridge becoming even more of a two-tier town.

Managing such growth pressures would be challenging enough, but tightly drawn city Council boundaries mean planning responsibilities are split, with much of the growth happening in neighbouring areas within the remit of South Cambridgeshire District Council. A collaborative

Cambridge

DWH '09

approach was needed, and it has been the innovative ways of planning that have been developed by the authorities, as much as the huge appeal of the town itself, that really make Cambridge stand out. Both the university and the city recognised the challenge early on and in the late 1990s established a partnership called Cambridge Futures to investigate different growth scenarios. A political consensus emerged in favour of an ambitious but carefully managed growth strategy whereby the wider county would grow in a planned way, with housing supporting economic growth, matched by infrastructure. Northstowe, in the South Cambridgeshire District area, was identified as a new settlement along with a series of major urban extensions in the green belt, some of which straddled administrative boundaries.

The process was based around building 73,000 new homes with £4 billion of infrastructure spending, including a guided bus system. To help secure the highest quality, principles were set out in the *Cambridgeshire Quality Charter for Growth* with themes of Connectivity, Community, Character and Climate, and a crosscutting theme of Collaboration. Cambridgeshire Horizons, an independent not-for-profit delivery body, was set up with financial support from the government to bring the authorities together through a range of partnerships and capital funding. Even with all of this, progress has sometimes been slow, especially in Northstowe, where the owners of key sites have frustrated progress. An important requirement of the new neighbourhoods is that they be accessible to people at all income levels. Choice and affordability could, however, suffer if growth isn't matched by further investment in sustainable transport. The redevelopment and expansion of Cambridge's central shopping development has made this even more of a regional shopping hub, and alternatives to the car, such as the guided bus system, have become more important than ever.

But despite these challenges, few places offer more scope for tapping into local knowledge and expertise and applying it to solve problems like reducing congestion and carbon emissions. There has been a lively debate on the merits of following London's example by introducing congestion charging. With its low rainfall and generally high levels of sun and wind, Cambridgeshire could also demonstrate the feasibility of zero-carbon housing. Judged by British standards, what has been achieved so far has been a huge success, both in terms of attracting investment and delivering high-quality developments such as Accordia, the 2008 Stirling Prize winner (see page 116). Cambridge already has some exceptional cultural

facilities, including the Fitzwilliam Museum and Kettles Yard, a tradition of world-class music-making, from the college choirs to the renowned Cambridge Folk Festival, and large open green spaces near the heart of town. This quality of life is critical because Cambridge is no longer just competing against regional centres such as Peterborough or Norwich; other world-class universities and cities are also trying to attract and retain the same top talent. And at just 50 miles north east of London, Cambridge is an easy commute to the capital. This market town knows it is in a competitive world marketplace. Like many successful places, it has recognised that partnership and planning will be more fruitful than politicking.

Above: With its large student population, Cambridge is one of the few British towns that can compete with Denmark for levels of cycling.

Few places offer more scope for tapping into local knowledge and expertise and applying it to solve problems like reducing congestion and carbon emissions

Chester

Shortlisted 2010

Above: Chester's half-timbered buildings with their first floor 'Rows' or walkways were designed in the 19th century by the architect John Douglas.

If you want plenty of future, lashings of past
And a present that's glowing with promises
Here's to a location that's growing so fast
With modern and old Roman premises!
It's a town built with class on the banks of the Dee
Like all riverside places, it rocks!
The stone where you're standing dates back to BC!
Look left and you'll see working locks
On the Cheshire canal; on a bright summer's day
You can understand Chester's longevity:
A mixture of beauty, and learning and style
Of nous, gravitas and felicity...
And if you don't believe me then you're best ter
Get on the next express to Chester!

Many towns include the word 'chester' in their name. All of them were founded as fortified Roman towns, which is what 'chester' means. But the fact that there is only one place that is just called Chester says something about how important it was to the Romans. Chester was the camp of Legio II Adiutrix – 'Legio' meaning 'Roman Legion'. They pitched camp in AD 79, setting out their accommodation around four streets – Eastgate, Northgate, Watergate and Bridgegate – surrounded by a wall. Two thousand years later these elements still form the street plan of the city. The camp was to grow into the largest fortified military settlement in Britain with an amphitheatre just outside the city walls that could seat 10,000. This has led some historians to speculate that Chester had been intended as the capital of the Roman province of Britannia, rather than London. The history of the UK could have been very different had that alternative history unfolded.

After the Romans left in AD 400, the history of Chester mirrors that of many other towns in this book. The church that would become the cathedral was founded in 907 by Ethelfelda, daughter of King Alfred. It was largely rebuilt by the Normans after their

occupation of the town. They persuaded Abbot Anselm to come from Normandy to found the cathedral and monastery. The monastery was dissolved by Henry VIII but, after a clever piece of politicking, the abbot and monks managed to retain their positions by turning it into an Anglican cathedral and assuming the positions of dean and canons.

Walking through Chester today, around the top of its walls, down its streets of half-timbered 'Elizabethan' buildings and along its medieval Rows, you might think you were in the perfect historic city. Chester Renaissance, the not-for-profit company set up to promote the city, aims to make it a 'must-see' destination on the European tour, alongside the medieval towns of Germany and the hill towns of Tuscany. Indeed Chester has been identified as one of north-west England's four 'attack brands' capable of attracting international tourism to the region.

But all is not quite as it seems. The black and white, half-timbered buildings that are so much part of Chester's character date from the late 19th century rather than the 1500s. They are a product of the Gothic Revival that swept through Victorian England at the height of the Industrial Revolution. A society terrified by the pace of technological change and degradation of urban areas sought refuge in an earlier arcadia of English Gothic architecture. This was introduced to Chester by the

architect Thomas Mainwaring Penson, who built a half-timbered shop in Eastgate in 1850. However, its main exponent was John Douglas, a local architect who became the favourite of the Duke of Westminster. This was a good move business-wise because, in addition to Mayfair in London, the Duke owned Eaton Hall near Chester and with it most of the town, including the cathedral. Douglas went on to design many important buildings in Chester, including the Grosvenor Hotel and City Baths, in an ever more exuberant, some might say eclectic, style and became particularly well known for his trademark twisted brick chimney stacks.

These Victorian buildings did, however, retain a feature that is unique to Chester: the Rows. These are raised walkways set within the buildings down each of the town's four principal streets. Their origins are unclear but it is speculated that the timber medieval town was built on top of the retained stone ground floors of the Roman city, creating a pedestrian circuit for shops to trade above the mud of the street. It is a building form much evoked by the developers of modern shopping malls but never successfully recreated. Very few of the original Row buildings survive in the city but the walkways have been incorporated into Victorian and more recent structures, a good example of Chester's approach to conservation.

Today we take for granted the conservation of towns like Chester, but it wasn't always the case. Back in the 1960s historic cities were felt to be in need of modernisation, while architecture like Douglas' was seen as cheap Victorian pastiche. In 1967 the Ministry of Housing and Local Government responded to concerns about the destruction of our heritage by promoting the Civic Amenities Act that introduced the idea of Conservation Areas. They also commissioned four town studies for York, Chichester, Bath and Chester. The Chester study, undertaken by Donald Insall and published as *A Study in Conservation*, becoming one of the formative documents of the conservation movement. As Insall said, 'conservation is for marmalade', arguing that cities like Chester should not be set in aspic but must be allowed to grow and develop while retaining their character. This approach has not only transformed Chester but has also created an ethos for the whole heritage and conservation movement in the UK. It has meant that Chester has prospered while remaining true to its Victorian idea of what a medieval city with Roman roots should look like.

> Chester has prospered while remaining true to its Victorian idea of what a medieval city with Roman roots should look like.

Chichester

Shortlisted 2009

Look behind me, hear the Romans talking
And the Saxons laughing and as I'm walking
By the cathedral
You can hear medieval voices singing this song!

Look around you, feel the glow of history
Get close to this city's eternal mystery;
Beauty's defined
As you hear divine voices singing this song!

The city's walls keep nothing in except a sense of tradition
The city's walls let ideas seep through: call it innovation!
This mix of old and new is hard to pull off, it's really tricky!
But this place has succeeded in a way that's really
Chichestery!
The Festival Theatre and the galleries and the shops are
Places that define this city, the throbbing heart of Chichester!

Look around now, take in a heart that beats
Across several hundred years of West Sussex streets
Chichester's living
Chichester's showing us the future so sing along!

Chichester is also a Roman town. Like Chester its streets were laid out by the Romans, in this case when they established the city as a beachhead after their invasion in AD 43. From its gates, roads were built to London and to the north and the city, then called Noviomagnus Reginorium, became their regional capital with a forum and fine baths. However, Chichester's finest feature, the one that dominates the plain between the South Downs and the sea, is the spire of its cathedral. The great cathedral was built 1,000 years after the Romans. Construction was started by the Saxons and completed by the Normans in a mix of Gothic and Norman architecture. It has dominated the city ever since, both architecturally and socially; it was said that so large was the cathedral compared to the city, that the entire population could attend a service. The cathedral's most dominant feature, its tower, is not as old as the main building. It was first built in the 14th century and was repaired by Christopher Wren in the 17th century, but then collapsed in 1861. The current spire was designed by Sir George Gilbert Scott, a few feet taller than the original.

The town plan is, however, Roman, as can be seen by visitors walking the city walls (which were rebuilt for show in the Georgian period). The cruciform of lively Roman streets, simply called North, South, East and West, contrasts with the relative calm of the historic quadrants in between: the Pallants, Little London, St Martins and the Cathedral precinct. While suburbs have been built around the old city in recent years, it retains its compact legibility and its flat terrain makes it a very walkable small city.

In the planning of the town nothing has been allowed to compete with the spire. The river's flood plain and designated Areas of Outstanding Natural Beauty limit the scope for outward expansion, creating pressures to increase densities. However the planners have maintained a height limit of four domestic storeys and imposed an approach to design that may have been a little reactionary. There is now a recognition that this led to too much historical pastiche, and the planners are now more confident with contemporary design, as can be seen by a number of recent housing schemes and cultural buildings. This confidence is also expressed in the design of new spaces like Eastgate Square and New Town Square, with their simple designs and quality materials.

The city is home to the world-renowned Chichester Festival Theatre, founded by Laurence Olivier as a forerunner to the National Theatre. The festival season runs from April to September and attracts thousands of people to performances at the theatre and in a variety of indoor and outdoor venues. The Novium Museum, opened in 2012, displays remains of the

Roman baths, while the Pallant House Gallery, behind its distinctive 'dodo' gateposts, houses one of the best collections of 20th-century modern art and won the 2007 Gulbenkian Prize for museums and galleries. The University of Chichester and Chichester College add a lively student population into the mix and the area's creative economy has been fuelled by the South Coast Design Forum, chaired by Wayne Hemingway.

A twice-monthly farmers' market enlivens the central pedestrianised streets and has introduced independent food retailers as an antidote to the dominance of fashion retailing and national chains. The mix of culture and shops, and proximity to the South Downs and the coast, as well as the Goodwood racetrack, make the town a desirable place to visit and to live. The number of retirees has created challenges, with an ageing population and house prices that are 20% higher than the south-east average. The council has responded by promoting mixed-tenure developments, the largest being a 750-home zero-carbon development on the site of the former Graylingwell Mental Hospital through the agency of a Community Development Trust.

The environment was rated as the best thing about living in Chichester in a survey by MORI. The district's Biodiversity Action Plan aims to improve parks (each of which has a local friends group), adapt to climate change and create green corridors. Peregrines have nested in the cathedral and the skies are full of swifts encouraged by the council through the inclusion of nest boxes in its buildings.

As with many towns in this book, people use words like 'unique', 'lovely' and 'beautiful' to describe Chichester. It attracts people, often in their retirement, who bring with them skills and experience, creating an articulate, engaged community. The city may have grown beyond the point where everyone can fit into the cathedral, but the community is keen to preserve its intimacy and human scale. As one resident told MORI; 'a nice friendly place with a sense of ease' a place where 'people come and never go back'.

> So large was the cathedral compared to the city, that the entire population could attend a service

Derry~Londonderry

Winner 2012

Left: The view into Derry~Londonderry up Shipquay Street leading through the city walls from the river.

Let's consider the walls of this walled city
And what they keep in and what they keep out:
They keep in a feeling that this is a place
Where you know every face, reflect every smile.
They keep out the people who just shake their heads,
Say 'Derry's not ready, Derry's not right'
and we know that they're talking... detritus!

Let's consider the fact that Derry's to be the City
of Culture! Stand on the walls and shout it out:
This is a poetic place, a dancing, an arty place
Place with a history as wide as the smile
Of greeting you get here, the nods of the heads
That say 'Derry's arrived!' and 'Derry's just right!'
And forget all those who just chunter... detritus!

Veteran broadcaster Gerry Anderson, known to his friends as Gerry-LondonGerry, ran a programme on Radio Ulster for a number of years called *Stroke City* – referring to the '~' between the city's two names. Because Derry-Londonderry is a city that can't decide what it is called. The majority of the Catholic/Nationalist community call it Derry, the place where the civil rights movement started. The majority of the Protestant/Unionists call it Londonderry and venerate it as the home of the Apprentice Boys who saved the city in 1688. The use of one name or the other is therefore a political act.

Before the 1960s the Londonderry name had, in reality, largely fallen out of use. That was before the 'Troubles' when 'Free Derry' became the centre for the civil rights movement in Northern Ireland, a response to discrimination against the Catholic population. Widespread protests came to a head on 30 January 1972 with the Battle of Bogside on what became infamous as Bloody Sunday. British soldiers shot 26 unarmed civilians, 14 of whom died, during rioting in Derry's Bogside neighbourhood. The Troubles were to scar Northern Ireland and indeed the whole

of the UK for the next 25 years as Derry-Londonderry once more became a fortified town with ugly army watchtowers built on top of its original city walls.

Those walls have given the city yet another name, 'Maiden City' (since they were never violated). It is one of only three European cities with an intact city wall. The walls date from the rebuilding of the city in 1608, which was done with financial backing from the Livery Companies of London, in recognition of which the city was renamed Londonderry in 1613. The fortification was part of the Plantation of Ireland, the settlement of its 'unpopulated' northern province by English and Scottish Protestants. The residents of this unpopulated region were not best pleased and the resulting conflict rumbled on for decades. The defining moment came in December 1688 when a Catholic regiment marched on Londonderry and the town was saved by 13 apprentice boys who raised the alarm and barred the gates. The army of King James II laid siege to the city for 105 days during which time half of the population were to starve. The barring of the gates and the lifting of the siege have become the two most important dates in the calendar of Northern Ireland's Protestant community, with 231 Apprentice Boys Marches each year marking both the barring of the gates in December and the lifting of the siege in July/August.

Between this ancient conflict and the more recent Troubles Derry-Londonderry was a prosperous place. Economic growth was based on trade from its port on the River Foyle and textiles as the city became known for shirt-making. Austin's, which still stands on the main square, is reputed to be the oldest department store in the world, having opened in 1830. The town also provided the main administrative centre for the north-west of Ireland, including County Donegal which, of course, became part of another country following partition in 1920. Derry-Londonderry grew to become the second largest city in Northern Ireland and the fourth city on the island of Ireland, with a city population of 100,000, and a catchment population of 350,000.

This prosperity suffered as tensions rose through the 20th century, but particularly in the 1970s and 1980s, as the city became embroiled in the death and destruction of the Troubles. Sitting in the cafe of Austin's on the main square in the 1980s and early 1990s could be a surreal experience as people went about their daily lives, while heavily armed British soldiers patrolled the same pavements, taking cover behind street furniture as they would in any other war zone. The conflict permeated everyone's lives and the physical effect is evident in historic buildings lost and the poor design of some of their replacements.

As is often the case, it was at the city's low point that the seeds of its recovery were planted

Left: The Academy assessment team being shown bomb damage in the city centre.

Above: Austin's on the main square is reputed to be the oldest department store in the world.

Below: The view down Shipquay Street.

Opposite: A view of the town from the eastern bank of the river.

As is often the case, it was at the city's low point that the seeds of its recovery were planted. It was in 1981 that Paddy Doherty started the Derry Inner City Trust with the intention of buying buildings that had been damaged by bombing or had fallen into dereliction. Using unemployed young people, these buildings were refurbished and put to community use, creating new shops and business space and low-cost housing. It is because of the trust that there remains a tradition of living over the shop in the city centre. The work of the Inner City Trust continues but, does not have the profile that it did in the 1980s. Then it was held up as the best and certainly the bravest example of community-led regeneration in the UK, inspiring many other building preservation trusts to emulate the model.

Adversity tends to work like this; it breeds resilience and creates opportunities for people to try something new. In Derry~Londonderry it cemented a society of tight-knit extended families and communities known for their ready warmth and quick wit. It forged politicians like the Nobel Peace Prize winner John Hume and the Deputy First Minister of Northern Ireland Martin McGuinness. It created authors like Seamus Deane, Jennifer Johnston and, of course, Seamus Heaney. It also nurtured a lively counterculture and music scene personified by the band the Undertones. This cultural resilience not only helped the people of Derry~Londonderry to survive the Troubles, it also laid the foundation for the city's recovery once peace had been secured.

The symbol of this culture-led recovery was Derry~Londonderry's designation as UK's first City of Culture for 2013. The year saw the city host a huge range of cultural events in theatre, music and film, symbolically marking the city's rebirth. As Ed Vulliamy wrote in the *Observer* newspaper; 'beneath the surface of cultural prestige, the resounding achievement of Derry's year as City of Culture lies in the way it not only refused to airbrush the Troubles and Bloody Sunday with arty-farty gloss, but engaged in a reckoning with the recent past'. This

renaissance of the city has also included the opening of a pedestrian crossing, the Peace Bridge, over the River Foyle and new cultural institutions like the Millennium Forum and included the recovery of the city's economy based in part on the digital economy and a high-capacity transatlantic IT link that has encouraged US companies like Seagate to base themselves there.

The city's regeneration strategy is set out in Derry City Council's *One City, One Plan, One Vote* regeneration initiative, which includes a vision of 'a competitive, connected, creative and caring city'. The council has been particularly innovative in its involvement of young people, creating a new post of Children and Young People's Co-ordinator to help embed the rights of children and young people in strategic planning, policy and decision-making arrangements at a local level. The strategy has seen the ongoing restoration of the city centre and the extension of development across the Peace Bridge to the Ebrington Barracks. This was an American naval base during the war but more recently was the home of the British Army and was therefore off-limits for most of the population. The new bridge has opened this up as an emergent new quarter for the city with housing, workspace and leisure facilities.

One of the ongoing frustrations lies in the higher education sector. The city's promotional literature highlights the University of Ulster's Magee Campus in the city. However, in reality the long campaign to establish a University of Derry has not been successful, not yet at least. Instead, when the University of Ulster was established in 1968 it's main campus was built in Coleraine with only a satellite campus of some 3,500 students in Derry~Londonderry. This was one of the grievances that sparked the civil rights movement. While Derry~Londonderry has discovered a new prosperous future, this lack of a major university and student body remains a legacy of the city's history that risks holding back its further development.

Falmouth

Shortlisted 2013

Falmouth is a great name for a place that sings
And speaks and talks but here's an idea
Let's rename the place: FalEye, FalEar;
Got a certain something, hasn't it? It rings

With poetic truth, I reckon: FalEye
Because the things can you see here
Gladden the heart, and FalEar...
Just listen to the laughter drift across the sky

From the beaches and the thronging streets
And how about a town called FalNose
Taking in the fish and the sweet wild rose
On the heights? Your sensory tour's complete:

FalEye, FalNose, FalEar...Falmouth, I guess
Is the best name for a town that never fails to impress!

To those on the land, Falmouth might seem to be a peripheral place, a small town on the south-west tip of Britain. But viewed from the sea, it is the hub of the nation's maritime trade. Ship's masters who had been at sea for many months headed straight to 'Falmouth for orders', to report their safe arrival and get instructions on which port to take their cargo. Given the natural advantage of its deep-water harbour, it is perhaps surprising that Falmouth only really dates back 400 years. Its history reflects the rise of British sea power and its layout and character are rooted in this maritime legacy. So to understand Falmouth you need to do what those sailors did and get out onto the water.

Head out on any of the small ferries to the nearby villages of St Mawes, Mylor or Flushing and your sense of scale shifts. In the world of the Fal estuary, Falmouth becomes the big town. In one sweep from right to left, the town's story is laid out, from the elegant Georgian homes of those ship's captains upriver down through the stone and slate town wharves and waterside pubs to new developments at Discovery Quay and the National Maritime Museum Cornwall, and finally the busy commercial and naval dockyards. From the sea, you get a better view too of the rows of terraced houses climbing past the railway station towards the town's long sandy beaches of Gyllyngvase, Swanpool and Maenporth, hidden from town beyond the headland of Fort Pendennis.

Back on land, the sinuous stone-fronted main street changes its name several times as it progresses past some of the usual features of a Cornish town: the tall granite tower of the town church, the Seven Stars pub, pasty shops, art galleries and surf shops amongst the factory outlets and a new Wilkinson's plugging the gap where Woolworth's once stood. There are some distinctively Falmouth landmarks too, such as the King's Pipe, a tall brick chimney where contraband tobacco was burned, and the 19th-century headquarters of the Royal Cornwall Polytechnic Society, which is now the Poly Arts Centre. Established by the Quaker Anna Maria Fox, the Poly is doubly responsible for the cultural dynamism in town. In 1902 an art college was founded as an offshoot of the Poly, and just over a century later it became a university, making considerable investment in a campus above town and sealing Falmouth's reputation as a creative hub.

Not all the students in town are artists. Falmouth Marine School, part of Cornwall

College, can also trace its roots back a century and continues the local maritime traditions. Falmouth still earns its living from its maritime location. 1,400 of its 20,000 people are employed in the docks, building and repairing ships and super-yachts, in businesses that are internationally competitive.

Its remoteness from London has meant that Falmouth has always been keen to manage its own affairs. The town's first resident royal agents, the Killigrews, husbanded the profits of trade to the benefit of the town far from the gaze of London. The same spirit today sees businesses, community groups, educational institutions and councils taking a practical approach to working with limited resources through the Town Forum and Business Improvement District. When tourism funding was withdrawn, the local partnership set up its own Visitor Information Centre. This has taken over promotion, events and marketing with initiatives such as the Mussel Card for local ferries and buses. These activities serve visitors and locals, adding to the quality of life for the whole town. This led to investment in new shops and restaurants, including an outpost of the Padstow Stein empire, alongside independent shops and cafes.

Falmouth achieves what many towns strive for – a clear and shared vision, with a focus on sustainable growth and a distinctive identity that seems to be able to buck the trend experienced in other peripheral places. Falmouth may be a long way from our big cities, but it's far from being a backwater.

Galway

Winner 2013

If you open this Galway oyster carefully, carefully,
You'll find more than one pearl inside, truthfully
You'll find a handful of pearls from this jewel of a city.

This first pearl is the bedrock of Galway, the history:
A medieval town by a river, buildings in harmony
That face to the future with pride and with dignity.

This second pearl is music, reel through to symphony,
Choirs lifting their voices, pub sessions sing endlessly
Variations on tunes that have verve and longevity.

This third pearl is language, of prose and of poetry,
Of street conversations ringing with euphony
So words are a huge part of this city's scenery.

This fourth pearl is landscape, more complex than 'scenery'
More nuanced than postcards of water and greenery:
Here's land and here's water; here's people, here's empathy.

Galway has a scale so intimate in its medieval heart that it has all the good characteristics of a great town: compact, lively, a strong sense of place and wellbeing. But if that sounds rather too cosy, it isn't; this modern city where the River Corrib meets the sea is also a gateway, not just to the wild scenery of western Ireland and the Gaeltacht, but to people and ideas that have been flowing in and out of this part of Ireland for centuries. In a nation that prides itself on its welcome, Galway's reputation stands out, whether you're just visiting for the festivals – arts, oysters or horse racing, take your pick – or have chosen Galway as your new home, like the hundreds of students at National University of Ireland Galway and the thousands born outside the country. It is the fastest growing city in Ireland.

Having said that, city walls were generally not built to welcome visitors. Galway's 12th-century fortifications were built on the east bank of the Corrib not to protect it from the sea but from the other direction. Galway is a Norman town, consolidated under Richard de Burgo, who built its stone walls to protect the fledgling town from the native Irish. It grew and thrived as a sea port and

arches were built into the walls for traders to pay taxes on returning from France, Portugal and Spain, of which only the Spanish Arch remains. Columbus himself passed through in 1477 en route north and mentioned Galway in his jottings a few years later.

In 1484 Richard III granted 14 Norman merchant families – the 'Tribes of Galway' – the right to choose their own mayor and bailiffs and bypass the influence of the de Burgos, effectively making Galway an independent city state. In the same year the Galwegians successfully petitioned Pope Innocent VIII to grant religious independence to St Nicholas Church so that English rites could be used by its vicars. Trading with France and Spain covered every commodity medieval merchants could think of, but the most important by far was wine. The Tribes went to great lengths to protect their wealth and influence – passing laws to prevent inter-marriage or mingling with native Irish and only speaking and writing in English. Their loyalty to the crown was rewarded by successive monarchs and their success was apparent to anyone visiting Galway then – and now – from the splendid buildings they commissioned, such as Lynch's Castle.

But beware, this is a city of storytellers and all is not always what it seems. Druid Lane, where Galway Civic Trust has restored the medieval

Top left: The Spanish Arch.

Top right: The beach at Salthill is a popular place for watersports even though wetsuits are required.

Opposite: The main street running through the town to the port.

Left: The Galway Museum by the architects Ciaran O'Connor and Ger Harvey.

Below: Views of the town.

Hall of the Red Earl, must, for example, be an ancient place? Not so. The street has been through several names in its history and was only given its present name by Galway City Council in 1996. This was to commemorate the 21st birthday of the Druid Theatre Company which was set up by a group of NUI Galway graduates and was the first professional theatre company outside Dublin, with a mission to bring world-class theatre not only to the citizens of Galway, but to people across Ireland.

The fact that the theatre company that is not even named after ancient Druids but rather the *Asterix* books fits the Galway story perfectly. It is just one of many creative organisations that have flowered in the ambitious and independent air of Galway; indeed, this love of creativity is an important part of its identity. Annual cultural highlights include the Arts Festival where Macnas, another Galway-born theatre company, leads the Macnas Parade, bringing the arts to the wider community through processions and spectacle, and the Cúirt International Festival of Literature, which is held every spring at Galway Arts Centre. Music you can find year-round, in pubs and venues such as Monroe's, the Quays and the Crane, and Galway itself is often the subject of song, most famously in The Pogues' 'Fairy Tale of New York' and Steve Earl's 'Galway Girl'.

Galway's independent spirit can also be found in its retail sector, which bustles with life and is still dominated by independent shops. The high street, part of which is called with admirable simplicity Shop Street, runs through the town to the Spanish Arch and is lined with brightly coloured shops and thronged with shoppers. Around a busy weekly farmers' market in St Nicholas' Square is a hardcore of good food shops including Sheridans cheesemonger, on the square itself and local institutions Colleran butchers and traditional deli McCambridge's, founded in the 1920s.

Next to the Spanish Arch embedded in the town walls stands the recently completed Galway City Museum. This gives an excellent introduction to some of the many stories of Galway, not always focused on the centre itself. These include Galway's love affair with the dance hall and the cinema.

Several of these institutions were in the city's seaside suburb of Salthill, which is still home to Leisureland and another renowned deli and food institution, Mortons. Salthill stands on the southern side of the river through the Spanish Arch and along the often windswept promenade, the 'Long Walk', a favourite weekend stroll for Galwegians.

Galway's location on a narrow neck of land through which all east–west traffic is channelled, together with poor public transport to Salthill and the outer residential suburbs, has created some problems with traffic congestion. The city is investing heavily to promote cycling, although the weather sometimes doesn't help. New developments are being designed to be more walkable and older developments are being densified and stitched back into surrounding neighbourhoods, but it's a long process for some of the car-focused suburbs. While the recession has taken a heavy toll here, as elsewhere in Ireland, Galway had boomed under the Celtic Tiger and is considered to have weathered the downturn better than most, thanks to a strong base of investment from technology and biomedical companies. Support for new investment is seen as key to that success, whether it comes from abroad or from homegrown companies.

Looking to the future, the city has been working on a shared vision and objectives for planning. The City Development Board's 2000 Vision has been succeeded by Galway 2040, looking towards a more distant horizon and encouraging a wide-ranging dialogue with citizens. Some opportunities, perhaps, have yet to be fully realised. Despite the sense of water everywhere, Galway does not fully exploit its relationship with its harbour. There is a long tradition of marine science here and it is home to the national Marine Institute, but EU investment offers greater opportunities in this sector. There are also ambitions to increase capacity in the harbour itself. Investment in the port for the 2009 visit of the Volvo Ocean Race attracted over 650,000 people and generated over €55 million, rising further when the race visited again for its finale in 2012. Now the Harbour Board plans to create a new deep-water terminal where cruise ships can dock and freight can be unloaded.

Infrastructure is essential for a place that is so remote from the rest of Ireland, never mind the rest of Europe, and Galway has some major questions to tackle about how it connects with the outside world. The M6 motorway linking Galway to Dublin was completed in 2009 but the last section connecting Galway to Shannon Airport, to support the aspiration for an Atlantic Enterprise Corridor, has taken much longer. Completion dates also keep being put back for the much-anticipated Galway City Outer Bypass.

What is certain is that people have a deep attachment to Galway – to its traditions and landmarks, to its tolerance and enterprise and a pride both in its culture and that it is one of the safest places in Ireland. The personal scale of the place helps ensure that partnerships here work in practice. It would seem that in the next chapter of Galway's life water might play a much stronger part, whether from research into renewable power generation or bringing new people to this most welcoming city.

Hebden Bridge

Winner 2011

Town with a tissue that's quite unique;
Town where history's strata show
Alternative visions cheek to cheek,
Different plants allowed to grow.
In a world where towns are pallid clones
Hebden Bridge stands out a mile,
As the sun lights up West Yorkshire stones
And the sky is as bright as a smile;
You walk through the streets and the voices rise
Like steam from a coffee emporium
And very quickly you realise
This whole town's an auditorium!
Hebden Bridge is theatre, so let's all clap
The wizard's cloak behind the new flat cap!

Nestled on the hillside midway between Halifax and Burnley, Hebden Bridge is just like many of the towns along the Calder Valley and yet it is also completely, almost defiantly, different. After a long period of hardship in the latter part of the 20th century, Hebden Bridge's story seemed to be writing itself: a former mill town on its uppers, struggling to find an economic role. Since then Hebden Bridge has not only survived but thrived, and was recently described by *High Life* magazine as the 'fourth funkiest place on the planet'. The story of a Yorkshire mill town's transformation into a bohemian hotspot, shows that there are no simple models for regeneration and it's not the materials that you have to work with that matter but how they are used and who puts them together.

Hebden Bridge may be concealed in a fold of steeply sloping Pennine hills, but its history is all about its connections. The town grew initially because of the bridge where the hilltop packhorse routes carrying wool across north the of England dipped into the steep valley to cross the River Hebden. The valley is one of the only east–west passes over the Pennines and so became the route of one of the first roads between Yorkshire and Lancashire. Later the same path was chosen for the Rochdale Canal that opened in 1804 linking Manchester and Liverpool to Sowerby Bridge (see page 234) and onwards to the Yorkshire wool centres and the east coast ports, becoming a vital trade route. A few years later the railway threaded its way along the same valley. It is this rail line that explains the town's regeneration because it allows an easy commute into both Manchester and Leeds, but we are getting ahead of ourselves.

These transport connections and the surrounding steep and (often) wet hills meant that Hebden Bridge developed its own textile industry. Water-powered mills were built to exploit the fast-flowing streams and the ready supply of wool as the town grew into a thriving industrial centre. The canal connection allowed cotton to be imported and Hebden Bridge became known for its fustian cloth that clothed the workers of the north, particularly below the waist – hence Hebden Bridge becoming known as 'Trouser Town'. Housing for its workers was built up the steep hills around the town, giving rise to its distinctive 'over-and-under' housing – with houses facing onto the upper street being built on top of those facing onto the street below. This all came to an end

The town has become a magnet for a 'motley mixture of artists, writers, photographers, musicians, alternative practitioners, teachers, green and New Age activists.'

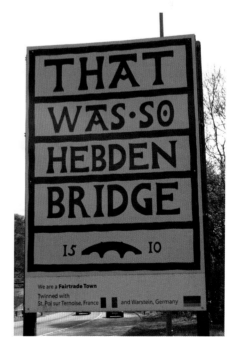

Left: Hebden Bridge's 'over and under' housing. The housing in the smaller picture forms the upper two floors of the street in the larger image.

Bottom: A view across the town and its valley in winter by local resident Anders Hanson.

Opposite: David Fletcher outside his mill leaning on his electric car that is charged from the hydroelectric Archimedes screw that he installed in the river.

after the Second World War and by the 1960s the town was experiencing severe depopulation and economic decline with many of its shops empty and its houses abandoned.

As often happens, this provided the catalyst of revival. The cheap housing started to attract what became known as the 'Hebden Bridge hippies', people searching for an alternative lifestyle. A public meeting in May 1965 at the civic hall attracted 100 or so people who decided on a four-part strategy for the town: to clean up the environment, to promote events to attract visitors, to convert these visitors to full-time residents and to protect industrial buildings so that they could be used for new employment. One of the people at that first meeting was David Fletcher, who can still be seen driving around Hebden Bridge in his electric Renault, powered by the hydroelectric Archimedes' screw that he installed in the river. In 1972 David, a lecturer at the Architecture School in Manchester, was trying to save Hebden Bridge Mill, the oldest building in the town (indeed, the town was named after the mill rather than vice versa). With no other option he raised a mortgage and bought it himself, spending the next few years working every available hour to refurbish the building. This is the

core of Hebden Bridge's revival and David, now in his 80s, still has his lunch every day in the mill's cafe. Back in the 1970s he became Chair of the Calder Civic Trust and helped establish Pennine Heritage in 1979 with a group of local conservationists. This development company and charity would go on to buy Nutclough Mill and raise £1 million to convert it into workspace. It is now occupied by Calrec Audio, a high-tech company employing 150 people. Pennine Heritage has since undertaken a number of schemes across the region but back in Hebden Bridge its most ambitious project and base is the Birchcliffe Centre. This was a large Baptist chapel perched on the hillside that closed in the 1970s. It has been converted to a community centre, venue and home to Pennine Horizons, a digital archive of more than 60 photographic archives of the region.

The final decades of the 20th century saw a complete change in Hebden Bridge's fortunes. In addition to the physical works, the strategy to attract visitors and turn them into residents has been a huge success. The Hebden Bridge Arts Festival has been running for many years and the annual calendar also includes a piano festival, a burlesque festival and many other smaller events. The visitors really have become residents as the town has become a magnet for a 'motley mixture of artists, writers, photographers, musicians, alternative practitioners, teachers, green and New Age activists and, more recently, wealthier yuppie types' to quote HedWeb (billed as the UK's first community website). The open and tolerant atmosphere has also led to the town's more recent billing as the 'lesbian capital of the north'. The town centre is full of independent shops selling arts and crafts along with alternative therapies and coffee such that it was described by the New Economics Foundation as the 'least cloned town in Britain'. In 2006 it was also granted Fair Trade Zone status.

This is a model of town regeneration that will not suit everywhere. However, like some of the other towns in this book, such as Stroud and Skipton, Hebden Bridge has successfully transitioned from a run-down industrial centre with no apparent future into a thriving town. It has done this by becoming somewhere distinctive in order to suck wealth and people along the train line out of the surrounding cities. The trick is to do this without becoming a dormitory, which is the real key to its success.

Richmond

Winner 2009

How to make Richmond...
You need a river; preferably one that can hold the light
Of the setting sun in autumn; you need a castle,
A nice big dominant one that holds half the sky,
That percolates your thinking if you live here.
You need a theatre, one where the performers on stage
Are almost sitting in the audience, where the words you speak
Seem to hang in the air like lights. You need a history
That doesn't poke you in the eye, but rather walks beside you,
A companion, a guide pointing and explaining. Cobbles are good,
And a range of museums. And the language has to be local,
Has to sound like it's made of things like cobbles, and the river,
And the shadow of the castle, and the impossibly beautiful
Skies of North Yorkshire with just the odd cloud sailing...

is the mother town of this worldwide family. It is a town blessed with a spectacular setting above the Swale Valley, a gateway to the Yorkshire Dales. But its greatest charm is that, while it has retained much of its distinctive architecture and original character, it has remained a working market town.

The layout of the town radiates from the castle and is characterised by wide streets interconnected by narrow wynds. In the Middle Ages the town became an important ecclesiastical settlement and it received its market charter in 1441 when the town was home to 13 craft guilds. Richmond developed as an early industrial town based on nearby lead workings and a wool industry supplied by the sheep on the surrounding hills. The craft guilds included knitters who produced caps and stockings.

R ichmond is apparently the most popular place name in the world, with some 57 towns and cities across the Americas, Africa and Australia called Richmond. The residents of Richmond-on-Thames believe that theirs is the original town, but even that is named after Richmond in Yorkshire. However, even this is not the full story because Richmond in Yorkshire is named after Richemont in Normandy.

This is because Richmond is a Norman town. Many of the towns in the book have Norman castles, often a threatening presence on the edge of the town built after the Conquest to keep an eye on the locals. Richmond by contrast *is* the castle. It was founded in 1068 by the Breton noble Alan Rufus, the first Comte de Richemont. He built the castle on a defensible bluff in a crook of the River Swale. Today's marketplace was the original castle keep and the castle grew to become the town.

The title Earl of Richmond brought with it great power and wealth. At one point the title was held by King Henry VII, who built his Royal Palace on the Thames in a place that he also named Richmond. Later Earls of Richmond were active colonisers and planters of towns that they also named after themselves. Nevertheless, Richmond in Yorkshire

Richmond's entire historic core has Conservation area status with over 450 listed buildings. The large marketplace and many of the minor streets even have listed cobblestones

The character of the town was formed in the Georgian period when it reinvented itself as a regional social centre where wealthy wool traders built fashionable townhouses. This was based around the local racecourse, military musters at the Caterick Barracks, 'assemblies and card parties'. It was this period that gave Richmond a well-to-do reputation, a bastion of Yorkshire Conservatives and until recently the seat of the former government minister William Hague.

The genteel town huddles around its sloping marketplace surrounded by 18th-century buildings with the Gothic medieval Trinity Church at its centre, and the clock tower at its head. Richmond's entire

historic core has Conservation area status with over 450 listed buildings. The large marketplace and many of the minor streets even have listed cobblestones. In the centre of the marketplace stands an obelisk, erected by the Georgians to replace the market cross. This was part of a programme of civic improvements and is built over a 12,000-gallon reservoir fed by nearby springs to provide the town with a reliable water supply. A few years later the town would build one of the world's first gasworks, using it to provide street lighting.

This mix of heritage, gentility and technology sums up Richmond. It does not live in a heritage bubble but instead has a long history of innovation and civic partnership. This has continued in recent years through collaboration with the Countryside Agency and regional bodies through the Richmond Swale Valley Community Initiative. Indeed, perhaps the secret to Richmond's success today lies in the way that the local community, often working with public agencies, has faced threats and challenges to its livelihood and found very modern solutions. One of these challenges was the loss of its railway station, a victim of the Beeching cuts in the 1960s. A community-led initiative has now seen the old station building reborn as an arts, business and leisure centre. The Grade II* listed building reopened in 2007 with a new extension and houses a two-screen cinema, an exhibition space, meeting rooms and conference facilities, as well as a bakery and a microbrewery.

An earlier project saw the restoration of the beautiful Georgian Theatre Royal. This was originally opened in 1788 by the actor Samuel Butler when Richmond was at its most fashionable, but closed in 1840 and was for many years used as a warehouse. It was reopened as a theatre by a local group in 1963 and then in 2003 with Lottery money was restored and extended, with the addition of contemporary public space providing cafe-bars, meeting rooms and a second performance space alongside the original Grade I listed building.

In 2001 the town faced one its gravest threats when it was virtually quarantined during the foot and mouth epidemic. It lost three quarters of its tourist income, leaving behind 18 empty shops.

The crisis galvanised public agencies and the wider community into action. Vacant shops were re-let, some for traditional services such as a cobbler, investment was made in the appropriate redesign of shopfronts, windows and improvements in the public realm and new residents were encouraged to move into the previously empty upper floors of town centre commercial buildings. The weekly outdoor market in the marketplace was also supplemented by a farmers' market every three weeks.

This programme of improvements – prompted by foot and mouth – has regenerated the whole town. It now attracts around a million visitors a year and has a prosperous population of just under 8,500. Unemployment is low and the town's attractive environment, good schools, low crime rates and strong local community attract both visitors and residents. This brings with it the challenges of an ageing population and like many towns in rural areas, Richmond educates far more young people than it retains as young talent migrates to the cities. It does, however, benefit from the nearby Catterick Garrison, which is set to expand to house 25,000 troops and support staff and is the largest British Army base in the world. The garrison started life in Richmond Castle and the barracks were established by local Richmond resident Robert Baden-Powell after the First World War. It has since grown to become a major part of the town's economy.

The strategy has been heritage-led and consensus has been key. Even a proposal to fell over-mature trees to reveal some of the early 19th-century views of Richmond painted by Turner has found cross-community consensus. Above all, people are passionate about their town, and are extremely conscious of its historical legacy; they hold it in great affection and have demonstrated that they will intervene to protect it.

Scarborough
Winner 2010

Tide of visitors in, tide of water out
Tide of water in, tide of visitors up
To the shops and the cafes for a cake and a sup
While the kids on the sand play
beach cricket and shout
And the trains go out and the trains come in
And the sun turns the sky a marine kind of blue.
If this town is a boat, then we're all the crew,
And the Scarborough fun can begin!
Sea Life, Rotunda, a boat ride, a theatre
The best fish and chips that you'll ever chew
A town close to perfection and pretty near ter
Nirvana for people just like me and you.
It's a promise, a fact, but it's no empty boast
That Scarborough's the jewel of the
East Yorkshire coast!

It is not easy being a seaside town in the north of England. The coastline may have an austere beauty, and the great Victorian seaside resorts, of which Scarborough is perhaps the best, have a brash confidence, but, given a choice between sunny Spain and a biting wind off the North Sea then what are you supposed to do? Scarborough in its heyday was a resort that managed to balance the civilised charms of its spa and its Grand Hotel with the more earthy delights that drew whole factories of workers from Yorkshire mill towns on specially commissioned trains for their Wakes Week holiday. This is a world that disappeared with the rise of the cheap package holiday and for a while Scarborough struggled to adapt. To make matters worse, the town's other industry – fishing – was in decline, and the impact on the local economy was profound; businesses were struggling and unemployment was high, creating a whole range of social issues. Three wards in Scarborough made the top ten per cent nationally on the index for multiple deprivation. Meanwhile, Victorian Scarborough, built to welcome those seeking the bracing sea air, had not enjoyed being exposed to this air, wreaking havoc on its genteel architecture.

Then in 2001 Scarborough was selected as a 'Renaissance Town' by the regional development agency Yorkshire Forward. In the belief that the region's economic success depended on its towns and cities, the Renaissance programme developed an intensive system intended to empower places to manage their own regeneration. The idea was to assemble a panel of international experts for the region that could be called upon to work with local communities, businesses, politicians and officials through 'Town Teams'. The Town Teams with their experts would draw up a strategy and would thereafter become the focus for its implementation. It was not a system that worked everywhere, but in Scarborough it was transformational. In part this was due to the manager of the Crown Spa Hotel, Nick Taylor, who, having come along to the early Town Team meetings, decided to change careers and become the town's first Renaissance Manager - a post that he holds to this day.

The first stage of the Renaissance process – 'rethinking' – involved the Town Team working with their expert panel to understand the town. The panel included John Thompson (the first Chair of the Academy of Urbanism), Adrian Geuze from Dutch firm West 8 and Alan Simpson from Yorkshire Forward. A community planning weekend attracted over 1,000 people – compelling evidence of the passion and strength of feeling for the town – and provided broad agreement of the need for change. The Scarborough Renaissance Partnership was born and the material from the planning weekend was turned into two documents: a *Renaissance Charter* and a Strategic Development Framework, entitled *Kissing the Sleeping Beauty*. The first of these documents was a manifesto for the town and, like the town charters of old, was signed by all of the town's leading people as a mark of their commitment to its transformation. The Strategic Development Framework turned this vision into a strategy aimed at making Scarborough the hub of the Yorkshire coast, introducing green gateways to welcome visitors, linking together the seaside assets, improving streets, squares and public spaces and generally breathing life back into the town.

Scarborough's origins are those of a small fishing town on the North Yorkshire coast. All that changed with the discovery by a certain Mrs Farrer of bitter, brown spring water trickling from the rocks on the South Bay in 1620. Spas were not a new phenomenon – places like Bath and Buxton were much older – but word spread of the medicinal properties of Scarborough's spa and it became the country's first coastal spa town. This was boosted in the 18th century when William Buchan published

'Did you know that the hotel we stayed at had a tower representing each season, a chimney for each week of the year and a room for each day?'

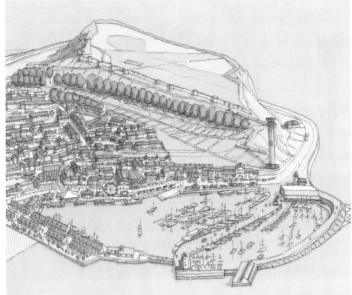

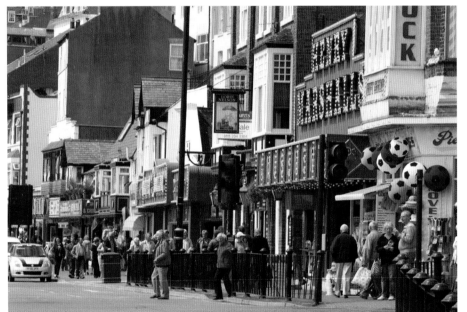

Above: An illustration by JTP from the cover of the Renaissance Charter.

Above left: The public realm scheme for the waterfront.

Left and below: Scarborough retains its traditional seaside attractions.

Below left: The spa.

his book *Domestic Medicine* advocating the benefits of seawater. This led into a whole new trend of sea bathing, although most people opted to do this in summer, rather than winter as Buchan had advocated 'for maximum impact'. Scarborough was the first resort to introduce bathing machines, wooden changing huts that were wheeled into the sea so that Victorian ladies could immerse themselves in the healing waters of the North Sea while maintaining their modesty.

The arrival of the railways caused trade to boom and Scarborough became one of the first seaside resorts. The Grand Hotel, completed in 1867, was one of the first purpose-built hotels in the world. Its critical dimensions were made to be recounted in stories of family holidays: 'Did you know that the hotel we stayed at had a tower representing each season, a chimney for each week of the year and a room for each day?' People still came to take the waters but the spa had other attractions to offer. The Grand Hall, originally built by Joseph Paxton, fresh from his success on the Crystal Palace, was rebuilt in the 1880s. Later the Sun Court, a sheltered open-air terrace, would play host to the legendary Max

Jaffa and his Palm Court Orchestra. Meanwhile, up in the town Wakes Week trains would arrive every weekend through the summer, disgorging the working classes of Yorkshire for their one week of sun (hopefully) and freedom. Scarborough's magic was its ability to maintain its respectability in the face of this working-class invasion, unlike its grubbier cousin Blackpool.

Max Jaffa died in 1991, by which time the spa had been closed down by public health officials, its waters being declared as unfit for human consumption. Holiday patterns changed and Scarborough's visitors were likely to be elderly and to be visiting for the day, or at most a weekend, the hotels were struggling and the attractions were looking tired and dated. The problem with the British seaside is how quickly its cheerful, boisterous charm can start to look depressing when decline sets in. This is fatal when your economy is based on making people happy!

It was in this context that the Town Team went to work. The plan was to take the town back to its slightly more upmarket roots, the 'Cannes of Britain' as the Yorkshire Post put it – The spa has seen a £3 million refurbishment, with a view to recapturing the conference market (the Conservative Party held their annual conference there in the 1980s). A major public realm scheme has been completed along the quayside, separating the fishermen's clutter

from the tourist promenades. The designs by LDA narrowed the road (to discourage boy racers), while improving pavements and creating long sinuous benches. This has set the quality standard for public realm improvements elsewhere in the town, including Trafalgar Square, which had become a focus for anti-social behaviour and was refurbished in partnership with local residents. Elsewhere £4.8 million was spent to refurbish the Rotunda Museum, with its internationally renowned geology collection. The Woodend Creative Workspace, originally the family home of the Sitwells and more recently a natural history museum, has been converted to support the growth of digital and creative industries, providing a gallery together with office and workshop space to over 50 organisations.

Of course, not everyone was ready for 'cappuccino culture' (to quote a BBC News report). There have been particular concerns about the redevelopment of the North Bay where a new holiday apartment scheme saw the loss of the Art Deco 'Corner Cafe'. Local campaigning group the Sons of Nepture, bemoan the loss of the North Bay's comfortable, if slightly shabby character. Next door there are plans for a major all-weather waterpark and leisure complex. This was put on hold during the recession and has recently received financial support from the council voted through by a single vote.

Altogether £200 million has been spent as part of the Renaissance programme, including grants from Europe and the Heritage Lottery. However, the majority has come through private investment in a concerted effort by everyone associated with Scarborough to reinvent the British seaside resort. And it is working: visitor numbers are up since 2006, and their average age is down. There is now a surf scene on the beach and the town has developed its university as a centre for digital media. Because of this, there is a growing cluster of digital businesses locally and a more educated workforce that is proving attractive to other employers. Amazingly, it was voted the Most Enterprising Town in Britain and then beat off stiff competition from cities like Valencia and Prague to win the European title in 2009. The conference market is growing and the town has developed a strong presence in the short break holiday market, such that the average occupancy of the Grand Hotel is now 90 per cent.

Scarborough continues to manage a tricky balancing act. While still feeling like a classic English coastal town should – kiss-me-quick hats and candy floss – it has modernised and diversified what it offers. Not content to only deliver regeneration – although it has done this by the bucket (and spade) load – it has also recognised the importance of a change in attitude as much as a lick of paint.

Shrewsbury

Shortlisted 2013

This is a rhyming rhapsody
About the town of Shrewsbury
Just between me and you-sbury
It's a jewel of a place!

This town's name has melody
And it just goes to shows-bury
That a town like Shrewsbury
Puts a smile on your face!

Medieval streets in harmony
With modernism: true-sbury,
It's a prime example, Shrewsbury
Of development with grace!

It's not swamped by history
It doesn't start to doze-bury,
It's wide awake, is Shrewsbury
To the future's bright embrace!

To be a proud Salopian is to be happy with the way that things are. When Henry VIII said to the people of Shrewsbury that, having dissolved their monastery, they could have a cathedral, a bishop and all the prestige and trappings that comes with it, their response was 'Thanks but no thanks'. They were content to remain the 'first of towns' and didn't fancy the upheaval. Salop is another name for Shropshire and Salopian is the name given to the citizens of its county town, Shrewsbury, and indeed to the pupils of its prestigious private school.

A town so limited in its 'ambitions' that it never even got around to building a ring road

This contentment and resistance to change could be said to sum up this town of 70,000 just a few miles from the Welsh border. The nearby village of Wroxeter was once the fifth largest Roman civitas in Britain but was abandoned after the Romans left. Nearby lay a much better site, a small hill at the narrow neck of a meander on the River Severn. This became a fortified town; some say it was once the capital of the Welsh Kingdom of Pengwerm, although by the time of the Saxons it had become part of the Kingdom or Mercia. It was a border town fought over for centuries; its Welsh name Amwythig means fortified place, while its English name means 'fort in the scrubland region'. Rather wonderfully it was, for a while, called Shrubtown, which is very appropriate for a town that now hosts one of England's largest horticultural events, the Shrewsbury Flower Show.

Shrewsbury stood at a strategic position and, in more peaceful times, it thrived economically. It's early woollen industry grew because the town controlled the trade routes for Welsh wool into England along the Roman road Watling Street. The road is today known as the A5 and in 1815 an Act of Parliament was passed to extend the route to Holyhead, linking Dublin and London. Thomas Telford was engaged in what was then the largest road engineering project since the Romans. Shrewsbury was at a crucial point on this route and its economy developed to serve the coaches travelling to and from Ireland.

The scene was set, you would think, for Shrewsbury to grow into a major industrial centre. You can get a sense of the town's potential at that time from the Ditherington Flax Mill. Built in the 1790s as the world's first iron-framed building, it may have been just five storeys tall, but is the acknowledged grandfather of all modern skyscrapers. It was bought for £64,000 in 1804, yet 80 years later was sold for just £3,000, by which time the Industrial Revolution had passed Shrewsbury by.

The proud Salopians were happy as they were, without any of that economic development stuff. Shrewsbury slumbered through the Industrial Revolution and beyond. It was a town so limited in its 'ambitions' that it never even got around to building a ring road! While the future was being built in Telford New Town a few miles away, Shrewsbury retained its inefficient historic streets and outdated medieval buildings. Of course today this doesn't seem quite so backward. Shrewsbury achieved the useful trick of becoming less important but remaining quite prosperous – as a market town, a centre for agricultural industries and an administrative centre. It benefits from being a substantial place a long way from any other large centre. A large, rural hinterland extending deep into Wales looks to Shrewsbury as its local metropolis and this has shielded it from the competition of the major regional cities. Alongside its independent shops and bustling indoor market, it has seen investment in new retail and hotel developments, a new museum and the recently built Theatre Severn. This is not a radical place; the proud Salopians can be a little risk averse and conservative, with a small c. The cultural offering and quality of life, dare we say, are a little middle class and middle aged – the year's big event being the Flower Show. This is a town that knows itself; the Salopians are happy with the way things are as well they might be.

Stirling

Shortlisted 2009

Trying to describe Stirling...
Newest city in an ancient land; place to sit and listen.
In the castle's shadow I drink espresso; Stirling sky is a colour
Just the red side of blue, tonight.

How do you describe a city like this?

Old Town in name only; stand and look
And on Graduation Day students flock like birds
Coming home to roost in the nest of learning.

How do you describe a city like this? I'm trying.

At the 'top of the town' I look out over the city
And somehow the city looks back at me; I'm reflected
By a place and Albion have won three nil; I'm smiling.

How do you describe a city like this? I'm trying my best.

Describing the essence of Stirling is like trying
to hold the water of St Ninian's Well in your open hands;
it's a feeling somewhere between fresh air and birdsong...

Oh, how do you describe a city like this?
Come and live here!

From the ramparts of Stirling Castle, sat atop a crag commanding the town, you can see half of Scotland – well not quite, but it feels that way. The castle looks down on the 'wee town but bigger than its boot', as the head of planning put it, that stands at the crossroads between the Lowlands and the Highlands. Stirling stands in a gap where the River Forth cuts through a ridge of hills, the Campsie Fells to the south west and the Ochil Hills to the north east. Until the 1930s it was the nearest point to the sea at which the Forth could be crossed, meaning that most of the traffic between the north and the south of Scotland had to pass through the town. This may account for it's name, because Stirling in the local dialect means 'a place of battle, struggle or strife'. It has been the fulcrum on which every war in Scotland has pivoted and its castle, standing virtually impregnable above the town, has dictated the fate of kings.

This history goes back a very long way. The Randolphfield standing stones within the town show that it was an Stone Age settlement. The Romans built a fort on its crag and 600 years later a siege of the castle is described in the chronicle of Bede. One of the myths of the medieval town tells of a wolf that howled to warn the townspeople of invading Vikings. However, it is a slightly more recent myth that draws tourists today. The Battle of Stirling Bridge in 1297 saw Andrew de Moray and William Wallace defeat the English. Wallace went on to briefly become Guardian of Scotland before defeat at Falkirk the following year. The story has been mythologised twice: first 200 years after the event by the minstrel Blind Harry whose romanticised version of events has held captive the imagination of the Scots ever since, and second by Hollywood in the 1995 film *Braveheart*. The Wallace Monument overlooks the town and draws more than four million tourists a year. This, however, was not even the most important battle in Stirling's bloody history. Less than 20 years after Wallace, the king of the Scots Robert the Bruce was lain siege in Stirling Castle by a formidable English army under Edward II. The siege failed and an English force of 16,000 was defeated at the Battle of Bannockburn. This is the iconic battle in Scottish history in which independence was gained from the English.

Meanwhile, the long-suffering citizens of the town in the shadow of the castle struggled on as the wars raged around them. The town's first Royal Charter was granted in 1130 and Stirling has remained an important town ever since. It was a busy port trading timber with the Baltic and tea with India. Its Mercat Cross stood at the heart of its market, which served the surrounding lands. Indeed, to this day its shopping centre serves a huge catchment area. The railways, however, put paid to the port, by stealing its trade and

Stirling University was built in 1967 on a greenfield campus. It has just under 12,000 students and has generated a range of spin-off businesses in its Innovation Park. The town's attractive setting and excellent road and rail links mean that it is increasingly seen as a commuter centre for people working in Edinburgh and Glasgow. As a result, it has one of the fastest growing populations in Scotland and this level of growth is one of the major challenges it now faces. Also looking to the future, the recently introduced Going Carbon Neutral Stirling project is working from the grassroots up to bring about a significant reduction in the town's carbon footprint and has attracted £2 million in government funding.

The historic city's topography creates a linear layout not dissimilar to Edinburgh's Old Town, with the compact core clustered around the 'tail' of the castle's crag. The ravages of 20th-century planning have arguably done more damage that the previous 2,000 years of conflict. The gem of a train station opens onto an expanse of roads and the shabby rear end of the high street. A dual carriageway severs the town from its river, although plans for the 40-acre former army barracks at Forthside will provide a new civic square and open up the river front with a new footbridge.

Stirling's relatively small size (just 45,000 people) and intimacy ensures that it is a city on a human scale, where local worthies are commemorated in the names of its streets and where the castle no longer dominates the town but hosts events like the Scottish Fashion Awards. As the pressures for growth come to bear on the town perhaps bravery is called for again, as Stirling faces new challenges for a sustainable future and opportunities to reconnect and rediscover itself.

building a bridge build downstream that restricted the size of the vessels that could reach the town.

Today Stirling's economy is based on tourism as it draws visitors from all over the world. The challenge is to encourage visitors to explore beyond the castle and the Wallace Monument. Work has

> Meanwhile, the long-suffering citizens of the town in the shadow of the castle struggled on as the wars raged around them

been undertaken as part of the Vital Stirling Framework for Action to improve Port Street by creating a lively pedestrian area with high-quality granite paving, street furniture, lighting and tree planting. The street now hosts farmers' markets, planned and impromptu musical performances and family-centred celebrations such as Tartan Day. The Orientation and Interpretation Strategy aims to raise the city's profile and encourage visitors to explore further by helping them navigate their way around. Within the city core the level of vacancy has been kept below the Scottish average, supported by initiatives such as a Business Space Strategy and a Management and Maintenance Manual to ensure the quality of the urban landscape. There is a good deal of housing within the centre, much of it social housing, including new schemes knitted into hilly streets, a Living over the Shop initiative and historic building renovation grants aided by the Stirling City Heritage Trust, funded by Historic Scotland.

Stroud
Shortlisted 2011

Say it with a kind of dashing loudness:
There's something here we all call Stroudness!
Built round a mix of cloth and wool
When the hills turned noisy and industrial
This town thrives on reinvention,
Changing direction and intention;
Creativity's the key round here,
Because there's strength in a pint of local beer
And joy in the sort of local store
When they know who you are when you walk through the door;
Yes, Stroud's a town with an aura about it
You can't define it but you just can't doubt it
So stand and say with Stroudish proudness
There's something here we all call Stroudness.

And never, unless you're being rude
Refer to the town as flipping Strood.

The Industrial Revolution didn't start in the great cities of the north but in places like Stroud. Nestled below the western escarpment of the Cotswold Hills at the meeting point of the Five Valleys, Stroud started life as a textile town of woollen mills powered by its fast-running rivers and supplied by Cotswold sheep from the encircling hills. It was known for the production of military uniforms of Stroudwater Scarlet and its reputation drew Huguenots and later Jews fleeing persecution and bringing with them skills in tailoring and the cloth industries. To get the town's produce to market and to import coal for the new-fangled steam engines, an Act of Parliament was obtained in 1730 to make the River Frome (or Stroudwater) navigable over the 12 miles to the Severn Estuary. However, the mill owners objected to the canalisation of the river that they used for power and the canal wasn't completed until 1779. Then in 1820 the Kennet and Avon Canal opened and in 1845 the Great Western Railway. However, by then the Industrial Revolution had long left Stroud behind.

This historic dithering stands in stark contrast the 'Stroud way' that characterises the town today. When the Academy of Urbanism assessment team visited as part of the awards process, they were told that there is a certain mindset in the town that just gets things done in the face of opposition or indifference. Today Stroud is a town of 32,000 people and sits within its steep valleys surrounded by the Cotswold Area of Outstanding Natural Beauty. Its historic community of stubborn mill owners has been supplanted by incomers attracted by its beautiful setting and the easy links to London. This is a mix that we see in a number of the towns that have been nominated for the Academy awards. Professional people, often from elsewhere, many retired with time on their hands, have applied their considerable skills and experience to campaigning and practical projects that have transformed the town. This has made Stroud into what the *London Evening Standard* called, rather unfairly, 'Notting Hill with wellies'.

A good example of this is the Springhill Cohousing scheme visited by the Academy team. This scheme of 35 homes built around a common house, where communal meals are cooked three times a week, was started in 2000 by David and Helen Michael. They had moved from London a few years earlier and had started looking for a site for what would be the first new-build cohousing scheme in the UK. This independent spirit is typical of Stroud and can perhaps be dated to the mid 1970s and campaigns by locals against Gloucester County Council's plans for a new ring road. A little later proposals to demolish 18th-century buildings in the heart of the town led to

rooftop protests and a High Court battle, out of which emerged the Stroud Preservation Trust. The Trust took on 32 High Street, which had been threatened by roadworks but turned out to be a medieval hall and the oldest structure in the town. It has been converted into three shop units, offices and a courtyard. The Trust have since completed the renovation of Withey's Yard, Cainscross Toll House, Arundel Mill House, the Anti-Slavery Arch and the Brunel Goods Shed.

This is just one of many campaigns in the town. In 1989 a midnight operation to fell 13 trees for another road scheme was thwarted following a stand off that lasted until dawn. In 2000 locals prevented the demolition of the landmark Paul Hill Building, later selling enough community shares to take an option on the building and pass it on to a developer. Since then there has been a long list of remarkable achievements by the community,

A midnight operation to fell 13 trees for another road scheme was thwarted following a stand-off that lasted until dawn

from the annual fringe festival with over 400 free events over the August Bank Holiday to the International Textile Festival. It includes practical initiatives like the evening bus services to take young people to the cinema and clubs, the restoration of the canal, the farmers' market, Made in Stroud initiatives, artists' studios and support for local shops. It seems at times that the Stroud community is actively involved in almost every aspect of the life of the town and can overcome most problems and ensure the provision of many facilities that would be inconceivable in other places. The 'Proud to be Stroud' label seems to be completely justified and there is an obvious sense of civic pride throughout the town.

Above: The Springhill Cohousing scheme.

Totnes

Shortlisted 2012

A heavenly town, a smart addres
A place in which I must confes
I feel the opposite of stres
In fact I glow with happines:
Streets are tidy, there's no mes;
Shouts are of joy, not of distres.
The sun shines down and seems to bles
A town that's built around a 'Yess'.
The architecture seems to dres
To energise and to impres,
The opposite of dry blandnes
Antithesis of boringnes;
What this town has, nothing les
Is a fine abundance of Totnesnes...

Halfway between the red sands of Paignton and the green hills of Dartmoor, Totnes has stood at the highest navigable point of the River Dart for over 1,000 years. The street leading from the river through town to the castle may be steep, but never mind, you can take a rickshaw – and don't worry about your carbon footprint – chances are it's running on cooking oil. Here in Totnes 'transition' means much more than the usual process of urban change.

Urban change there has been, of course. The town, founded as a Saxon burgh in 907, became a flourishing Norman fishing port and then in medieval times one of England's richest trading towns, where cloth and tin merchants displayed their wealth in their fine houses climbing the steep main street under Eastgate. It can sometimes seem that there has been very little urban change since then. Two colourful weekly markets and independent shops still sell fresh produce from the surrounding parishes, and as you climb the streets through the town you will pass hardly any chain stores. There is an equally ancient tradition of governance; Totnes' 'Witan' (or council), established in 1018, predates the motte and bailey castle built by William I to control the region. The council, which still meets in a Guildhall built in 1553, is at the heart of a community in which most of the 8,000 people seem to be involved in some way in the life of the town. It is a place that has worked hard not to change.

The catalyst was the arrival in 1925 of Dorothy and Leonard Elmhirst. They had a vision of a rural utopia and created a centre for educational and agricultural research at the nearby Dartington Hall. As a centre for sustainabilty, creativity and learning, it became a magnet for those pursuing alternative lifestyles in the 1960s. Many of the graduates settled in the town and the pursuit of consumerism, so normal elsewhere, was rejected. Then in the early 2000s the environmentalist Rob Hopkins returned to Britain from Kinsale in Ireland where he been working on the issue of peak oil and community action on climate change. In Totnes this evolved into the 'Transition Town' concept, a movement that in little more than five years had given rise to more than 350 other Transition Towns worldwide. Totnes has created and, more importantly, implemented England's first Energy Descent Action Plan.

Totnes, of course, is not immune to the problems of other market towns. It suffers from traffic congestion, unemployment, low wages and a shortage of affordable housing. The town's economy is largely based on tourism and public-sector employment, and many people commute to Exeter, Plymouth or even London for work. The hilly terrain limits the potential for growth, although recent development has seen former wharf buildings being converted into apartments and cafes across the River Dart. A further mixed-use development with affordable housing is planned as one of a number of sites included in an 'Enquiry by Design' masterplan promoted by the town council, supported by South Hams District Council.

Totnes' reputation as the 'capital of New Age chic' makes it seem superficial but this is a serious place seeking sustainable solutions to global challenges. The town has created an ethos of creative mutuality, based on a strong philosophy, but also the ethos is commercial and practical. Initiatives include the local currency the Totnes Pound and the Totnes Healthy Futures Project promoting local food production and wellbeing. Fruit and nut trees have been planted and photovoltaic panels installed on homes and public buildings. Indeed, the town is full of practical community-based action as part of a 'transition' to a low-carbon future.

If it sounds rather worthy, it isn't; in Totnes the serious business of saving the planet is mixed with fun and celebration. It is this that makes Totnes important. Transition Towns may be a work in progress, but progress there certainly has been. The citizens of Totnes have embarked on a journey that may yet provide the route map for more of us to create a sustainable future.

> Totnes reputation as the 'capital of New Age chic' makes it seem superficial but this is a serious place seeking sustainable solutions to global challenges

Westport

Shortlisted 2011

About Westport there are so many things to say-o:
It's a town by the water in gorgeous County Mayo
And if you come to Westport we know you'll want to stay-o
For more than an hour or two and longer than a day-o!
Settled in the mountains it's been Ireland's tidiest town
Its bars are lively and its architecture is profound:
Georgian with echoes of how Normans marked the ground
Feel history running through you as you wander slowly round.
I want this poem to feel as welcoming as Westport;
To make you smile; give you moments of acutely deep thought
This town ensnares you: any stay here has to be far too short
Westport hurls its net and you can't struggle 'cos you're caught!
My rhymes might be clumsy but my feeling's not:
Westport's the most amazing town County Mayo's got!

Right: The town architect's colour scheme design service has resulted in some bold statements.

William Makepeace Thackeray, the Victorian novelist, produced a travel guide entitled *The Irish Sketchbook* in 1842. He was generally very rude about Ireland and therefore very popular with his English readers. However, in Westport he suspended his cynicism and wrote: 'The most beautiful view I ever saw in the world. It forms an event in one's life to have seen that place so beautiful that is it, and so unlike other beauties that I know of. Were such beauties lying on English shores it would be a world's wonder perhaps, if it were on the Mediterranean or Baltic, English travellers would flock to it by hundreds, why not come and see it in Ireland!"

There is a story about Westport, told to us when the Academy team visited, that shows a different side to this idyll (although it doesn't appear in any of the online histories). This tells that between the wars the townspeople decided to thumb their noses at their former masters by building a crescent of council housing on the front lawn of Westport House. There is a certain symmetry to the story, assuming it to be true, because the Browne family, who built Westport House in 1780, demolished the old town because it was in their way. They built the new Westport a little way inland, thereby creating one of the very few planned towns in Ireland.

The Browne family still own Westport House and are one of the last of the great Anglo-Irish families. They made their fortune in the slave trade, although, as the museum in Westport House suggests, the family redeemed themselves to an extent by playing

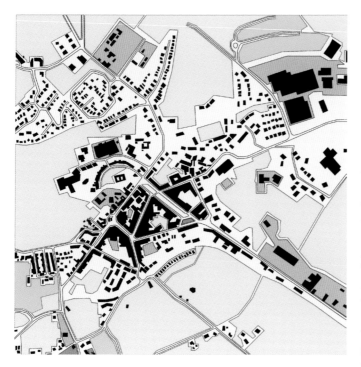

When the play was staged triumphantly in the rector's home town, it caused a riot as the townspeople recognised themselves in the characters

an important part in its abolition. Following the demolition of the original settlement, which had been called Cathernamart, the family commissioned James Wyatt to plan a new town. This was done on Norman principles with a grid of tree-lined streets. The most notable feature is the Mall, a canalised section of the river with streets on either side that has been incorporated into the grid.

The town was built to house estate workers but also attracted visitors due to the nearby mountain of Croagh Patrick, which sits like Mount Fuji as a backdrop to the town. This strange conical mountain, known locally as the Reek, has been a place of pilgrimage for thousands of years and, because of this, St Patrick spent 40 days fasting on its summit in the 5th century. Ever since pilgrims have climbed to the chapel at its summit and there is a mass pilgrimage on the last Sunday in July, known as Reek Sunday.

At the foot of the mountain Westport grew very little as one of scores of small towns on Ireland's west coast. There is a lovely story about the playwright George Birmingham, who was a Protestant rector in the town. He wrote the satirical play *General John Regan* about a small town that is duped by a trickster into erecting a statue to one of its natives who apparently led a revolution in South America. The play was a great commercial success in London and New York. However, when it was staged triumphantly in the rector's home town, it caused a riot as the townspeople

recognised themselves in the characters.

For much of the 20th century Westport was that sleepy, rather parochial small town isolated on the far west coast of Europe. Simon Wall, the town architect shows slides of Westport in the 1980s that, were it not for the few beaten-up cars, could have been from the 1880s. The people of the town decided to do something about this and commissioned a plan – Westport 2000 – to set out a vision for its future. This, of course, is something that many towns have done and most of their strategies remain little more than reports gathering dust. Ireland, however, has a system by which each town appoints a town architect as a sort of one-man/woman planning department and regeneration agency. Many towns no doubt end up with ineffective town architects, but when you get a good one like Simon in Westport, then incredible things can be achieved. He started with the easy stuff: a campaign to remove all of the unauthorised signs that cluttered every road junction in the town. He prepared a set of approved designs that businesses were 'encouraged' to adopt through a licensing system. He also offered a colour scheme design service to shops, thereby encouraging the repainting of many of the premises with bright colours. Another scheme insisted that PVC windows be replaced as part of any works to buildings and created strict guidance for new shopfronts.

This worked because of the arrival a year or so after the plan's adoption of the Celtic Tiger. This was an extraordinary Irish property boom that resulted from a strong economy in the early 2000s combined with tax breaks for investment in property. In Westport the result was a rash of new housing schemes, many designed by the best architects in Ireland. It saw the buildings of the town refurbished and infill development take place on brownfield sites within blocks to create new pedestrian shopping closes. In many parts of Ireland the Celtic Tiger left in its wake a trail of ill-considered and often incomplete schemes, but in Westport, with its strong town architect, it pretty much allowed the whole town to be refurbished and expanded.

For all of this Westport remains tiny; it is by some distance the smallest town in this book with a population of 5,500 - rising to 12,000 with summer visitors. Yet it is the liveliest place you could ever want to visit, full of independent shops, really good pubs and a range of civic institutions. Compare this to a new town with a similar population that would struggle to support a single pub and corner shop, and you get a sense of how miraculous this is. The economic life of Irish towns shows us what we have largely lost in English towns bled dry by superstores and bypassed by highway engineers. This economic diversity is like an ancient forest that once felled will never grow back. Ireland's 'wilderness years' allowed these unique commercial ecosystems to survive and long may they thrive.

Neighbourhoods

Back in 2011 the British government passed the Localism Act, which was intended to devolve power to local communities and allow them to draw up neighbourhood plans. This begged the important question about what we mean by a 'neighbourhood'. It is a question that planners have been struggling with for years and the 15 neighbourhoods described in the following pages illustrate the difficulties of pinning down a definition.

Part of the definition is geographical: a neighbourhood is a part of a larger settlement. Towns and cities have town and city centres around which neighbourhoods are arranged. In this respect a neighbourhood is similar to a district, or maybe an arrondissement if you are in a French city. In America you have precincts, which are electoral subdivisions like the wards we have in the UK. Then there is the idea of a quarter, which derives from the original subdivision of a Roman town into four districts divided by a crossroads, but which has now come to mean an urban district or neighbourhood. Or maybe we should be thinking of a neighbourhood as a suburb, somewhere less urban and more residential with a clearly subservient relationship to the town or city of which it is part.

All of these terms imply both place and identity. They refer to somewhere that has a name and that people identify with, as residents or visitors. Sometimes the identity relates to an original village that has been engulfed by an expanding city (although there are no examples in this book). Sometimes it comes from the parish church, as in St Pauls in Bristol, or from a marketing brand given to the scheme when it was first developed, like Bournville. Sometimes it comes from the activity that once took place there, like the Lace Market or the Jewellery Quarter. One might also say the same for Ropewalks in Liverpool, except that its name is a modern invention inspired by an activity that took place in the area for a very short time. Indeed, a lot of the names of these neighbourhoods are recent inventions. The Northern Quarter in Manchester is not even to the north of the city and refers to an area that had no distinct name until regeneration started in the mid 1990s. The Cathedral Quarter in Belfast is a similarly recent invention, as is Coin Street, although, of course, there has been a relatively minor street of that name for many years. Accordia, like Bournville, is a housing scheme given an evocative name as a marketing device.

Sometimes these places are defined by administrative boundaries or postcodes but often their definition is quite fuzzy. It is often the case that people are reasonably clear about where the centre of a neighbourhood is to be found, but less clear about its edges. Neighbourhoods overlap, or even sometimes nest within each other. Popular neighbourhoods tend to expand, particularly when people in surrounding areas claim that their house or business just 'falls within' or 'is on the fringes of' the area.

Geography is, however, only part of the definition. Neighbourhoods are, or at least should be, places where people relate to each other as neighbours. This is much more problematic as a definition, particularly when you are not just analysing what exists but also seeking to create new neighbourhoods. Planners have for years been trying to create neighbourhoods, generally with little success. The planning theory of the 20th century, from Clarence Perry's neighbourhood unit onwards, saw the neighbourhood as the building block of towns and cities. Each neighbourhood would have its allotted quota of shops, facilities and open space normally based around the catchment area of a primary school. The problem was that these formulas were not very good at predicting how people would live together and what type of communities they would create. There are just two neighbourhoods in this book that have attempted this trick of creating new neighbourhoods, at least in recent years; Coin Street in London and Accordia in Cambridge. The unique history of the former, arising out of a community struggle to stop the commercial development of the site and to build affordable housing in the heart of London, really does mean that a community of neighbours has been created in a newly constructed neighbourhood. In the latter it is perhaps too early to tell.

There are older residential neighbourhoods in this book that were built from scratch: Bournville in Birmingham, Stocksbridge in Edinburgh and Pollokshields in Glasgow. These are places that have had time to put down roots and to build social capital. They are true neighbourhoods in both senses of the word, a distinctive geographical identity and a strong local community. They are good places to live, with attractive environments and a rich array of local facilities. They attract middle-class families, pushing up prices, which can make them quite exclusive. Can a good neighbourhood be socially exclusive? If not, then there are some built-in contradictions with our ideas of a good neighbourhood.

Nowhere is this more true than in the large inner-city neighbourhoods. Brixton in London and St Pauls in Bristol were once well-to-do middle-class neighbourhoods but have evolved over the years into much more diverse places with strong Afro-Caribbean communities (both, of course, also experienced riots in 1980). As much as this diversity may be seen to have enriched these neighbourhoods, it only exists because they fell on hard times. These close, if sometimes embattled, communities have made these neighbourhoods their home but they are now under threat from gentrification. The invasion may not be by the genteel middle classes of Bournville or Stocksbridge, but rather the army of urban hipsters seeking a bit of grit and excitement. The effect is the same; the success of the neighbourhood and the attractions that it offers push up prices and squeeze out existing families and businesses. This damages the very things made the place so attractive – the dilemma, as we say, of a successful neighbourhood. Both St Pauls and Brixton have once more experienced riots in recent years, but this time the targets were gentrification and yuppies.

The difficult question for the Academy is whether its awards are a recognition of the strength of the original communities in these neighbourhoods or of the process of gentrification. Would the black Brixton with its saltfish shops and Jamaican barbers have been nominated were it not for the Brixton Pound, its Transition Towns Group and its multi-ethnic restaurants and farmers' market? We don't know, of course, since the nominations are done by means of a vote, but it is an important question nevertheless. These are just the sort of characteristics that the Academy tends to value, as seen in many of the places in this book. But there is a deeper, older form of neighbourhood urbanism in places like Brixton which took root at a time when the area was not fashionable and which is now threatened by its success.

This brings us to the largest group of neighbourhoods in this book: the creative quarters. These are places where the process of gentrification is perhaps more benign because it has been a force for regeneration in neighbourhoods that were in need of it. Seven of the places in this section could be described as creative quarters, sometimes literally, as in Folkestone which, like Margate, has used creative industries to reinvent its role as a seaside town. Others are resurgent industrial quarters, from Nottingham's Lace Market to the Northern Quarter in Manchester, Ropewalks in Liverpool, the Cathedral Quarter in Belfast and the Jewellery Quarter in Birmingham.

All these places share a similar history. They started out as well-to-do residential neighbourhoods before being taken over by a particular industry and being redeveloped with factories and warehouses. In each case the industry disappeared (the exception being Birmingham's jewellry industry) and the area fell into decline and dereliction. In some cases there was talk of demolition and in all of them fine buildings were lost to fire or neglect. However, gradually the cheap vacant spaces started to attract activity such as small businesses, artists and musicians. Developers like Urban Splash in the Northern Quarter and Ropewalks started to see the potential and public agencies set up initiatives that have gradually brought the quarters back to life. Such quarters can now be found in all British cities and, far from being economic anachronisms, the businesses that they house are seen as increasingly important to the city's economy and its ability to attract young qualified people. But are these places neighbourhoods?

In the Academy of Urbanism's second book, *Urban Identity,* we discussed three other big city creative quarters: Grainger Town in Newcastle, Temple Bar in Dublin and the oldest of them all, Soho in London. We concluded that they were not really neighbourhoods; indeed, in some respects they were places that you went to escape your neighbours. Creative quarters are places that thrive on life and activity and the interaction of strangers. The anonymity of life in a large city is what gives people the freedom to be creative and draw on diverse influences. This is not impossible in a respectable neighbourhood, but it is much easier in a creative quarter. So we maybe need to rename this category; rather than great neighbourhoods, the places that the Academy has been most likely to recognise in the past are great urban quarters.

Then again, maybe it is time that we turned our attention back to real neighbourhoods because these are where most of us live. Having celebrated the urban quarter in the early years of the Academy, we should perhaps now focus on the good neighbourhood. Maybe even that rarest of places; the good neighbourhood built in the last 25 years. We know how to do creative quarters and now need to find ways of creating equally good new neighbourhoods.

Accordia, Cambridge

Shortlisted 2012

The name of this place plays soft mood music;
And it sounds like Utopia or Shangri-la
But it's real. Real as the people who walk its streets
From the old nuclear bunker to Hobson's Brook
And it could be Nirvana and it sounds like Arcadia
But life is lived here from breakfast to bedtime
From evening to morning the lifestyle hum
Of curtains being drawn and kettles boiling
Doors opening and closing, people coming and going
And still the name sounds like something amazing
Something from a future so close you can touch
Something from a present so real it just sings…

Architects are fascinated by housetypes. A house is the simplest of building forms: a couple of reception rooms, some bedrooms and a kitchen and bathroom. There are only so many ways in which these elements can be arranged. The four or five standard housetypes built in the 1920s – when single-family homes came to the fore – are essentially the same as those used by housebuilders today. Architects' fascination with reinventing this particular wheel comes partly from a conviction that there must be a better way of doing a house. But there is also a sense of this being architecture at its most basic; doing housetypes is like a musician doing scales or a designer doing chairs – the purest form of their craft. It is easy to create architecture out of a museum but can it be done with the mundane, everyday ingredients of a house?

Well it clearly can, because the Accordia scheme in Cambridge won the 2008 Stirling Prize, the highest accolade UK architecture can bestow. The scheme, by Fielden Clegg Bradley Studios (FCB) together with MaccreanorLavington and Alison Brooks Architects, was designed for Countryside Homes. They built the first phase, to which the Stirling Prize relates, before selling the site to Redeham Homes. In total the masterplan covers 9.5 hectares and includes 378 homes at a net density of 47 units per hectare. Of these 166 are apartments and 212 are houses with a range of one bedroom to five bedrooms

The site was originally occupied by a house in extensive grounds. Brooklands House still sits on the main road at the northern end of the site and serves as the regional offices of English Heritage. The house and grounds were acquired by the government and were used for many years by a variety of government departments, many in Nissen huts. Beneath it a nuclear bunker was built, which would have been the regional seat of government in the event of attack. All of this was decommissioned in the 1990s, with the government offices being moved into new offices on the southern part of the site. The council prepared a planning brief in 1996 and the site was marketed, eventually to be bought by Countryside Homes in 2003, who appointed the three architectural practices to develop the scheme.

The masterplan was prepared by FCB who also designed 65% of the homes. MaccreanorLavington designed a row of four storey

It is easy to create architecture out of a museum but can it be done with the mundane, everyday ingredients of a house?

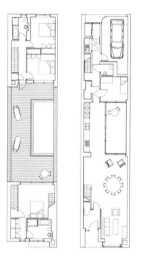

terraced houses, while Alison Brooks designed a set of semi-detached villas on the main road. All three practices explored new forms of housing layout. The plans to the left show one of the FCB courtyard houses. This occupies the whole of the plot with a front door onto the pedestrian walkway (at the bottom of the plan) and a garage at the rear. The living space occupies the whole of the ground floor with a light well and a 'courtyard' on the first floor accessing the bedrooms.

Just one of the many housetypes developed from the scheme, this is the sort of housing that is common in the Netherlands (where a book is published annually of new housetype plans) but rare in the UK. The early 2000s was, however, a time of experimentation in the housing market. Mainstream housebuilders like Countryside were interested in exploring these new types of product and it looked for a moment as if housing in the UK would become a lot more interesting than it had been. It never happened, of course. While the public reaction to housing like this was generally very positive, people remained conservative when making the biggest investment of their lives. For the developer, the costs were slightly higher and the values slightly lower so that as the recession hit they retreated to their standard product. The question is whether schemes like Accordia were a one-off, or whether interest in this type of innovation will return as the market gets stronger.

The fundamental issue from an urbanist perspective is that the form of the housetype affects the shape of the neighbourhood. It determines the density of development, the spacing of roads and the degree of permeability. It's like getting a new set of Lego pieces; all of a sudden more things become possible. We know from the experience of housing innovation in the 1960s that the result is not always positive. However, we will never build strong urban neighbourhoods if all we have to play with are the standard housetypes of the volume housebuilders. We need new and different types of Lego piece and Accordia shows a few of the possibilities.

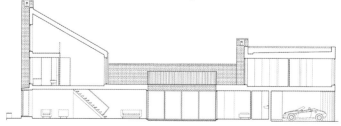

Borough/Bankside, London
Shortlisted 2012

Walk where Shakespeare walked,
sit where Dickens sat,
Feel Chaucer's stories surround you in the market
Watch the river flow with all the Bankside set:
Dreamers and poets who were there when it started
And who are watching the Shard grow, glass in the air
Not a sonnet's length from where Pepys saw the fire.

Here by the water taste regeneration
Hope in a hard hat, a full skip, a crane:
The past and the future seen through the prism
Of buildings and people, of singing and stone
Of thinking as wide as those alleys were narrow
Of Bankside and Borough embracing tomorrow...

Right: The Academy visit took place as the Shard was being built nearby.

Like all good double acts, Bankside and Borough is a neighbourhood of contrasts. Nestled along the banks of the River Thames, Bankside has experienced significant development that has seen it transformed from a dingy industrial backwater into a new urban quarter. Borough, further from the river beyond the railway lines has remained a more typical inner London district – a dense, fine-grained mix of homes, businesses and industry with less evidence of the glass and steel that has been reshaping its glitzier partner. The best-known feature in the area, the wonderful Borough Market, won the Academy's Great Place Award in 2007. These two very different places have developed a shared approach to working with the new development that has been thrust upon them to create a successful, liveable neighbourhood in the heart of London.

Borough was first settled by the Romans and was for centuries outside the jurisdiction of London. It had a reputation for both bawdy behaviour and creativity. In Elizabethan times it was a heady mix of theatres, taverns and brothels. The late 18th century saw Bankside develop as an industrial district of riverside wharves and warehouses, in touching distance of St Pauls but isolated on the far bank of the wide Thames. It was home to an impoverished community, living in overcrowded and unsanitary conditions, made worse when the railway companies sliced through the district with a series of viaducts in the 1860s.

The area remained a backwater until the 1970s when a pedestrian route was opened up along the river as part of the Silver Jubilee Walkway. To the west the South Bank Centre and Coin Street (page 128) were coming back to life, but through Bankside the walkway couldn't simply run along the water's edge; it had to wind its way around obstructions, although this did allow people to discover the hidden gem of Southwark Cathedral, hemmed in by railway viaducts. The next step in the rebirth of the area came with the opening of the Shakespeare Globe Theatre in 1997, following a 20-year campaign by the American actor Sam Wanamaker. While it is not on the site of the original Globe, it is faithful to the design of the theatre in Shakespeare's time.

A few years later the neighbouring Bankside Power Station, designed in 1947 by Sir Giles Gilbert Scott, opened as the Tate Modern gallery. When the power station closed in 1981, there was a long and nearly unsuccessful campaign to reuse the building (at one point demolition had started). The Tate appointed Herzog & de Meuron as architects following a competition and the £132 million project opened its doors for the Millennium. At the same time the Millennium Footbridge finally overcame the area's isolation (except for a two-year hiatus when it was closed to fix its wobble). These works transformed Bankside into one of London's tourist hotspots. To the rear the once dreary Southwark Street has been transformed with new schemes by the architectural practices Allies and Morrison and Rogers Stirk Harbour. The final piece of the jigsaw is an extension to the Tate, also by Herzog & de Meuron, that opened in 2016.

However, what is impressive is the way that the local authorities and other partners have harnessed this growth and spread the benefits from the river back into Borough. This has been done through a strong planning policy framework, enabling significant developer contributions to be directed towards public-realm improvements, projects such as the Tate Modern extension, a new public square at Flat Iron along Union Street and the Thameslink Borough Market extension. North–south routes that had been lost to the railways are being reopened, improving connections. The Bankside Open Spaces Trust has championed parks and gardens, notably Red Cross Garden, with the aim that 'wherever you are in Bankside you will see something green'. The Bankside Urban Forest group has been undertaking projects that bring life to outdoor spaces, using inventive engagement with residents and businesses. Drawing on ecological language, meandering north–south streets have been classified as 'streams' while busier east–west streets are 'rides' and open spaces are 'clearings', all combining to challenge assumptions of what a forest could be in an urban setting.

This has all been co-ordinated through Better Bankside, the area's Business Improvement District, which uses a proportion of business rates to pay for a staff team to manage the area and co-ordinate projects. It is this co-operation between businesses, the local authority and the Neighbourhood Forum that has made Borough and Bankside work. Many areas would have buckled under the onslaught of such development pressure, but Bankside has forged it into a thriving place to work, live and visit.

The Millennium Footbridge finally overcame the area's isolation (except for a two-year hiatus when it was closed to fix its wobble)

Above: North–south routes are being improved to overcome the severance caused by the railway viaducts.

Bournville, Birmingham
Shortlisted 2013

I can't resist it, I have to say it: life is sweet here,
Sweet as chocolate. The air is Bournville-clear,
Clear with a clarity of thought and design,
That says 'Being here means a chance to shine
Like the silver wrapper on a chocolate bar!'
Sorry, can't resist it, but this is where we are:
Bournville, streets built from philanthropy
Constructed with love and with sympathy, empathy
For artists and bowling clubs and cycleways
A place to spend your evenings, celebrate your days,
Play chess, volunteer, make a difference, just be.
Bournville is that kind of place, it seems to me,
Born from a vision, it's marvellous, it's belting:
It may be built on chocolate
but Bournville isn't melting!

Birmingham was no place to make chocolate in the 1870s. It was dirty, congested and unsanitary and the brothers Richard and George Cadbury, who had taken over their father's cocoa factory in 1861, decided that they needed to move. Both devout Quakers, Richard was the businessman and George the social reformer. Their decision to build a 'factory in a garden' outside the city would please both of them, being both good for business and at the same time creating humane conditions for their workers.

Their chosen location was Bournebrook House and its surrounding estate in Worcestershire. This was entirely rural at the time. But, being next to the canal and with a newly opened railway station on the Birmingham West Suburban Railway, it was not isolated. The factory they built was a model of its day with modern working conditions and facilities. This was something that many industrialists were doing at the time, including Josiah Wedgwood in Stoke, Titus Salt in Bradford and the Lever brothers on the Wirral. However, if you build a factory outside the city, you need to think about where your workers will live. These industrialists all therefore started to plan worker housing and, once more, a mix of business acumen and social concern caused them to rethink the type of residential environments that they should create. Healthy, happy workers were, after all, more productive and loyal to the company.

In 1895 the Bournville brothers purchased 330 acres of land and engaged the architect Alexander Harvey to build an estate. The specification indicated that each plot was to be at least a sixth of an acre and no house was to occupy more than a quarter of the plot, which was also to include six fruit trees. The three-bedroom houses were built for £50 or less and were sold at cost price on 999-year leases to... 'make

it easy for working men to own houses with large gardens secure from the dangers of being spoilt either by factories, or by the interference with the enjoyment of sun, light and air'. The estate was not, however, just for workers; anyone could buy a house. George Cadbury's aim from the start was not to house his workers but to influence policy-makers to reform housing conditions.

In 1899 Richard Cadbury died of diphtheria and George moved to secure their legacy by gifting the land and the new homes to the Bournville Village Trust. This was established in 1900 and continues to manage the estate today, in conjunction with the Bournville Village Council, which was established two years later. In 1906 the trust leased a further piece of land to Bournville Tenants Ltd, a housing co-operative that built a further 398 homes and in 1913 the trust built an extension to the garden suburb aimed at white-collar workers. In the 100 years since then the trust has developed and expanded the estate until it covers 1,000 acres, with 8,000 homes, 25,000 people and 100 acres of parkland.

The result is a really good suburb, one that is actually not that different from Birmingham's other really good inter-war suburbs. Bournville's significance is that it was the first. It is less formal that many of the other early garden city schemes and was probably therefore more influential in creating a template for inter-war suburbia. What really sets it apart are the governance structures and community ownership and management of the estate. With the exception of Letchworth, it is the only place where these mechanisms, so important to the garden city movement, remain in place.

> George Cadbury's aim from the start was not to house his workers but to influence policy-makers to reform housing conditions

Opposite: The Cadbury factory viewed across the sports field.

Below: George Cadbury.

Right: Alan Simpson from the Bournville Village Trust showing the Academy assessment team around the village.

Brixton, London

Shortlisted 2013

Essence of a city, this; city in a city,
Spend your Brixton pounds here,
This pulsing village in a city
Buy all you want in the market
In this idea of how a city in a city
Can be. Down at the Academy
Music rises through the city
As you rise from the tube like
Excitement rises in the city
In a city that Brixton is. Pretty?
Maybe not, though in this city
In a city there's a kind of beauty
That you really can't define
Although I think a city in a city
Like this is going places
And the place this city in a city
Is going is all the way to the future
When maybe every city in a city
Will feel like Brixton...

neighbourhood rather than the trendy bars or even the Brixton Pound. We hope that Urban 75 are right when they say it is not under threat.

In 1948 when the ship the *Empire Windrush* docked in London, it bought the first 492 immigrants to the UK from Jamaica. The group was initially housed in a shelter in Clapham and instructed to sign on at the nearest labour exchange on Coldharbour Lane in Brixton. In the years that followed this seed community started to move into the surrounding streets and, as further immigrants came, they made Brixton into the first and largest Caribbean community in the UK. They came into a Brixton ravaged by war and poor housing.

Most of London's local centres grew from villages absorbed into the growing city. Brixton is the exception. It was an area of forest that remained undeveloped until relatively late in London's history. Not until the construction of Vauxhall Bridge in 1816 did ribbon development start to stretch along the Clapham Road and the Brixton Road (both of which are Roman in origin). However, it was the opening of the Chatham Main Line railway in 1860 that caused the area to develop. Indeed, the next 20 years saw a huge building boom from which Brixton emerged as

Urban 75, a popular online forum based in Brixton, says on its site that there are some who worry that a 'slew of swanky bars and restaurants is threatening the very essence of Brixton'. They go on to say, however, that 'it'll take a lot more than a few sushi bars to kill off the colourful, exciting and unique character of Brixton'. This, it seems, goes to the heart of the question about what makes a good neighbourhood. Brixton is now the trendiest of south London neighbourhoods with a 'boho' arts scene, farmers' market and, yes, plenty of sushi bars, along with restaurants of just about every other nationality. It was also one of the first places to apply the Transition Towns philosophy at the neighbourhood scale (see Totnes on page 108), hosts one of the country's largest urban green fairs and has adopted the Brixton Pound as its local currency, all the things that secures a neighbourhood a nomination in the Academy of Urbanism Awards.

But there is another side to Brixton and one that has perhaps given it an even better claim to the title of great neighbourhood. This is the Brixton where the community has come together to battle poverty and poor housing, gangs, riots and rampant street crime. It is the resilience and character of this older community that makes Brixton a great

Young professionals are attracted to places like Brixton because of its grit and authenticity. They are keen to protect its diversity and culture but their spending power and tastes inevitably damage the thing that they found so attractive.

a fashionable middle-class suburb. In 1877 James Smith of Tooting used his racecourse winnings to build the UK's first purpose-built department store in Brixton, which he called Bon Marché after the world's first department store of the same name in Paris. Two further department stores opened and soon Brixton was rivalling Oxford Street as a shopping destination. Electric Avenue opened in 1880 as an arcaded shopping street, the first in London to be lit by electricity.

The middle classes were not to stay long. By the end of the 19th century it had become a much less genteel place, known as home to entertainers like Dan Leno and even Charlie Chaplin for a time. Decline in the inter-war years led to the middle-class villas being subdivided into bedsits. During the Second World War Brixton was heavily bombed and in the post-war years, as the leases on its

houses fell in, the area was subject to extensive slum clearance. Eventually, this led to the construction of six large council estates that were to accommodate a large part of Brixton's population, particularly the Caribbean community.

This community brought with it some of the less pleasant aspects of Caribbean life. Brixton became the base for two notorious Jamaican 'Yardie' gangs, the Firehouse Posse and the Kartel Crew, gaining a reputation for street crime and drug dealing, and this gangland culture has been part of Brixton ever since. As recently as 2012 the BBC called Brixton's GAS the most notorious gang in London. At the time GAS was at war with Brixton's other gangs, The Murderzone, Poverty Driven Children and Organised Crime and it was estimated that half of all shootings in the capital were gang related.

Back in April 1981 a similar surge in street crime in the Brixton area prompted the Metropolitan Police to mount an exercise code-named Operation Swamp (which was presumably to be drained). Over the course of six days they stopped and searched almost 1,000 people, mostly young black men. On the seventh day the area erupted into some of the worst rioting seen in London for years. It is estimated that around 5,000 people took to the streets and there were 324 injuries, 279 of which were to police officers, who also saw 56 of their cars burnt out. The rioting spread to 12 other towns and cities, including Toxteth in Liverpool and St Pauls in Bristol. The focus of anger was the 'sus law' introduced by the Conservative government that had given police powers to stop and search individuals based only on reasonable suspicion that a crime might have been committed. This was seen as a measure to persecute the black community, a view shared by Lord Scarman, who chaired the public enquiry into the riots. The sus law was repealed within months

and the Scarman Report led to new codes for police behaviour in the Police and Criminal Evidence Act 1984 and also the establishment of the Police Complaints Authority in 1985.

These were not the last riots in Brixton. A riot took place in 1985 triggered by the accidental shooting by the police of Dorothy 'Cherry' Groce. There was further rioting in 1995 and the area did not escape the London-wide rioting in 2011. The 1995 riot was also triggered by a police shooting; however, a quote by a local resident in the radical magazine SchNEWS suggested that the problems went deeper: 'Local people are not only pissed off with the death of Wayne Douglas but the whole gentrification of Brixton. Council houses and houses occupied by squatters are being sold off the local pub, the Atlantic, run by black people, was opened last week by yuppies as The Dog Star. In anger this was smashed, looted and burnt out. The £33 million City Challenge development including CCTV is only of benefit to big business not local stall-holders'.

Yuppies were, of course, the target of much of the radical politics of the 1980s and 1990s. This does, however, bring us back to where we started. The people of Urban 75, who were not worried by sushi bars, are more likely to have frequented the Dog Star than the Atlantic. Today the players in the story are hipsters rather than yuppies but the narrative is the same. Young professionals are attracted to places like Brixton because of its grit and authenticity. They are keen to protect its diversity and culture but their spending power and tastes inevitably damage the thing that they found so attractive. Local shops become sushi bars, house prices rise and the area becomes gentrified. Brixton has not quite been changed to the extent of other hipster enclaves like Hoxton and Shoreditch because of the presence of its large council estates. However, London is a city where the enclaves of wealth have grown and merged, leaving islands of poverty. The righteous indignation of Brixton's black community may not be as visible as it once was but that doesn't mean that it has dissipated.

Is Brixton therefore a great neighbourhood? Whether the members of the Academy of Urbanism who voted it as such did so because of its working-class Caribbean roots or its more recent gentrification we will never know. The tensions between these communities are, however, playing out across London as the city's economy and property market overheat. If Brixton can find an accommodation between these old and new ideas of what makes a great neighbourhood, then it really will have discovered something significant.

Cathedral Quarter, Belfast

Shortlisted 2011

There's a renaissance here: come and catch it!
There's a groundswell powered by art,
Hear it, taste it, touch it, watch it:
A transformation in a city's heart.
Of course you need money to make change last
And commerce helps to turn things round
But art makes sense of the glorious past
So the future's on solid creative ground.
Galleries and bars and espresso to savour;
A fiddle tune and an abstract construction
This quarter's a feeling, a notion, a flavour,
A place of delight and of subtle instruction
So come and write a sonnet
or raise a glass of porter
In the artistic hub:
the Cathedral Quarter!

Right: Former linen warehouses now used for cultural uses

Like their continental cousins, cities in the British Isles have old towns and new towns – their ancient cores with tightly-knit streets and their grand extensions with avenues and vistas. With the notable exception of Edinburgh, this is not how we tend to understand our cities. It does, however, help to explain Belfast's old town, known as the Cathedral Quarter. Built on the banks of the River Farset (that gave the city its name) where it meets the much larger River Lagan, Belfast was extended at the end of the 18th century. The river was culverted under the newly built High Street with the ceremonial axis of Donegall Place leading to the new City Hall – which replaced the original While Linen Hall – set within a grid of streets named after English lords and kings.

This extension saw the old town fall into a long period of decline. It initially became a place of linen warehouses, a slightly disreputable quarter on the edge of the grander new town, the haunt of writers and artists (Trollope wrote his first novel when working as a civil servant in the area) and a base for newspapers and satirical magazines like the *Northern Whig* (commemorated in the name of one of the area's best-known pubs). Much later, when Belfast was riven by the Troubles – including 'Bloody Friday' in 1972, when the Provisional IRA detonated 22 bombs within the city centre – the historic streets and buildings of the old town faced the twin threats of bombing as well as neglect. There was a real concern that the

It became the capital of Northern Ireland but was never a county town. The Catholics had a bishop and a cathedral, built on the Falls Road in the 1860s. But there was no Protestant cathedral until 1899, when work started to convert the parish church of St Anne into a cathedral (albeit one without a bishop) in the heart of what was once the old town and would soon be called the Cathedral Quarter.

Today this is one of the liveliest parts of Belfast. To the north stands the University of Ulster including its Arts School. Nearby North Street has long been one of the liveliest in the city with bars like the Front Page and Giros notorious during the punk era. Low rents in nearby streets attracted arts organisations like Northern Visions TV, the Safehouse Arts Gallery and the Belfast Print Workshop. Each spring since 2000 it has hosted the Cathedral Quarter Arts Festival encompassing comedy, theatre, art and music. The festival combines established acts with emerging talent and it has grow from 5,000 people in its first year to 60,000 attending more than 150 events.

area might not survive. But survive it did, being designated as a Conservation Area in 1990 and then in 1997 the Laganside Corporation made it a cultural quarter. One of the first projects was the refurbishment of Custom House Square, a major public space that sits on the edge of the Cathedral Quarter and links it to the waterfront. The site has traditionally been the focus for political meetings, and has been transformed into an outdoor venue hosting live music and events throughout the year. Beyond this the Cathedral Quarter stretches to the north and west.

There was no cathedral until 1899 when work started to convert the parish church of St. Anne into a cathedral (albeit one without a Bishop)

'Cathedral Quarter' is a bit of a misnomer. Belfast is not an ancient city; in 1610 John Speed's map of Ireland described it as an 'insignificant village'. It started to grow when it took over the rights to levy duties on imports that had previously been held by Carrickfergus (hence the significance of the Custom House). As its trade grew, so did its population with an influx of Scottish Presbyterians. One of these, William Richie of Saltcoats, brought with him his trade of shipbuilding, completing his first ship the *Hibernia* in 1791. The company he founded would grow into Harland & Wolff, the world's largest shipbuilder with 35,000 workers at its peak. By 1900 this Protestant city had grown into the largest city in Ireland with a huge influx of Catholic workers. The tensions this created would flare up throughout the 20th century and can be seen in the 'peace walls' that continue to scar the city to this day.

The young city straddled the Lagan, the boundary between the counties of Antrim and Down.

This grassroots regeneration via local arts organisations happened alongside mainstream regeneration initiatives that have focused on the public realm and the refurbishment of the area's buildings. Warehouses have become restaurants, managed workspaces and venues, while streets, laneways and public squares have been upgraded. Public art, much of it by local artists, has been installed through the Laganside public art strategy. The culmination of this work is the Metropolitan Arts Centre, a purpose-built venue that has recently opened on St Anne's Square. This is the largest public-sector cultural investment in Northern Ireland and will significantly increase the Cathedral Quarter's cultural capacity, raise the profile of the area and contribute to the evening economy.

In many ways this is a classic story of regeneration partly through the attraction of arts and cultural activities to an area that no one else wanted, and partly through public-sector mainstream regeneration. It is a mix that does not always work and the fragile balance of anarchic independence and top-down intervention can easily go wrong. However, while the Cathedral Quarter is still a work in progress, it is well on the road to regeneration.

Coin Street, London

Winner 2010

Newly-minted place, place of great worth
Not far from the banks of the mighty river
New ideas conjured up from ancient earth
To inspire, renew, rebuild and deliver.
A place to look and eat and drink
A place pulled right back from the edge
A place to walk or sit and think
A promise and a future and a pledge
That living in a city can help you grow
And not in the shadow of an office block;
Renewal and hope are what got sowed,
And something marvellous grew on London rock.
This neighbourhood can dazzle and can amaze
It overflows with riches, to Coin a phrase.

Coin Street, just a few miles north of Brixton (page 122), is also a story of a community in London taking on the power of the market. However, in the case of Coin Street the adversary was a million square foot office scheme and Europe's tallest hotel, rather than a battalion of hipster eateries. The official history of Coin Street is an inspiring story of a local community taking on the power of London's encroaching property market and winning – a community that subsequently bought the land over which it had been fighting and who has since used it to build a series of housing co-operatives, workspaces and a park, and are now planning to build a community swimming pool. However, extraordinary as it is, this official history does not tell the whole story.

The eight sites owned by the Coin Street Community Builders sit on the south bank of the Thames between Waterloo Bridge and Blackfriars Bridge. Geographically this is in the middle of London, except of course it isn't. When London Bridge was the only crossing over the Thames, much of the South Bank was a backwater. The heart of Southwark at the southern end of London Bridge became a riotous stew of brothels

'Any strategy that is sustainable has got to have something that brings in money and recycles it – it's a Robin Hood approach'

and theatres beyond the control of the London authorities. The fields to the west, where Coin Street now stands, remained open save for a few villas until the early 18th century. Blackfriars Bridge was opened in 1769 and Waterloo Bridge in 1807, finally linking the south bank to the city, and the area developed as a dense mix of industry and wharves, cheek by jowl with working-class housing. The history of the South Bank was described in the Academy's second book *Urban Identity*. For our story here we can roll forward to the late 1970s when the industry and wharves were largely gone and the office market started to see opportunities on sites south of the river. Enter the million square foot office scheme and the hotel tower.

The Coin Street Action Group was set up in 1977 to oppose these proposals. As part of its campaign it drew up alternative plans for the site, which it submitted as a planning application alongside the developer's scheme. This resulted in two public enquiries to consider both the developer's scheme and the community scheme, with the result that both were granted planning permission. The developer was, however, unable to proceed because part of the land was owned by the Greater London Council (who had originally supported the commercial scheme). In the early 1980s there was a change of heart and the GLC designated the land as a 'Community Area', a policy that had been introduced across London to protect residential districts from the commercial pressures of the city. The developer saw the writing on the wall and admitted defeat, selling their land to the GLC who subsequently sold it to the newly established Coin Street Community Builders. The sale included restrictive covenants limiting the use of the land but also reducing its value to just £1 million – money that the Coin Street Community Builders borrowed from the GLC and the Greater London Enterprise Board. Rarely can there have been such

a comprehensive victory of community activism over commercial 'greed'. The result was that the Coin Street Community Builders now owned one of the most significant pieces of real estate in the capital. To generate money in the early years the group allowed temporary parking on the sites. Next to the river they worked with Eric Reynolds of Urban Space Management to set up an area of craft workshops and restaurants using cheap prefabricated concrete garages. Gabriel's Wharf, as it was known, was only designed to be a temporary use but is still thriving 30 years later. Meanwhile, the group set about delivering on its promise of affordable homes for local people. The Coin Street Community Builders set up a secondary housing co-operative able to access grant money for social housing. This has since promoted four housing schemes, each of which has been passed on to a management housing co-operative, controlled by its residents. Mulberry was the first co-op to be completed in 1988, followed in 1994 by the Palm co-operative in the Broadwall scheme (by Lifschutz Davidson Sandilands Architects), and in 1996 by the Redwood co-operative in the Oxo Tower, and finally in 2001 by the Iroko housing co-op scheme designed by Haworth Tompkins Architects. In addition to this the group created Bernie Spain Gardens (named after Bernadette Spain, one of the original committee members) and are currently working on controversial plans to build a public swimming pool funded through the construction of a private residential tower.

The issues raised by this residential tower are not new to the Coin Street Action Group. When they undertook the £20 million refurbishment of the Oxo Tower, an iconic structure on the South Bank of the river, they rejected the option of working with a development partner and decided to do the scheme themselves. However, in order to generate value, there was a need to create commercial uses, including a Harvey Nichols restaurant on the top floor. As Iain Tuckett, long-term director of the Coin Street Community Builders, says: 'one of the greatest failings of social enterprise is to confuse what your social objectives are with your commercial requirements. Unless... you are willing to cater for people with money, if you are only going to cater for people in poverty, you will never get to viability. Any strategy that is sustainable has got to have something that brings in money and recycles it – it's a Robin Hood approach'.

The swimming pool scheme is nothing more than the application of this principle.

This is an interesting inversion of the politics that built Coin Street. The aim of the original GLC policy was to take a very expensive piece of real estate and to destroy its market value, thus creating the conditions under which it could be developed by local people for social housing, workspace and a park. The modern-day Coin Street, by contrast, is exploiting the market value of the site to act as Robin Hood. What would the original Coin Street Community Builders have thought of this? Well it is easy enough to ask them because many are still involved. Their philosophy, as Iain Tuckett explains above, is to play the system to the benefit of local people.

Which brings us back to the parts of that early history that do not tend to form part of the good practice case studies. Back in 1981 there was a stormy meeting of the Bermondsey Labour Party at which the long-term Labour council leader John O'Grady was deselected as a candidate for his own seat. He complained of a takeover by the 'far left' at a time when nationally there was concern about the Militant Tendency's entryist tactics in the Labour Party. The local GLC councillor, George Nicholson, countered that the local party had become moribund and all they had done was to introduce new members, who were more radical in their outlook (this all sounds very familiar in 2015 with the election of Jeremy Corbyn as Labour leader). In May that year the Labour Party won the GLC elections and within 24 hours the moderate Labour leader Andrew McIntosh was replaced by Ken Livingstone in what parts of the press called a 'Marxist takeover of London'. By 1983 George Nicholson had risen to become chair of the planning committee that would designate Coin Street as a Community Area and agree the deal to sell the land to the group. He was also a founder director of the Coin Street Community Builders and remains on the board today.

This, of course, is democracy at work: a local community faced with the prospect of being pushed out of its own neighbourhood by commercial developers, using the democratic process to put its own people in positions of power and thereby securing the decision that it wanted. Today it would be called 'localism'. It is, however, impossible to imagine any community doing today what Coin Street did in the early 1980s. There are many inspiring community-led developments across the UK but none that have carved out a territory in the face of such commercial pressures. Today these commercial pressures have swept over Coin Street and have it surrounded. But the Coin Street Community Builders have created a structure that cannot be undermined or taken over and hace thereby secured their community in perpetuity.

Creative Quarter, Folkestone
Shortlisted 2013

Scent of the sea, of making and dreaming;
Sound of a gallery door, a university with rooms
Where, just listen, you can hear them thinking
Things like 'This is Folkestone so let's assume

We're at the centre of things, a quarter like this
Can put this town right back on the map.'
A quarter's a fraction, it's partial, a piece
But I know this quarter can turn on the tap

Of regeneration, of confidence, cash
To make a new destination;
the cobblestones ring
With the sound of an idea made real,
made flesh,
So raise Folkestone voices
and let's hear them sing

of the Creative Quarter, a place like no other
to live and to work in; play in and discover!

For people of a certain age Folkestone will always be associated with Channel ferries – those grainy Kodak days of endless summers and the Sealink and Townsend Thoresen ferries that ploughed back and forth across the Channel. Today you can once more get a ferry from Folkestone but there was a period after 2000 when there were no services as the port lost out to its neighbour Dover after the opening of the Channel Tunnel. Losing its main industry has, however, been character-forming for Folkestone. Its path to reinvention leads through the Creative Quarter with its emphasis on the arts but also its ambitious programme of 21st-century philanthropy, which has created an artistic hub that is now a visitor attraction in its own right.

Folkestone is not a natural harbour town. It started life as a fishing community but the unforgiving shingle beach, battered by storms, was not the best place to bring up boats. But the town persisted and a stone harbour was built at the beginning of the 19th century. Following the arrival of the railways in the 1840s, the South Eastern Railway Company purchased the harbour and the town became the principal packet station for continental traffic to Boulogne. Folkestone thrived, becoming an attractive Georgian resort. By 1849 it was serving 49,000 passengers and the service grew to a zenith in the 1970s when its two newly commissioned ships *Hengist* and *Horsa* were carrying over a million passengers. By 2001 that figure was zero.

For Folkestone the announcement of the Channel Tunnel was like being given a terminal diagnosis: you have ten years to live while we build the tunnel, but after that your main industry will disappear overnight and your town will die. There was at least time to plan but what should the town do? One possibility was the arts; Margate had built the Turner Gallery (see page 142) while Hastings had built the Jerwood Gallery, both towns using these flagship projects to change their image to appeal to a more discerning (and wealthy) type of visitor and to attract artists. The model seemed to work but did you really need a flagship gallery? Folkestone thought not.

One of the town's biggest businesses was Saga Holidays. Roger de Haan, who had taken over the company from his father in 1984, sold it in a management buy-out in 2004 for £1.34 billion. He used part of the money to buy Folkestone Harbour, reopening ferry services, while further money was put into his charitable trust. Folkestone's original fishing village, just behind the harbour, is a distinctive tight network of streets within the Old Town Conservation Area. The Roger de Haan Charitable Trust started funding the purchase and refurbishment of run-down properties in the area through The Creative Foundation. This was set up in 2002 and now has a staff of 19 (20 if you include Baxter the office dog). Since that time 300 jobs have been created and a remarkable 90 buildings have been restored. These include the Quarterhouse, a performance venue hosting music and theatre alongside a wide range of studios, shops and business spaces. The charitable trust leases refurbished space to the Creative Foundation at a peppercorn rent, allowing them to rent it at affordable rents to artists while also generating an income. The income has been used to run two internationally-acclaimed Art Triennials, an annual book festival and a year-round performance programme. The Creative Foundation has also developed Folkestone Artworks, a permanent contemporary art collection of growing significance.

The creation of an ersatz cultural quarter from scratch using the wealth generated from selling

> You have ten years to live while we build the tunnel, but after that your main industry will disappear overnight and your town will die

holidays to old people shouldn't work. Creative quarters surely need to be forged through the struggle of artists colonising space that no one else wants, not cosseted in expensively refurbished buildings? But in a world of austerity when public funding for the arts is disappearing fast, the Creative Quarter in Folkestone is a remarkable beacon of excellence and artistic independence. The quarter has filled with artists and businesses and they are now making the area their own. Not every town has such a sympathetic benefactor, but Folkestone's Creative Quarter shows that there is a route to arts-led regeneration that doesn't require a Lottery-funded gallery.

Above: Views of the Creative Quarter. Many of the buildings have been refurbished by the Roger de Haan Charitable Trust. These include the orange and timber fronted properties on the right of the lower view, which were designed by Foster Gearing, a collective of architects and artists based in Folkestone.

Opposite top: The focus for the Creative Quarter is the Triennial that has been running since 2008 and has become a major event in the national artistic calender.

Jewellery Quarter, Birmingham

Winner 2009

TALKING TO SOMEBODY ABOUT THE JEWELLERY QUARTER

This place shines. It really shines. Put that in your poem: it shines.
I'm scribbling as fast as I can, but this place is many faceted,
Like a jewel, you mean? Very clever. Don't forget: it flippin' shines.
It's a kind of multi-faceted and gleaming and, yes, shining, asset
To a city that's already full to bursting with ideas and places.
Put this in your poem: it's been here for two hundred years
And have you mentioned the Big Peg? Not yet but I will, I will,
It was a place where jewellers with their gleaming faces?
Yes, if you like, gathered in this city ... am I making myself clear?
It kind of moves, this places, it dances, it shimmies, it's never still.
Shimmers. I like that. That's really helpful, thank you very much.
No, shimmies, mate; it dances, this place really moves and shines
A bit like a jewel does; Thanks, thanks ... It sparkles to your touch
The Jewellery Quarter: craft and art and business meet. Sublime!

Jane Jacobs has a chapter in her book *The Economy of Cities* entitled 'Birmingham Good, Manchester Bad'. Writing in the late 1960s, her point was that Manchester, a city of mills employing thousands of people, was ill-suited to an age where economic growth would come from the innovation of entrepreneurs and small firms. Birmingham, by contrast, was a city of tradesmen and meisters running small workshops creating and manufacturing all manner of metal products. The Jewellery Quarter epitomises this. When Jacobs was writing, 8,000 people were still employed in the Jewellery Quarter in 900 firms. This, she argued, was why the car industry found the Midlands so attractive and why Birmingham would always outperform Manchester (not that it worked out like that, as we discussed on pages 44-47).

Birmingham, it is said, is a city of a thousand trades. Its speciality is small-scale metalwork: buttons and buckles, toys and badges, guns and locks, and of course jewellery. The jewellery trade developed in the 18th century and expanded rapidly after the opening of the Birmingham Assay Office in 1773. By the mid 19th century Birmingham jewellers had cornered the market, eclipsing jewellery centres in Derby, Edinburgh and even London. In 1845 a delegation of Birmingham jewellers presented jewellery worth 400 guineas to Queen Victoria and by 1850 half of the gold sold in the jewellers of London carried the Birmingham assay mark.

The jewellery industry in Birmingham predates the Jewellery Quarter. The land to the north east of the city was originally used to extract sand for use in the moulds employed in the metal casting process (part of the area is still called Sandpits). In the mid 18th century the grounds of a large house (New Hall) became available and the area started to develop as an upmarket residential district with a grid of streets on either side of Newhall Street. In 1779 St. Pauls Church was completed, sitting within a fine residential square, by which time the quarter had become home to some of the city's most prominent industrialists such as James Watt and Matthew Boulton. The latter was instrumental in lobbying for an assay office in Birmingham and the site chosen was on Newhall Street. This, together with the opening of the Birmingham and Fazeley Canal in 1789, meant that the new residential area would become the centre

The production line was the street and the means of transport the pockets of the jewellers

for the city's jewellery business. In this book there are many stories of genteel Georgian neighbourhoods being taken over by industry or colonised by the working classes. The story of the Jewellery Quarter is slightly different. Because of the value of their products and the small scale of production, many of the master jewellers continued to live on site as the industry expanded. As a result the quarter became a productive industrial area while also remaining a respectable place to live, something that was unheard of in the cities of the north.

The making of jewellery is a complex process, as pieces are cast, worked, engraved, plated, set with stones, lacquered, polished and finished. The reason for the proliferation of businesses in Birmingham is that each part of the process was undertaken in a different workshop; the production line was the street and the means of transport the pockets of the jewellers. The majority of companies had fewer than 50 employees and nine out of ten business owners had started as craftsmen so they knew the trade and understood their product. Such a diversity of specialist businesses created a climate where innovation could flourish. George Elkington, for example, invented the process of electroplating and established the Elkington Silver Electroplating Works on Newhall Street, while in 1862 Alexander Park invented Parkesine, the world's first man-made plastic.

The peak of the Jewellery Quarter's prosperity was just before the First World War when around 30,000 people were employed in the area. During the war, production changed to military buttons and medals but the profitability of the trade was undimmed. The inter-war years were, however, more difficult. The growth of the trade and the development of larger factories meant that the area became overcrowded and the environment suffered. The fragile balance between living and working was disrupted; the residential population declined while some of the larger companies moved to other parts

of the city where they could find more space. In the Second World War the quarter was bombed because of its munitions production, so that by the late 1940s and 1950s it had been identified by the city council as a district in need of modernisation. In 1953 the council declared 23 hectares of the quarter as being beyond repair and drew up plans to zone the industrial and retail uses. Opposition meant that it wasn't until the early 1970s that the scheme was implemented, and even then on a much smaller scale. The Hockley Centre, an eight-storey flatted factory block, was completed in 1971 and a series of workshops with parking on their roof a few years later. Neither was a great success because the rents were too high and many of the companies displaced by the development either disappeared or found premises elsewhere, causing the council to abandon further plans. Decline continued and 25 years after Jane Jacobs written so glowingly about the city's economy, workforce of the Jewellery Quarter had halved.

In the 1980s the emphasis changed from modernisation to regeneration with a recognition of the importance of the quarter's heritage. Industrial improvement area grants and support from English Heritage saw almost 300 buildings refurbished and schemes were promoted to bring new housing into the area and even – because it was the 1980s – a wine bar. However, by 1990 a quarter of the space was still vacant. In that year the regeneration company URBED established the Jewellery Quarter Action project, promoting the refurbishment of buildings like the Argent Centre for small managed workspace. Later in the 1990s the quarter was designated as an Urban Village, leading to the establishment of the Jewellery Quarter Urban Village Regeneration Partnership. This developed a strategy to promote the quarter as a centre for creative business. The Hockley Centre has become the Big Peg and now hosts the British School of Jewellery and numerous small business spaces.

Throughout all of this long history the Jewellery Quarter has continued to make jewellery. Despite cheap foreign competition, cramped conditions, the modernising attentions of the planners and more recently an invasion of trendy young things, the jewellery trade has survived. There are complaints, as there always are, and in 2008 the Jewellery Quarter Association published a manifesto entitled *Time to Polish the Gem* to draw attention to the lack of progress in the regeneration of the area and also to the high rents that were pushing some firms out. However, unlike most historic quarters that have seen their original industries disappear, forcing them to reinvent themselves, the Jewellery Quarter still does what it always did, and in that respect it is indeed a rare gem.

Lace Market, Nottingham

Shortlisted 2009

Past, present and future in streets built on lace,
Built on lace and a capacity for invention,
A capacity for invention and a refusal to lie down,
A refusal to lie down when history comes knocking.

When history comes knocking you open the door,
You open the door and let rethinking in,
Let rethinking in and convert the old places,
Convert the old places to hotels and homes.

Hotels and homes and places to work in,
Places to work in, places to eat, places to think,
Places to think how the long-lost lace-makers,
The long-lost lace-makers would stand and applaud.

Stand and applaud the rebirth of a district,
Rebirth as a district, intricate as lace,
Intricate as lace in its delicate ecology,
Delicate ecology of past present and future...

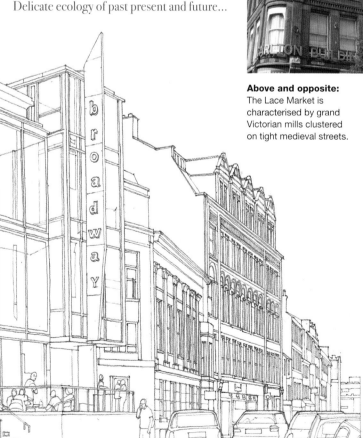

Above and opposite:
The Lace Market is
characterised by grand
Victorian mills clustered
on tight medieval streets.

When arriving at Nottingham Station, standing as it does on the low-lying ground known as Broadmarsh, you look up at a city on a ridge strung between two steep hills. Atop the western hill stands the Castle, home of that fabled baddie the Sheriff of Nottingham and once the centre of the French town. Atop the eastern hill crowds the Lace Market, a collection of grand Victorian buildings perched on top of a precipitous cliff of sandstone. Nottingham's city centre straddles the saddle of land between these hills but it was in the Lace Market, before it was called the Lace Market, that it all began.

Nottingham's original name was Tigguo Cobauc, which means 'place of cave dwellings' because the two hills are made of soft sandstone. The original city was underground, in a network of man-made caves that riddle the hillside. These were once home to thousands of people, as well as whole industries like tanning, and it wasn't until 1924 that the last family moved out of their cave home.

By the Saxon period, with a lamentable lack of place-branding advice, the city had been named Snotengaham, which just means 'the town of Snot's people'. It was a town of great halls, strung along its main street, High Pavement, which remains the main route into the Lace Market. The castle hill was occupied by the Normans following 1066, hence the French town that grew up around its base, and for years the two towns glared at each other from their respective hills.

By the 17th century the towns had merged and Nottingham (they had wisely dropped the 's') had become a prosperous city. It was at this time that the invention of the stocking frame revolutionised the production of hosiery. The towns of the East Midlands became the centre of this new cottage industry and by 1799 there were 149 hosiery manufacturers in Nottingham and six lace-makers (lace-making being a time-consuming handcraft). However, in the face of fierce competition from the textile centres of Lancashire, the Nottingham hosiers were forced to diversify by converting their stocking frames to lace-making. Increased production caused the price of lace to fall and it was incorporated into the fashions of the day. The Nottingham market boomed and by 1832 it had 186 lace-makers and just 70 hosiers. The lace-makers had started to concentrate on the hill around

Lace Market Heritage Trust. The building was very nearly selected as the national head office for English Heritage but eventually became home to New College Nottingham with a £16.5 million refurbishment.

The area's regeneration had started in 1989 when the Lace Market Development Company was established (the Lace Market Heritage Trust followed in 1993). Their strategy sought to protect the remaining lace manufacturers and resist the encroachment of offices. The area was designated as a National Heritage Area and tourism was promoted through the conversion of the Shire Hall and County Gaol as the Museum of Justice. The battle to save the lace industry was, however, something of a lost cause and the saviour of the area has been the very office development that the original strategy had sought to resist. The area is now part of Nottingham's Creative Quarter, together with Sneinton Market to the east. Its buildings have been gradually brought back to life, mostly for office and studio space together with some housing. On its northern fringe Goose Gate is a centre for the evening economy while High Pavement's role as a visitor focus has been reinforced with the opening of the Nottingham Contemporary gallery. The Lace Market is once more a functioning, fully occupied, normal part of the city, which must be the ultimate objective for any regeneration programme even if it no longer makes lace.

the medieval church of St Mary's which became known as the Lace Market. As with the Jewellery Quarter, the early trade was conducted in the merchants' houses, while the actual lace-making was a cottage industry in the surrounding areas.

This all changed with the invention of a series of lace-making machines. The first had been invented in 1813 by John Levers and then in 1846 John Livesey invented a lace curtain machine. As the patents fell in on these machines in the mid 19th century, the industry was transformed. Up until then Nottingham had remained a compact city. Unlike the other industrial cities, it was surrounded by undevelopable common pasture so that all its early growth had to take place within its walls (which is why its character is so different to other large British cities). Then in 1845 the Enclosure Act was passed, allowing the fields around the city to be developed. The lace merchants moved out of their cramped houses to suburban villas, redeveloping their former homes as mills to accommodate the new mechanised lace production process.

Over a relatively short period the medieval hilltop city became a forest of five- and six-storey warehouses, built by merchants with a bit of money to spend and a point to make. The grandest of these was the Adams Building, built by John Adams in 1855 as a trading and finishing house for lace products. The building was powered by a great steam engine that drove a hydraulics system running hoists and machines and providing heat through hot air ducts. The glazed top floors were used for lace-working while in the basement was a chapel that could seat 500, where prayers were said before each shift. The business closed in 1950, by which time the lace industry was in steep decline. For many years the Adams Building was subdivided into small business units but it gradually deteriorated until in 1996 it was acquired by the

> The medieval hilltop city became a forest of five- and six-storey warehouses, build by merchants with a bit of money to spend and a point to make

Northern Quarter, Manchester

Winner 2011

The ignorant say all of Manchester's 'Northern';
Not a quarter, not a half, but the whole Manc cake.
You should treat that kind of thing with Northern
    caution
'Cos there's a Northern Quarter here, make no
    mistake!

Its throbbing heart is beating on Oldham Street
And it dances round Tib Street and Shudehill
It's a real work-in-progress and it's not complete
And its creative heart is never, ever still;
If you want a definition of the cutting edge
Come to the Northern Quarter and feast your eyes
On a gaggle of streets that fulfils its pledge
To 'exist on work and play and surprise!'
If you want urban living that's delightfully vital
Come to the quarter with Northern in the title!

Affleck's has dressed, shod and shorn generations of Manchester's alternative youth

Above: Graffiti art from a Northern Quarter wall.

Top: Stephenson Square, where the former public toilets are programmed for graffiti artists.

Walk through the streets to the Northern Quarter in Manchester and layers of its history are revealed in its buildings. In places you can still see weavers, cottages with their long horizontal third-floor windows, behind which hand looms once worked before the Industrial Revolution. Next door you might find a terrace of Georgian houses, survivors from when this was an upmarket residential neighbourhood. Next to this, the looming presence of a six-storey Victorian warehouse from its boom years trading cotton. The uses tell the same story. Oldham Street, now occupied by vintage clothing emporiums and record shops, was once one of the city's main commercial streets, home to the imposing Affleck & Brown department store. The wholesale clothing showrooms and fashion businesses are an echo of the textile trade that once filled those six-storey warehouses. The hipster bars, with their upcycled furniture, include within their ranks venues from every stage of this history, like the Castle pub on Oldham Street built in 1776, where John Peel interviewed Ian Curtis of Joy Division in 1979. Or the legendary venue Band on the Wall that opened in 1975 as a jazz club and went on to become one of the city's main punk venues. Or Lammars, a bar named after Foo Foo

Lammar, the late, outrageous drag queen host of a eponymous basement cabaret club, with an opulent interior that stood in stark contrast to the area's dark, deserted streets long before its renaissance.

In the wonderful novel *The Manchester Man*, written by Isabella Varley under her pen name Mrs Banks, there is a description of the area now known as the Northern Quarter. Like Isabella herself, one of the main characters lives in a respectable house in what was then a well-to-do residential quarter. In one passage the book describes the scenes as the residents are disturbed by agitated crowds filtering through its streets on the day of the Peterloo Massacre in 1819. These roots as a Georgian residential neighbourhood are something that the Northern Quarter shares with many of the neighbourhoods described in this book. However, its gentility wasn't to last; within a few short years the Industrial Revolution had taken hold of Manchester and its Georgian past was swept away by bold, some might say brash, Victorian warehouses and mills (the Northern Quarter is, in fact, unusual in Manchester for having retained at least some of its Georgian buildings). The district became a place to trade in the cotton goods that were produced in the surrounding towns. The Northern Quarter was developed with what in Yorkshire would be called 'piece' warehouses – where samples were kept and trade was done – rather than with places to manufacture or store cloth. The legacy of grand buildings has allowed the Northern Quarter to be used as a stand-in for Manhattan in films like *Alfie* and *Captain America*. The city's cotton trade peaked in 1912 when

Left: A page from the graphic novel *Blood Blokes* by Adam Cadwell, in which the Night & Day bar is the venue where vampires party after dark.

Below left: A poem by Lemn Sissay set within the pavement by the ceramics artist Liam Curtin.

Below: A typical Northern Quarter scene.

eight billion square yards of cloth were traded. After this it entered a long period of decline as it lost out to cheaper foreign imports. But the trade never completely died and to this day there are clothing wholesalers in the area, although the sweatshops of the more recent past have largely disappeared.

By the 1980s the area was run-down and shabby. The streets behind Piccadilly were full of dark warehouses and, while few of them were completely vacant, most were in a poor state of repair. Further to the east and north there were vacant sites, used as surface car parks for city centre commuters while the northern part of the area had been dominated by the Smithfield Market. This was relocated in 1973, leaving some fine market buildings that lay vacant for years. In the late 1970s part of the market area was developed for the Smithfield Gardens housing scheme. Built as council housing with two-storey maisonettes over one-storey flats, this was the first new city centre housing in Manchester in the modern era and remains successful today. It was built around the former fish and poultry market that was converted into Manchester's Craft and Design Centre.

The birth of the modern Northern Quarter started at this time and can perhaps be dated to 1981 when Elaine and James Walsh opened Affleck's Palace. The model was simple enough: take a vacant building and let it to young entrepreneurs on flexible low-commitment terms so that they can start selling stuff. It quickly grew into a bazaar with more than 70 stalls selling all manner of fashions and alternative products. Created in the old Affleck & Brown department store that had become Debenhams and finally closed in the early 1970s, Affleck's has dressed, shod and shorn generations of Manchester's alternative youth. It has also spilled out businesses to populate the surrounding streets. One of these, a young graduate called Tom Bloxham started out running a poster stall in Afflecks, before leasing the neighbouring building, knocking through and creating the Affleck's Arcade. This was how Urban Splash started and one of their first large schemes would be the conversion of the neighbouring Smithfield Building.

In 1989 Factory Records opened a bar across the road called Dry (because at one point they thought that they wouldn't get a licence in time for the opening), with its Factory catalogue number

FAC 201. The chip shop next door evolved into the Night & Day cafe where Guy Garvey of Elbow played his first gig and where in a graphic novel by Adam Cadwell vampires party at night.

By the early 1990s these developments had created a kernel of activity in the lower part of Oldham Street, although much of the area remained as warehouses during the day and deserted streets at night. It was at this time that the name the Northern Quarter was coined, even if the area is more to the east than the north of the city ('northern' is more an attitude than a compass point, as Paul Morley points out in his book *North*). A study was commissioned and undertaken by a consortium of local consultants and architects led by Nick Johnson. Soon After the Northern Quarter Association was set up involving local business in the area's regeneration. An artist in residence was appointed: the ceramicist Liam Curtin, based in the Craft and Design Centre. He produced a range of artworks, including poems by Lemn Sissay set into the pavements. He also replaced all of the street name signs with versions made from ceramic tiles.

However, the regeneration of the area was not really something that was engineered. As Manchester's creative economy took off, the Northern Quarter was the natural place for it to be based and the whole district came back to life over the course of a decade. Streets that were once dark and forbidding are now lined with bars and cafes, and buildings once largely empty are now full of architects, graphic artists and tech companies. This is not so much a regeneration success story as an example of the natural cycles of decline and regeneration that happen in all successful cities. In the UK it seemed for many years that these natural cycles had stalled and that places like the Northern Quarter would never recover. However, with the renaissance of our provincial cities these cycles are once more at work.

Old Town/Harbour Arm, Margate

Winner 2012

Here in the heel of England, something stirs;
As the tide rolls in an artist takes her brush
And paints. And major cultural shift occurs
And preconceptions get crushed in the rush
And that's a good thing. What Turner saw
Was Margate water and Margate light
And this cultural quarter, this artistic core
Spreads Margate's wings. A town takes flight,
A town rethinks the way it views itself
Through art, the subtle connections that art
Can make with cohesion, inclusion and health
In the heel of England. That's more than a start...

Arrive at Margate by train and from the station forecourt a panorama is laid out before you. You could read it as the highs and lows of a love affair, proudly and painfully visible in the landscape of this Kent seaside town. In the background, around the sweeping bay, stuccoed Georgian crescents and Victorian terraces evoke the early, heady days of the 19th century, when a regular paddle steamer service from London carried eager crowds to seawater cures and society. Move forwards and the 20th-century Londoners' search for fun brought painted swing boats on the sands, a strip of flashing beachfront arcades and the rides and thrills of the Dreamland amusement park. And then the attractions of other holiday resorts beckoned and Margate languished unloved for 30 years. The high street hollowed out and many businesses, including Dreamland, were boarded up; some still are. So why is the rollercoaster of Margate's fortunes climbing once more?

The obvious answer lies in the striking focal point of this panorama: the understated, apparently windowless cubes sitting on the Harbour Arm – David

Chipperfield Architects' 2011 Turner Contemporary. Other towns and cities across Europe have looked to the opening of a new gallery to kick-start better times, but here it's only half the story. Not immediately obvious from our vantage point, but tucked away behind the tall terraces, is another neighbourhood, a tangle of intimate streets that almost turns its back on the sea the Old Town, where Margate's new life has already taken root.

This mix of old and new is key in Margate. It helps to create an air of expectation, which is just what coming to the seaside should be about. Now that sleek Javelin trains have joined Eurostar on the high-speed line from St Pancras, that anticipation can start as you race through the Kent countryside. Never mind that the Javelin's destination is the Isle of Thanet rather than the Île-de-France, because Margate's most famous visitor famously declared to John Ruskin that the skies over Thanet outstrip anything found in all Europe. J. M. W. Turner first came to Margate as a schoolboy. Later, attracted by the light, and by his landlady Mrs Booth, he had reason to return again and again and was eventually to depict the sweeping sands of Margate town and the coast nearby in around 100 paintings and drawings. When the resort was at its lowest ebb, local resident John Crofts and other members of Margate Civic Society recognised that this association with Turner was a unique endorsement by the master – of art as well as of self-promotion. And thus an ambitious vision was born: to celebrate the connection with Turner and fight back against the resort's decline.

Alongside plans for a new art gallery, Thanet District Council had also been developing some ideas. During the 1970s a number of reports had identified that investment in the increasingly derelict Old Town was key to Margate's fortunes – a complete about-face from earlier plans for its demolition to make way

Investment in the increasingly derelict Old Town was key to Margate's fortunes – a complete about-face from earlier plans for its demolition to make way for a ring road and car parks

for a ring road and car parks. With the listing of many of the Old Town's buildings in 1973, a vision emerged for public-realm improvements and building repairs. This continued through the 1990s when a Townscape Heritage Initiative and ERDF programme gave financial support to develop a cultural quarter. Kent County Council, later joined by Arts Council England and the South-East England Development Agency, also saw the potential for a culturally resurgent Margate to drive a wider regional regeneration.

Public and private sector-funded projects saved many buildings from demolition. These included several artists' studio developments in repurposed industrial buildings such as the Coal Stores on the pier and the former Pie Factory. However, what was so transformative was not the refurbished buildings but the critical mass of activity – cafes, bars, studios, galleries and vintage shops – that were attracted. Turner Contemporary, even before it opened, validated the town's creative credentials, attracting activity to the Old Town even while the nearby high street struggled. Architects, DJs, designers and artists helped to make Margate a credible cultural destination. Through partnerships like the Old Town Action Group, their energy and commitment has brought the area back to life.

Today Margate Old Town has a strong sense of place. Its enclosed, human-scale spaces are much more intimate than the rest of the town, wonderful places to sit and while away an afternoon, so that catching a glimpse of the open sea beyond can come as a surprise when it appears along a narrow street. Just a few yards from these fine-grained streets the promenade and beach open up to offer wide spaces and vast skies.

Across the road, at the entrance to the stone harbour and alongside the 1812 Droit House where customs were paid, the light, bold structure of Turner Contemporary was finally constructed. Fittingly, this place – known as the Rendezvous – is where Mrs Booth's boarding house once stood. With its entrance and cafe terrace facing the neighbourhood opposite, at first sight the gallery also appears to turn its back on the sea, yet once inside the quality of light that floods though the great North Sea-facing facing windows can be mesmerising.

The development of the gallery was hard won, with the original design abandoned in 2006 after costs spiralled. Before the final scheme was agreed, ideas were tested and exhibitions staged in several temporary homes, including the empty Marks & Spencer store on the high street and the Droit House

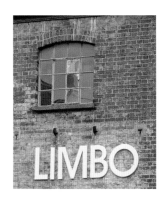

Opposite above: Turner Contemporary sitting on the harbour next to the Droit House, a former customs office.

Opposite below: Tracey Emin's neon artwork on top of the Droit House.

Above: Limbo is one of the new artists' studio spaces in the Old Town.

on the Harbour Arm. This meant that the principles and potential of the gallery were already growing in the community long before it opened, through fresh ways of consulting and engaging people about the design of the building and art more widely.

This relationship with the community is fundamental. Learning and cultural outreach are at the heart of the programme that emerged from Turner Contemporary's years of development. It extends beyond the artwork on display to offer employment, training and learning opportunities for local people, as well as reaching out to new, non-traditional audiences. Families with a CT9 postcode can attend weekend and school holiday workshops for free, while the grand sea-facing Foyle Room is becoming a popular venue for weddings. Turner Contemporary has already had a transformative impact, from the numbers of visitors and jobs created, to the adults and children that have taken part in learning activities in the vast bright Clore Learning Studio Room. Alongside the Turner collection contemporary artists have been shown such as Alex Katz and Margate's own Tracey Emin.

While Turner Contemporary has finally been achieved, Old Town is still a work in progress. A huge amount of physical conservation and regeneration has been achieved in the last 20 years. What's more, the energy and passion coming from the Old Town is spreading. More co-working and studio spaces, like Limbo, Crate and RESORT, are being opened to meet the demands of creative people drawn to the neighbourhood often after being priced-out of London. Successful Old Town businesses are expanding and looking elsewhere in the district – Cliftonville, Broadstairs, Ramsgate – to open new outlets. People with vision and nerve are even taking on the abandoned buildings of Margate High Street.

Attention is turning to planning issues too, with campaigns to sustain the quality of Margate's distinctive modern architecture and recognise the role that a lively public realm can play in reviving areas abandoned since the 1980s. A more confident sense has emerged of a place that celebrates its history in creative and contemporary ways. The council has played an important enabling role in this transformation but it is the businesses, residents and community groups who are making it real. Back towards the station, designer Wayne Hemingway is steering the 'retro' delights of Dreamland and its iconic Scenic Railway rollercoaster firmly into the 21st century. Like the Old Town and Turner Contemporary, it is part of a new, self-confident picture of Margate. As Tracey Emin's 2010 neon artwork displayed about the Droit House declares, 'I Never Stopped Loving You'. The secret to Margate's success will be falling in love with itself again.

Pollokshields, Glasgow
Shortlisted 2011

If you want a neighbourhood
with a neighbourhood feel
And a feel for the world and the future
Get down to the neighbourhood of Pollokshields.
It's a place where the people teach you
That regeneration begins in the heart
And spreads right through society
That the street where you live is the place to start
And the streets buzz with variety
That steps right up when you step off the bus
And shouts 'This is Pollokshields,
I'm proud to say!
And regeneration begins with us
From the Glasgow dawn to the end of the day'.
Bottle what they've got and take a sample
If you want a neighbourhood
here's a great example!

Two miles south of Glasgow's centre, on the wrong side of the river and bordered by motorways and railways, Pollokshields is an unlikely success story. A neighbourhood of two very different parts – each with its own outstanding architectural heritage – Pollokshields has managed to bring together a successful mixed community that offers a template for successful social and environmental stewardship.

The two sides of Pollokshields stem from its original design. It was planned by the Edinburgh architect David Rhind in 1849 for the Stirling-Maxwell family. The Scottish word for this type of planning is 'feued' which means 'to divide land up for rent' and has the same roots as the word 'feudal'. However, in the case of Pollokshields, the plots were sold with a ground rent to wealthy families who employed some of Glasgow's finest architects to build their villas. The character of the area differs on either side of Shields Road. The flatter, eastern side was set out as a grand grid of finely detailed tenement blocks, while the rolling terrain to the west allowed for spacious avenues, sweeping drives and bespoke villas on more generous plots.

There are other differences between the two sides of Pollokshields. The western part was

deliberately kept free of commercial activity while the busy eastern tenements are peppered with ground-floor shops. These were originally tightly controlled but as the area fell into decline in the 1970s, the eastern terraces became run-down. The cheap rents attracted a population of largely Pakistani origin and this community has bought the retail area back to life, such that it now has a reputation for Asian grocery that draws people in from a wide area.

The other side of Pollokshields also struggled. Like many early Victorian suburbs, houses built to be run by servants for wealthy families struggled to find a role in the 20th century. Many fell into decline and were subdivided into bedsits, converted to institutional use or slated for demolition. The villas along the northern edge of Pollokshields were cleared to make way for an ill-fated deck-access estate and a cluster of tower blocks. The community of this area now revolves around the community centre set up by the formidable Nan McKay. However over time, the quality of the Victorian heritage was recognised with its designation as a Conservation Area in 1973. This was the start of the area's recovery and Pollokshields is now a desirable residential area.

One of the key moments in this renewal was the conversion of the former Coplawhill tram terminus into the Tramway Arts Centre. This was done as part of Glasgow's transformational year as European City of Culture in 1990. The Tramway opened in 1988 with the

Houses built to be run by servants for wealthy families struggled to find a role in the 20th century

UK's only performances of Peter Brook's *Mahabharata* and is of a scale to stage international performance and exhibitions. This has become a symbol of the neighbourhood's regeneration and has played a major role in changing perceptions. It was recently extended to include the headquarters for Scottish Ballet.

Today a strategic framework is in place to guide the development of Pollokshields. This is supported by studies, action plans and guides developed by a partnership between Glasgow City Council, Glasgow Housing Association and the community including the Pollokshields Community Council and Pollokshields Heritage. The fruits of this partnership include the refurbishment of New Victoria Gardens, allotments that were once pleasure gardens. Because of this history, plot holders are required to grow flowers on at least a quarter of their plot. Maxwell Square Park, the neighbourhood's largest open space, has also been improved through the efforts of its friends group, who have been so successful in supporting biodiversity that the park has been designated a local Site of Importance for Nature Conservation. Perhaps the greatest success story is the Hidden Gardens. Opened in 1996, this is a sanctuary that delivers a range of initiatives and events designed to promote understanding between diverse cultures, faiths and backgrounds. These strong neighbourhood links have also been successful in delivering initiatives and events, such as the Eid on the Drive celebration that brings the community together to celebrate the end of Ramadan. This is symbolic of Pollokshields' journey from not so humble beginnings, using its historic legacy to become a thriving multi-cultural neighbourhood that looks both to its past and future.

Ropewalks, Liverpool

Shortlisted 2010

Sometimes living in a city is like walking on a rope
You can slip, you can tumble, you can end up falling down
Sometimes living in a city is just hanging on to hope
Walking every day between the grey sky and the ground
But Ropewalks is a vision of just how things can be
How regeneration alters more than just the view
And creates much more than buildings, more than you can see
And let me tell you that this much I know is true:
Ropewalks is renewal, that's a sculpture, that's a FACT
It's a place to sit and chill, it's a place to stand and think
It's a place for symbiosis, a place where opposites attract
But forget my theorising, let's just go and have a drink!
In a city where everybody sings and everybody talks
See them talking and hear them singing down the new Ropewalks...

Ropewalks is both Liverpool's creative quarter and the hub of its night-time economy. Like Temple Bar in Dublin, it is a place where both hipsters and hen parties are to be found. Home to cultural institutions like FACT and creative workspaces like the Tea Factory along with a number of arts spaces, it is also the place to find some of the city's largest bars and clubs. Add to the mix several thousand residents and a certain degree of tension is inevitable, if also quite a lot of excitement.

All of this so nearly didn't happen. Back in 1990 the area was in a sorry state. Many of its buildings were vacant, some falling into dereliction and others having been cleared to create car parks. What it did have going for it was the fact that it was almost entirely owned by the council. They had inherited a single land holding covering 80 acres and 388 buildings encompassing most of the quarter. It could have been a unique opportunity for regeneration but didn't work out that way.

In 1990 the council agreed to sell the land holdings to a company called Charterhouse Estates. This was not necessarily a bad idea; Charterhouse was owned by the architect Roger Zogolovitch, who was a partner in CZWG Architects with Piers Gough (and indeed a founding Academician of the Academy of Urbanism). They paid £10 million for the land and buildings and developed plans that would have turned the Duke Street Quarter, as it was then called, into an artist-led cultural quarter. Unfortunately, that was not what happened. An 1992 article by Rosie Millard in the *Independent* newspaper tells the story of artists left frustrated, not being able to agree leases on buildings and unable to invest.

The problem was that the country had gone into recession, one of the effects of which was that property values fell, leaving many homeowners in negative equity. Charterhouse may have been painted as 'big bad London developers', but their intentions weren't bad and they weren't big enough. They had bitten off more than they could chew and their bankers lost confidence, pushing the company into liquidation. Then the worst possible thing happened, the 80 acres were bought by a parking operator attracted by the area's potential for surface parking – surely ending any hopes of regeneration?

Today the quarter is known as Ropewalks, a name that only dates from the regeneration initiatives that finally got underway later in the 1990s. It is a good name, explaining its elongated blocks stretching uphill from the original 'pool' from which Liverpool takes its name. The pool was Liverpool's first enclosed wet dock, opened in 1715 to keep ships afloat when the tide went out. In order to maintain their ropes, merchants bought long strips of land up the hill. Within a few years the area was developed and the rope-working activities moved elsewhere. However, the long strips of land left their imprint on the quarter that subsequently emerged.

This was initially a quarter of grand houses for merchants and ship captains. Their houses included warehousing so that the merchants could keep a close eye on their stock. However, as the area became more crowded and less pleasant, the merchants decamped to the new neighbourhoods built on the ridges above the city (see Hope Street, page 178). This allowed their warehouses to expand and the area between Bold Street and Duke Street became a 'lively' dockside quarter. Chinese sailors jumping ship settled at the top of the hill, creating one of Europe's first Chinatowns.

Liverpool Rope Walks Partnership was formed to kick-start regeneration in 1997. Made up of stakeholders including Liverpool City Council, English Partnerships, private companies and community representatives, it commissioned an Action Plan that set out how the area might be tackled. However, what really made the difference was a deal with another developer. Given the experience with Charterhouse, it was maybe a surprising choice to go with a young Liverpool entrepreneur, Jonathan Falkingham, together with his associate Tom Bloxham in Manchester. According to Urban Splash's website Concert Square in Ropewalks was their first scheme. It included the extraordinary idea of a long bar serving directly onto the space that would be more at home on a beach in Ibiza than the north of England. Needless to say, it worked (who wouldn't want a bit of Ibiza in Liverpool?) and the square is now central to Liverpool's nightlife. Since that time Urban Splash have converted five buildings in the area, including the Vanilla Factory and the Tea Factory, to provide creative workspace and apartments. The public sector's contribution is to be seen in the public realm and in grants to aid the conversion of buildings. A comprehensive public-realm scheme by BDP has been used to transform most of the streets in the area with high-quality materials and street furniture.

In addition to Concert Square, five further public spaces have been created. Perhaps the most extraordinary of these and the one that best encapsulates the history of Ropewalks, is Wolstenholme Square. Originally a fine residential square, it declined over the years until it was an isolated space surrounded by tin sheds. This made it a good place for nightclubs because there was no one to disturb. The sheds were converted into a series of venues, the largest of which were the Kazimier and Nation. The latter is where Cream started as a residency before growing into a world-wide brand with clubs in cities across the world, a record label and a major festival called Creamfields. The square acts as a chill-out space for the bars and is dominated by the amazing *Penelope* sculpture by the Cuban-born artist Jorge Pardo. The history of the square, and perhaps also of Ropewalks, came full circle with the approval in 2014 of proposals for a large student housing scheme. Regeneration it may be, but it will also mean the closure of the clubs that have become central not just to Ropewalks but to the city's identity.

Then the worst possible thing happened; the 80 acres was bought by a parking operator.

St Pauls/Montpelier, Bristol

Shortlisted 2010

If you're looking for a jewel then let me tell yer
You want to get down to St Pauls/Montpelier!
It's a shining place, it catches the light
From artistic mornings to Italian nights
And the people on the streets feel part of a scheme
That's brighter than reality, more tactile than a
dream;
Somehow the future can be built from a past
That didn't fulfil this place's potential
But the streets and the squares are changing fast
It's a Bristol-type exponential
Expansion of a project into glittering reality
With the St Pauls/Montpelier can-do mentality
It's the opposite of a dismal failure
The runaway success of St. Pauls'/Montpelier!

The St Pauls area of Bristol shares a parallel history with Brixton described earlier in this section. Both have travelled a path from 18th-century affluence to 19th-century respectability and 20th-century decline. A legacy of large houses and unscrupulous landlords meant that both became areas where Afro-Caribbean immigrants could find a home in the 1950s. Both grew into strong black communities which also brought with them some of the less positive elements of Jamaica: Yardie gangs and drug dealing. In 1980 both St Pauls and Brixton erupted in some of the worst race riots ever to take place in the UK.

Meanwhile Montpelier, just to the north was described by the *Sunday Times* as one of the 30 coolest places to live in Britain, while just to the west lies the self-proclaimed 'people's republic' of Stokes Croft, where more riots took place in 2011 against the opening of a Tesco store.

There is irony in the fact that St Pauls, now home to a large Jamaican community, was originally built for slave owners. In the late 1700s the

architect Daniel Hague laid out Portland Square and designed St Pauls Church (at the very bottom of the map below). The architectural ambition of this early development was on the scale of the great London squares but the developer's aspirations were frustrated as affluent merchants were tempted by the even more genteel surroundings of Clifton. There is an urban legend that the origins of the black community in St Pauls date back to a black servant who inherited a house on Portland Square from his disgruntled master. This appears to have no basis in fact, although there were undoubtedly a large number of black servants in the early days of the area and at least one of them, Henry Parker, had become a housholder by 1850. By that time St Pauls was a mix of housing and small-scale workshops and, while still respectable, was no longer desirable.

Montpellier – meaning 'place with a beautiful prospect' – was developed a little later, at the end of the 18th century. It was originally pleasure grounds created by the entrepreneur Thomas Renisson. A directory of the time described it as having 'spacious baths and dressing houses, pleasant gardens and good accommodation'. By the mid 19th the area had been incorporated into the city as a modest middle-

class neighbourhood of two-storey terraces.

The key moment in the history of St Pauls came in the Second World War when the bombing that destroyed Broadmead caused extensive damage in the area. Parts were cleared and council estates built, while the remainder of the area was subdivided into bedsits, often by unscrupulous landlords. By 1951 the Ordnance Survey map described parts of Portland Square as being 'in ruins'. This was the area that met the Jamaican immigrants when they arrived in the 1950s: one of the poorest neighbourhoods in Bristol and the only place where they could find accommodation. The riots that took place in April 1980 followed a police raid on the Black and White Cafe on Grosvenor Road. Like the Brixton riots in the same year, the disturbances were blamed on heavy-handed policing, exacerbated by the poverty and lack of opportunity in the area. 130 people were arrested and 19 police officers had to be treated in hospital.

These tensions have not entirely eased since that time. St Pauls, despite huge improvements in recent years, retains a reputation for drug dealing and gang violence. Gentrification is taking place, particularly given the proximity of bohemian districts like Montpellier and Stokes Croft, but this is Bristol and the context is different to that in Brixton. In both areas the black community and a radical activist community have coexisted for many years and have gained strength from each other. In Brixton this mix is being threatened by the 'yuppies' and hipsters who are attracted to the area's radical chic but push up prices and squeeze out local people and businesses. This has not happened to the same extent in St Pauls – but, of course, there is still time.

By 1951 the Ordnance Survey map described parts of Portland Square as being 'in ruins'

Opposite above: George Ferguson on the Academy visit to St Pauls (he was later elected Mayor of Bristol).

Opposite: A before image of Portland Square from Historic England and the square today.

Stockbridge, Edinburgh
Shortlisted 2009

I like a place with 'bridge' in its name; it suggests movement,
Progression, a journey, no matter how small.

Well, take a journey to Stockbridge, walk the Colonies,
Gaze into the Water of Leith and see yourself reflected,

And that's what I call a journey, a journey into yourself,
And that's what Stockbridge offers, a time to reflect

On what can be done in a city; walk by St Stephen's Church
And past the Academy, wander up Ann Street, a street

That a better poet than me called 'the most attractive street
In Britain.' Sir John Betjeman, he knew a neighbourhood

When he saw one, these schoolkids, they know a neighbourhood
When they see one, these eaters, these drinkers, these thinkers

These walkers, these talkers, they know a good neighbourhood
When they see one: this one, with a bridge in its name...

Edinburgh has more great neighbourhoods than is entirely fair. It was built as a city of urban villages for its affluent residents, with fine houses of stone clustered around lively high streets that have, on the whole, retained their character and charm. Stockbridge is, and always has been, a comfortable, convivial, walkable place that has never really fallen out of fashion. Its history contains none of the dramatic highs and lows that we have seen in many of the other neighbourhoods in this book. This is a continuity that creates great places, if not great stories.

Stockbridge started life as one of a number of small settlements just outside the city. It stands just to the north of the celebrated New Town, and got its name – Stocc Brygg, Scots for 'timber bridge' – in recognition of its original crossing over the Water of Leith. It was known as a place to take respite from the city and its waters were thought to have healing properties. Lord Gardenstone, a wealthy Edinburgh judge, was so convinced of this that he donated funds for a new pump room to be designed by Alexander Nasmyth. The result, an elaborate Greek temple replete with its statue of Hygieia, the Greek goddess of health, was opened in 1789 and became known as St Bernard's Well.

At about the same time the New Town was taking shape and Stockbridge was overtaken and incorporated into the expanding city. The well was a great draw and there was a demand from the middle classes to set up home in the area. The painter Sir Henry Raeburn, who had been born in Stockbridge in 1756, set about servicing this demand. He bought the St. Bernard's estate and created a masterplan with the architect James Milne, replicating the financial model used in the New Town. He also improved its connections to the city (and no doubt its commercial prospects) through the construction of a more robust stone bridge.

In the decades that followed the area flourished. The Botanical Gardens was relocated to a large open space just to the north and the city agreed to the construction of a new independent school, the Edinburgh Academy. It was on the Academy's playing fields in 1877 that the first Calcutta Cup match was played between England and Scotland. This, the first ever international rugby match, was won magnificently by Scotland (even if, rather depressingly for some, England have won 71 of the subsequent 133 matches).

Stockbridge was also the site chosen to pilot a new type of housing, known as the Colonies, that went on to be built across Edinburgh in the latter part of the 19th century. These were a response to a severe housing shortage caused by a slump in housebuilding during a prolonged recession at a time of rapid industrialisation and population growth. The Reverends Dr James Begg and Dr Thomas Chalmers, Ministers of the Free Church of Scotland, campaigned to improve housing conditions for the poor and promoted the development of the Colonies between 1868 and 1911 through the Edinburgh Co-operative Building Company (set up by tradesmen locked out of a site in a dispute about working hours). In an era before mortgages the model offered the artisan classes the opportunity to own a property through subscription. So that each house could have a front garden, the Colonies were built as double flats that faced in different directions, the lower flat facing towards one street with a different address to the upper flat, which had its outside stairs and front garden on the next street.

Today Stockbridge is, in many ways, still a village – the sort of place that urbanists purr over but generally struggle to replicate. It is a tight-knit prosperous community within an easy walk of an enviable range of shops and facilities along Raeburn Place, its main street. One of the reasons for Edinburgh's embarrassment of strong neighbourhoods is the Scottish tenement. This

Given its easy character and location within walking distance of the city's commercial and banking institutions, it is hardly surprising that Stockbridge is pretty middle class

Top left: A popular Sunday market operates on Raeburn Place throughout the year.

Above left: The Colonies are a unique form of housing with a ground-floor flat facing onto one street and the upper-floor flat on to another.

is a housing model that achieves great density while also providing generous living spaces and remaining attractive to middle-class households. It is a form common in continental Europe but largely absent in England.

Given its easy character and location within walking distance of the city's commercial and banking institutions, it is hardly surprising that Stockbridge is pretty middle class. A popular Sunday market operates throughout the year on Raeburn Place serving the community as well as tourists who happen to wander down the hill from the New Town. You will have very little difficulty finding spelt bread and many other things come with the prefix of 'craft' or 'artisan' (the latter having very little to do with the early occupants of the Colonies). Despite this, there is a community that feels strongly about what it has got and is prepared to fight to keep it, having been galvanised by campaigns to retain local facilities like the library and swimming baths. As it always did, Stockbridge provides a place where stockbrokers and MSPs can escape from the city and there is nothing wrong with that, is there?.

Streets

What is the difference between a street and a road? In this section we describe the history of 15 great streets in Britain and Ireland, although four of them are in fact roads and three are other things: a hill, a market and an arcade. Whatever they are called they are the building block of any urban area. In the previous sections we may have talked about great cities, towns and neighbourhoods but the pictures we have used to illustrate these places invariably show their streets and squares (some of the latter appear in the last part of this book). Streets make up the majority of the public realm of every town and city; they are the stage on which the public life of these places is played out. Streets are the arteries of every town and city, the channels along which their traffic flows, like the blood in the arteries of our own bodies. At the larger scale the network of streets forms the shape of the settlement; the circulatory system becomes a skeleton. They are the most enduring element of any place; buildings come and go, but streets can last forever. There are streets in ancient cities that have existed for thousands of years, longer than even the most ancient of their buildings. Indeed, until the modern age and the advent of town planners and highway engineers, streets were pretty much immortal. When London burned down in the Great Fire of 1666, there were a number of attempts to replan the city, but the rights of ownership and the patterns of movement were impossible to change and the city was rebuilt on its original street plan.

So what *is* the difference between a street and a road? Historically the word 'street' referred to any paved road and because of this Roman roads in Britain were often called streets - such as Ermine Street that runs through Lincoln up Steep Hill. The word 'road', by contrast, derives from the word 'ride' and generally refers to a route between towns that would be ridden on horseback. Because of this, roads have come to refer to the open routes between towns while streets refer to routes within towns, paved and lined with buildings. Roads provide a quick and convenient route from A to B whereas streets are both routes and places where things happen, where people interact and where trade takes place. The stuff that happens in streets is both good and bad, as our language tells us as we talk about 'street life', 'street food' and being 'streetwise' but also about 'street gangs' 'streetwalkers' and 'street crime'. On the other hand, while 'road' might give us 'crossroads', it is also in 'ring road' 'road rage', 'road trip', and 'roadside uses'.

On the following pages we describe 15 streets of varying shapes and sizes. We start with Cardiff's wonderful arcades, which if you were being picky aren't really streets at all. The streets that follow take us from the planned streets of Brighton's New Road on the south coast to Aberdeen's Union Street in the north. In the west of England we go as far as Chapel Street in Penzance but still further to the west is St Patrick's Street in Cork. We have great commercial streets like Kensington High Streets and Byres Road and more quirky streets with independent shops like Portabello Road or Exmouth Market. Then there are the great set-pieces, like Hope Street, strung between Liverpool's two cathedrals, and

Grey Street, winding up to Newcastle's Grey's Monument. The variety is huge but they all do that thing that all good streets do: they are both routes from A to B and good places to be.

In these pages we explore the history of each of these streets. They split fairly evenly into streets that were planned and those that evolved. All streets, of course, are human constructs so that no street is entirely unplanned. However, six of the streets were once tracks that became roads, which were then incorporated into a town or city and became streets. You can spot these streets because they have a very particular geometry that they have inherited from the kinks and winds of the original paths from which they grew, as can be seen in Portabello Road or Chapel Street. Other streets based on former roads, like Kensington High Street and Byres Road, have been straightened and widened so that their origins are not quite so clear, but they still feel very different to streets that have been planned. Of course, many modern designers of housing estates seek to incorporate these 'natural' winds and kinks in their layouts to recreate the beauty of these informal places. But it is not easy; if you follow a path that has been worn by foot, then it responds in very subtle ways to topography and natural features. In the 1920s the amateur archaeologist Alfred Watkins produced two books, *Early British Trackways* and *The Old Straight Track* that sought to understand the way these tracks developed. This, he suggested, was a combination of ease of movement and line-of-sight wayfinding, so that tracks often pointed towards distant landmarks, even if they were not their eventual destination. Watkins used the term 'ley lines' to describe these routes but it wasn't until the 1960s that these were given mystical connotations. There isn't actually anything mystical about these lines; they are just the product of humans moving around and are at once very simple in their origin and very difficult to recreate convincingly in a new plan.

Seven of the streets described on the following pages have been planned on a drawing board and implemented – some might say imposed – through an act of will. Perhaps the ultimate example is Union Street in Aberdeen, which was cut like an arrow through the tangled streets of the old city, slicing the top off a hill and running for much of its length at rooftop level. It was an incredibly bold move that bankrupted the city, but today it has become the axis that gives clarity to the city plan. The plots on either side of the elevated route were sold off in the years following its completion, with two storeys built below the level of the new street forming a base for the grand new buildings with which it is now lined. This is the sort of grand planning of which Baron Haussmann would have approved, but it is very rare in the British Isles. In his book *Design of Cities*, Edmund Bacon contrasts the bold boulevards of Paris with the contorted line of John Nash's grand procession from Regent's Park through Portland Place and Regent Street, to Piccadilly in London (shortlisted in 2008). This book includes some more examples of this very British form of masterplanning. Grey Street in Newcastle, Cockburn Street in Edinburgh and St Patricks Street in Cork may all look 'natural' but they are in fact planned. Grey Street was the centrepiece of Richard Grainger's development of the grounds of a large house in Newcastle and follows the line of a brook up its gently curving valley. Today it looks effortless but the grand buildings lining the street are, at one point, less than 10 metres deep, little more than facades shoehorned into a difficult site. Cockburn Street may seem to wind drunkenly up the steep hill from Waverley Station to the Royal Mile in Edinburgh, but the curve is in fact carefully planned to create a walkable gradient. St Patrick's Street is also built over a river that was first canalised and then culverted to create a curving grand boulevard. The other type of planned street that features rarely in the following pages is the street created as part of a wider masterplan. In the Places section we talk about St Andrew Square in Edinburgh, laid out within the streets of Edinburgh's New Town on virgin land. But we don't really have any streets in this section that started life as the centrepiece of a grand plan. Hope Street and perhaps Exhibition Road might fit this description, but they sit within a patchwork of planned street grids and are hardly the Avenida Diagonal in Barcelona or even Buchanan Street in Glasgow (which won the award in 2008).

While the streets in this book vary hugely, they all serve as places as well as routes, something that has become increasingly difficult in the age of the car. As traffic volumes grew in the post-war years, the twin functions of streets as routes and as places were thrown increasingly into conflict. It is hard to imagine today that Northumberland Street, the main shopping street in Newcastle, was once part of the Great North Road, carrying all of the traffic heading up to Edinburgh. The response in many cities was to pedestrianise their high street, pushing the traffic onto ring roads and creating safe environments for retailing. The logical next step was the shopping mall, drawing inspiration from arcades such as those in Cardiff. It is telling, however, that, of the 15 streets in this book (and indeed the 30 streets shortlisted in all of the Academy of Urbanism's awards) the only pedestrianised streets are the upper sections of Buchanan Street and Grey Street (Cardiff's Arcades of course, never took traffic). Pedestrianised streets risk prioritising their role as places over their role as routes and while this may seem a good idea, it undermines something fundamental in their character.

But surely the alternative to pedestrianisation means that streets become clogged with traffic and parked cars, so fail in their function as places? Many of us as urban designers grew up with the beautiful drawings of Gordon Cullen, which are almost entirely free of cars (which was a conceit because there were plenty of cars around when he drew them). The drawings and photographs in this section do often feature the intrusive shape of cars and lorries. This urge to airbrush out these vehicles is still with us, but they are only the modern incarnation of the horse, cart and carriage. Were it not for these vehicles, we would not have the streets that we have, and removing them can harm the character of the place.

Some of the streets in this book have started to address these problems in a new way. New Road in Brighton is credited as being the UK's first shared space street and Exhibition Road is another early example of this approach. Both do away with the traditional geography of pavements and kerbs to separate pedestrians and cars. Instead, road users are allowed to mix on a shared surface negotiating with each other through eye contact – much as we did in the age of the horse. However, just as important is the approach championed by Kensington High Street and taken up by many of the other streets in this book. This approach retains pavements and kerbs but removes all of the other paraphernalia of the transport engineer designed to separate cars and people. This turns the street back into something much more traditional, allowing the functions of place and route to be put back into balance. These are important initiatives. Before they were developed, our streets were at risk of either having too much traffic or having none at all. If we lose our streets, we undermine a fundamental part of the urbanism of our towns and cities, so it is important that we get them right. The streets that follow hopefully provide some pointers as to how we might do this.

Arcades, Cardiff

Shortlisted 2010

There's something sublime about shopping;
Flitting from store to store on a mission
Carrying bag after bag and never dropping
One; and the shopper is always wishing
For somewhere great to use his plastic
Somewhere lovely to splash her cash
Well Cardiff arcades are just fantastic
Full of verve, wit, style and dash!
The arcades are theatre, showbiz, works of art
You can eat and drink and meet your mates
And in a city with the arcades at its heart
The present is shining and greatness awaits!
They're monuments, symbols and palisades...
Ladies and gentlemen: Cardiff Arcades!

For those visiting Cardiff for the first time, what sticks in the memory are its arcades. The arcades seem to be everywhere and to offer a complete alternative circulation system through the city centre, packed with interesting shops and bustling with interesting people. There are, or so it seems, arcades that twist and turn, that split and interconnect – portals entered in one part of town that spit you out somewhere quite different.

The academy assessment team's visit to Cardiff for the 2010 awards was able to get to grips with the geography of the city centre. Once you do this, it is clear that the Victorian arcades are not as omnipresent as they seem at first. Cardiff in fact has five Victorian arcades: Castle Arcade, High Street & Duke Street Arcade, Wyndham Arcade, Morgan Arcade and the Royal Arcade. Only the last two of these arcades link to create something large enough to feel like an alternative street network.

However, on the visit the council presented a much more radical notion of Cardiff as a city of arcades stretching from the Royal Arcade, built in 1858, to the Grand Arcade at the heart of the new St David's Centre (which was still under construction at the time of the visit). These mark either end of a continuum including the Victorian arcades, the covered market, some later arcades built in the 1960s and a series of shopping centres built from the 1970s through to the late 1990s. This raises the obvious question: are these really all arcades?

In a sense the modern shopping centres do the same job as the Victorian arcades. They provide a retail environment protected from the weather and extend the scope for retail frontage into the heart of the city's urban blocks. In actual fact, Cardiff provides a fascinating history of retail architecture over 150 years, which has come full circle with the new St David's Centre that seeks to learn from the Victorian arcades, albeit on a monumental scale.

But why does Cardiff have so many arcades? It is, in fact, a very young city. It remained a small town until the 1850s, after which it grew rapidly with the development of its port to export coal from the Valleys. The port was developed by the Marquess of Bute, one of the richest men of the time, whose lands covered much of the area on which Cardiff has since been built. The city was built under the Bute family's direction at a time when arcades were very fashionable.

Covered shopping streets have a long history. Ancient Rome had covered shopping streets and the 1,000-year-old Isfahan Grand Bazaar in Iran is perhaps the oldest shopping mall still trading today. The modern history of arcades is linked to the rise of the consumer society as a result of the wealth created in the Industrial Revolution. The first modern arcade was possibly le Passage du Caire, built in Paris in

1798, followed 20 years later by the Burlington Arcade in London, which had its own police force. Arcades provided a safe environment for middle-class ladies to indulge in the new fashionable activity of buying things they didn't really need. So taken were people with these new retail environments that there was an arcade boom in British cities, most of which have a number of arcades built in the second half of the 19th century. In Cardiff, where plans were being developed to build an entirely new city centre, it is hardly surprising that arcades were to be a central feature.

The streets of Cardiff city centre run north-south from the Bute family seat in the castle down the hill towards the docks. The arcades run east-west between these streets. These Victorian arcades are generally two storeys high. The ground floors are lined with small retail units that, because of the small unit sizes, tend to be occupied by independent businesses. The first floors are occupied by offices and small businesses, although in some cases a first-floor balcony would originally also have been lined with shops. The arcades are glazed and filled with natural light. Some are lavishly decorated, others are more plain, however, none are heated or air conditioned, making them feel like covered streets rather than shopping malls.

One of the unique aspects of the Cardiff arcades is that they bend and fork, creating interesting views and giving the impression that they go on forever. This is an inversion of the urban design principle of legibility. We are told that urban areas should be easy to understand and to find your way around. The arcades, by contrast, offer the opportunity to get lost, to wander, to be surprised.

This provides an interesting bridge to the design of the modern shopping centre, where the aim is to maximise 'dwell time' and deliver footfall to retail frontages. The huge St David's Centre casts a stark light on these questions, running almost the entire length of the city centre and providing only one east-west public route. This huge retail investment has been made possible by the size of Cardiff's catchment population: while the city's population is just 350,000, there are six million people within an hour's drive. The main mall, called the Great Arcade, runs north-south and is on the scale of the grand Galleria of Milan (another precursor of the arcade) with a smaller side arcade linking across to the Royal Arcade. This huge retail environment borrows some of the language of the arcades but the Academicians who visited remained sceptical about whether it really could be seen in the same tradition.

It is an even more moot point as to whether the other shopping centres in Cardiff, the Capitol Centre and the first phase of the St David's Centre, really can be considered in the great tradition of arcades. Their motives are the same – to get shoppers out of the rain and to extend the retail frontage – but the feel of the spaces is very different. The space feels sanitised and corporate, the air is conditioned and the materials are those of the boardroom rather than the street. Inside the malls you could be in any city in the UK; in the Victorian arcades you could only be in Cardiff. The developers of the St David's Centre have recognised this and have sought to take their cues from the Victorian arcades. The result is better – much better that the malls of the last few decades. If future generations really do start to see it as a continuum of the great tradition of Cardiff arcades, then the developers will indeed have done something very special.

Arcades provided a safe environment for middle-class ladies to indulge in the new fashionable activity of buying things they didn't really need

Byres Road, Glasgow

Shortlisted 2012

Start at one end hungry, begin your journey;
Chew your way through a map of the world
Sit with a bib on or glug from a flagon,
Down Byres Road the foody standard's unfurled;
Start at one end tense but follow your senses:
You'll relax as Byres Road unwinds.
Start at one end quiffy but then in a jiffy
You'll have a haircut as sharp as the sharpest minds
And you'll be sure that the best manicure
Awaits you: your hands will be gorgeous as jewels.
Stop reading. Get strolling: Byres Road is waiting
Making the future, rewriting the rules...

For a street that didn't really exist before the middle part of the 19th century, and that wasn't given its current name until the 1890s, Byres Road has had quite a journey to become one of the most important and well-known streets in Glasgow. At the heart of the city's West End, to many people Byres Road simply *is* the West End.

Byres Road may stretch for just half a mile but in that time it packs in all the ingredients that we expect of a great street: a diverse population, a wide variety of shops (including a good representation of independent and niche retailers), numerous community facilities and a host of cultural activities through the year. This multitude of uses populate the main street and spread symbiotically into the adjacent lanes. This is not just a great street; it is the life force of an entire neighbourhood, buzzing through the day, the evening and at night.

Given all this, it is perhaps surprising that Byres Road does not have a longer backstory. It originated as little more than a rural lane connecting the burghs of Partick and Hillhead. Then the rapid, insistent expansion of Glasgow in the mid 19th century swept westwards over the area. Byres Road, or Victoria Street as it was called at the time, became the axis for a grid-ironed hillside town as the fields were carpeted with classical villas and red and white sandstone tenements together with businesses and warehousing in the back lanes and alleys.

The housing was soon joined by Glasgow University, which relocated its entire campus to a leafy site on the hillside in 1870 to escape the overcrowding and poor conditions of the city centre. It was joined in 1874 by a new teaching hospital which, later expanded to become the city's Western Infirmary. The area thus grew to become an important part of Glasgow and in recognition of this, Hillhead was annexed by Glasgow City Council in 1891. This created a problem because, as the ever-expanding second city of Empire, Glasgow already had three Victoria Streets. Another one would just be confusing and so in recognition of the area's original name – the Byres of

retailers. The street's activity has spread into Ashton Lane, once a back street with stables and factories, now a popular hang-out with a range of bars and restaurants and a cinema, which are just as much part of the experience as Byres Road itself. The street has managed to maintain a diversity of uses and amenities without allowing any single use or user to become dominant (at least not for too long). It could easily have become an extension of the university campus but has managed to remain a vital path of the wider city.

This is helped by the month-long West End Festival, held each June. Now in its twentieth year, the festival has grown to become arguably Glasgow's largest cultural event. Community involvement is organised through the Friends of West Glasgow Association, which has been critical in bringing the communities and businesses together. Proud and passionate, the association provides a strong community-led input, collaborating with the local authority.

Success over such a long period does not happen by accident; great streets like Byres Road need all of these ingredients but they also need to be managed and cherished if they are to stay healthy. Byres Road is fortunate to be so loved.

Partick – Byres Road was born.

The final ingredient in Byres Road's success was its connectedness to the rest of the city. Glasgow introduced the world's third oldest underground system in 1896 (after London and Budapest), which included a stop at either end of Byres Road. This had the effect not just of linking Byres Road to the rest of the city, but, perhaps just as importantly, connecting the rest of the city to Byres Road. This gave its shops and businesses access to a much wider market and allowed it to develop into an upmarket retail street at the heart of a prosperous middle-class neighbourhood. And thus it has continued. As the surrounding streets have evolved from Victorian gentility to early-21st-century bohemia, Byres Road has prospered.

A number of factors have cemented its role as a great street. The first of these is the ubiquitous (by Scottish standards, at least) tenements. The mass of this building typology not only provides an appropriate scale of development, but ensures a density and variety of population that helps to support services and facilities. The flats also provide all-important activity, vibrancy and natural surveillance day and night. Added to this, shops on the ground floor provide a continuous active frontage, aided by the Victorian legacy of party walls that restrict the width of shops, keeping an enviable degree of variety and activity and a strong urban grain while also encouraging independent

As the surrounding streets have evolved from Victorian gentility to early-21st-century bohemia, Byres Road has prospered

Chapel Street, Penzance

Shortlisted 2013

Here on the toe of the country, a street like no other.
Stride it in all weathers, walking up from the water

And the people who are here today are sitting and eating;
You can hear the glasses clink and hear the cries of greeting
As we take advantage of the Gulf Stream and the al fresco seating
What are these people doing?
Yes, they're Chapel Streeting!

Chapel Street has excitement; you can see it in the eyes
Of those who live and work here. There is no compromise
Between work and rest and leisure here, each one wins the prize.
Why are these people smiling?
They're Chapel Street-wise!

Here on the toe of the country, a street to beat the rest,
A hidden gem, a talking point, Champs Elysses of the West!

When a Spanish raiding party rampaged up Chapel Street in 1585, burning 400 homes and three ships in the harbour, they were persuaded by their priest to spare St Mary's Church. Whether this is the chapel from which the street takes its name is the source of some dispute locally. Some argue that St Mary's stands on an ancient holy site that gives the town its name - 'pen' meaning 'headland' as in peninsular and 'sans' meaning 'holy'. Others argue that the street takes its name from the Chapel of St Anthony, the location of which has been lost. Either way, the street that runs along a ridge from the church on the headland towards the heart of the town was already ancient when put to the torch by the Spanish.

In the book *Treasure Island*, the narrator Jim Hawkins lives at his parents' inn, the Admiral Benbow, which can still be found on Chapel Street. One day a stranger, Billy Bones, arrives: 'This is a handy cove' he says, 'and a pleasantly sittyated grog-shop'. Billy Bones dies having been given the Black Spot by Blind Pew and Jim finds a chart in his sea chest, escaping the inn just before it is ransacked by pirates. So starts the story in which Jim, together with the local squire and doctor, set off to find the treasure marked on the map with a hired crew – who turn out to be pirates. This, at least, is the imagined history of Chapel Street, a haunt for pirates and smugglers in the wild south west.

But the Chapel Street of 1881, when *Treasure Island* was published, was already a very different place. Robert Louis Stevenson's den of pirates, if it ever existed, had long been replaced by something more civilised and Georgian. The street is one of the most unified Georgian streets in the country. Its youngest building, number 12, might just have been completed in the first few years of the 20th century; before that, the most recent facade belongs

to the Methodist Hall, which was enlarged in 1864, and a clutch of buildings including the rebuilt St Mary's Church and the Egyptian House from the 1830s. Most of the street, however, dates from the late 1700s, although some of these buildings are constructed on the bones of much older structures.

At its seaward end around the church, the street is residential in character. The row of brick-built cottages know, as the Rotterdam Buildings were reputedly built from the proceeds of privateering against Dutch traders, bricks being rarer and of a higher status in a town otherwise built of granite. One of these was lived in by Mary Branwell, who would later be mother to the Brontë sisters. Opposite this stands a classical building now occupied by the Penzance Arts Club but originally the Portuguese Embassy. As you walk towards the centre of the town, the residential character of the street gives way to more commercial buildings. In addition to the Admiral Benbow, the street includes the Union Hotel – within which survive the remains of a Georgian theatre dating from 1787 – where the victory of the Battle of Trafalgar was first announced. Of even greater antiquity are the Turk's Head, reputed to be the oldest inn in the town, and the Regent, which began life as a temperance hotel some 400 years ago. The most idiosyncratic building on the street is, however, the Egyptian House, designed in 1836 by the Plymouth architect John Foulston to house the geological museum of a local collector, John Lavin. This was built in the Egyptian Revival style that was all the craze in the 1830s following the discovery of the Rosetta Stone and the publication of prints from Napoleon's Egyptian campaign. The building is a gloriously eccentric landmark of the street, recently restored by the Landmark Trust.

The Egyptian House is Chapel Street's only Grade I listed building but there are a total of 50 buildings on the street, including four at Grade II*. However, as the historic building surveyor Ashley Baker says in his personal assessment of Chapel Street, 'the street is neither grand nor formal and with one or two exceptions its buildings are unlikely to figure in volumes of architectural history. It is in its subtle, lively variety of building forms and uses, grouped closely between the dome of the Market House and tower of St Mary's Church that the character of the street is established.' This is the beauty of Chapel Street: its gentle twist and curve that opens up to reveal a view of the church and the sea, its informal unity of architecture and style and its continued variety of uses and activities. All this is spoilt only slightly by a rather intrusive one-way traffic system, double yellow-lines and road signs, but then you can't escape the 20th and 21st centuries entirely.

Robert Louis Stevenson's den of pirates, if it ever existed, had long been replaced by something more civilised and Georgian

Cockburn Street, Edinburgh

Shortlisted 2012

Street of connections, street of diversions
Street of attractions, street of musicians
Street of decisions: this cafe, that shop
Street of collisions: that haircut, this top.

Street of palaver and street of kerfuffle
Street of hot coffee and street of cold trifle
Street of backpacker and worker and slacker
Street of street culture and Edinburgh weather.

Street of pulled suitcase on small squeaky wheels
Street of long scarves and big hats and high heels
Street celebrating, street laughing, street meeting
Street caught on camera or captured by tweeting.

Street of discussions, street of assertions
Street of commotions, street of emotions
Street of all nations: that language, this smile
Street from the station to the Royal Mile!

For those arriving in Edinburgh by train, Cockburn Street is as good an introduction to a city as you are likely to find. Running from the station to the Old Town, it draws you up its sinuous path: steep enough to tug at your calves, but not as steep as the medieval alleys that it was built to replace. Today it is thriving, thronged with people and lined with independent shops. However, this is recent and in the mid 1990s its decline was as steep as its gradient. Its shops lay empty and a poor street environment led to a general sense of neglect – a place to get through quickly rather than to linger and enjoy. Led by Edinburgh Council, working with the City Centre Neighbourhood Partnership, local traders and residents and a diverse range of stakeholders including Edinburgh World Heritage and Historic Scotland, a programme of sensitive improvements was put in place to restore Cockburn Street to its former glory and see it become a destination in its own right.

Cockburn Street is a relatively modern intervention; it was built in 1856 to provide a connection between the Royal Mile at the top of the hill with the new Waverley Station below. This was a commercial venture by the Edinburgh High Street & Railway Access Company. Their plan was to create a convenient street, thereby attracting people and allowing the backland closes of the area to be replaced with upmarket shops, hotels and apartments that would line the new street.

The dramatic change of level represented quite a challenge. The appointed architects Peddie & Kinnear carved out the new street as a wide, serpentine curve creating a relatively comfortable gradient. This was a vast improvement on the narrow closes that plunge directly downhill with an assortment of vertiginous steps. The architecture was picturesque, dictated by the Edinburgh Improvement Act of 1827, which set a standard for new development, but was also designed to attract benefactors. The buildings are Scottish baronial style, towers and turrets being used both to articulate and punctuate the arc of the street.

The curve may be a functional response to the slope but it is also a thing of beauty. There is no point on the street where both ends can be experienced simultaneously and once you are enveloped into the folds of the street, neither end is visible for much of its length. This discreteness – at odds with the normal urban design principles of visibility, connectedness and clarity – gives Cockburn Street its own microclimate, acting as a sensory buffer separating the swirling bagpipery of the Royal Mile above from the hisses, whistles and announcements of Waverley Station below.

The recent improvements have been made with a light touch given the sensitivity of the historic environment. Buildings have been refurbished and shopfronts improved with grants that have enabled the retention of original features. Subtle alterations have been made to the public realm; the pavements have been widened and street clutter removed, while vehicle traffic has been reduced by introducing a one-way system. Without altering the essential character of Cockburn Street, these improvements have led to greater pedestrian footfall and activity along the street, helped by the fact that the extra room has enabled cafes to spill out to add vibrancy to the street scene. The work has also forged a strong sense of community between businesses and residents, and a greater pride in the street and its place in the city. Today it combines the best aspects of Edinburgh: topography and townscape populated with independent shops, galleries, restaurants and community uses. Cockburn Street is a very British type of urban design. Created at the same time as Hausemann was slicing boulevards through the medieval fabric of Paris, Cockburn Street looks almost unplanned, insinuating itself into the fabric of the Old Town as if it has always been there. It is an example of the art of British masterplanning, (see also Grey Street in Newcastle, page 174) that we need to rediscover.

> Cockburn Street looks almost unplanned, insinuating itself into the fabric of the Old Town as if it has always been there

Exhibition Road, London

Shortlisted 2013

Let's face it, this is more than a road, it's a route
Bringing knowledge like the old Silk Road did
All those years ago. More than a road, it's a path
That leads to enlightenment, lifting the lid
On science, art, history. More than a road: a way
That thousands of people expand their knowledge;
Every day; more than a road, it's a walking-space
To a kind of open-minded open-hearted college
That welcomes everyone. Look how full this road is
Of people, a bustling, a throng, a more-than-a-road
Leading to civilisation; it's an Exhibition. Exhibition Road.

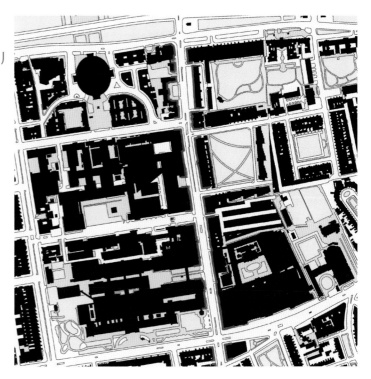

The Victorians really knew how to put on a show. Over 150 years ago the surplus – yes, surplus – generated by Prince Albert's Great Exhibition of 1851 was used to create 'Albertopolis', an extraordinary assembly of world-class arts, science and educational institutions in west London. These stretched from the twin goliaths of the Victoria & Albert and Natural History museums in the south to the Royal Albert Hall facing Hyde Park in the north. Linking the two was Exhibition Road, unfolding like a grand procession of learning and exploration, with the Science Museum, Imperial College and the Royal Geographical Society advancing up the hill in stately convoy.

Albertopolis was the granddaddy of every learning and innovation campus in the world today. But if the institutions were evolving, the road itself wasn't keeping up. By the 21st century Exhibition Road was more of a sideshow: a traffic-dominated dual carriageway with cluttered, poor-quality public space and narrow pavements. Luckily, the Victorians had thought of this too, building a pedestrian tunnel underneath the road from South Kensington station – although this can get stiflingly hot in summer and arguably had only encouraged the tyranny of the car.

It was a redesign of the one-way traffic system around the station that proved to be the catalyst for the transformation of Exhibition Road. By returning the streets to two-way traffic and creating pedestrian spaces outside the station, the area no longer felt like a vehicle-dominated racetrack. This also had the effect of reducing traffic volumes along Exhibition Road by around 30%. This was a radical move, but when it came to tackling traffic, the Royal Borough of Kensington and Chelsea had form. About a decade previously, they had taken a drastic and ultimately successful approach to the redesign of nearby Kensington High Street (page 182), removing the barriers that had made it into 'some ace caffs with a quite awful racetrack attached' (to horribly mangle the V&A's famous 1980s slogan). Now it was Exhibition Road's turn to be 'rebalanced' and an architectural competition was launched, with a brief to integrate vehicles and pedestrians in an attractive environment without unduly compromising the road's role as a key transport link.

> When it came to tackling traffic, the Royal Borough of Kensington and Chelsea had form

After long consultation, particularly with disability groups, engineers and planners, the winning design by Dixon Jones Architects saw the pavements removed along the road's length to create an expansive multi-functional shared space. Instead of kerbs, colour, texture and scale were used to indicate to different users how the street worked and how they should move through it. A four-metre-wide 'safe area' for pedestrians is marked by a continuous strip of corduroy paving, helping the visually impaired to negotiate the space. A diagonal pattern of grey and pink granite setts claims the whole of the street as a place for strolling and exploration rather creating separate lanes for pedestrians and traffic. Soaring LED lighting masts provide an elegant three-dimensional structure to the space.

A walk along the road reveals a series of quarters with subtly changing character. To the south, around South Kensington station, spaces are softer and have a high level of mixed-use interaction, with pavement cafes full of life. Beyond Cromwell Road – which remains a major east–west artery – the road becomes more formal around the museums where it perhaps lacks the earlier intimacy and character. The real success of this space, however, lies in how traffic and pedestrians now interact as equals.

Arguably, like the original Albertopolis, this was a project of its time. It was a grand statement on the scale needed for Olympic London in 2012 and it rightly received national and international recognition, including an RIBA Award. Appropriately for the place that Imperial College calls home, the rebirth of Exhibition Road demonstrates how a clear vision, strong leadership and clarity of design can bring about a creative engineering solution where 'normal' rules and regulations have been successfully challenged. Extensive and ongoing community consultation throughout both design and construction phases also helped in the generally wide acceptance of such an ambitious project. It is certainly an inspiring scheme, though with a construction value of over £26 million it is hard to see how many other public places like this can be replicated in the near future. When it was built, Exhibition Road exemplified the Victorian understanding of 'legacy'. At last the road can live up to its name again.

Exmouth Market, London

Shortlisted 2011

Exmouth Market, take note of the word,
Take note of the mouth in the market's name:
Exmouth Market's at its best when heard,
When the complex rules of a market's game
Are shouted or sung in the market's voice,
An aria of stalls, fine restaurants and bars
A song of plenty and a ballad of choice
A chorus of shopfronts shine like stars.
It could have been Exeye Market, I guess
Because this really is a sight to behold
Where commerce and streetlife coalesce
As the city's lights turn the evening gold.
To be alive in Exmouth Market is
Experiencing the closest you'll get to bliss!

The woman who turns to her companion sounds unconvinced. 'Is that it?' she asks. Why does this small street in Clerkenwell have such a big reputation as one of London's must-see thoroughfares? What is it about this small assortment of shops and restaurants, bookended by a chain of coffee shops at one end and a small supermarket at the other, that justifies its billing? Yet despite its rather unassuming demeanour, Exmouth Market really does have a strong claim to being a great street.

Both Starbucks and Pizza Express dipped a toe but decided that it was not for them

These days, when a row of central London shops supports both a bookmaker and a bookstore we prize it as something special. So add in a chemist, bike shop, tattoo parlour, craft shop, jeweller, hardware store, hairdresser, wine merchant, designer menswear and record shop, and you get Exmouth Market - a street that can boast the variety we used to take for granted on high streets. Yes, one or two of the units are national brands, but most are independents. Indeed, this small pool of retailing in a corner of London EC1 is bucking the trend. Both Starbucks and Pizza Express dipped a toe but decided that it was not for them. Today the part-pedestrianised street, lined with business frontages and sheltered from the heavy traffic of Farringdon Road and Rosebery Avenue, is thriving. Appearances can, however, be deceptive; this has not been an unbroken story of commercial success and the mix of independents isn't as effortless as it might seem.

The two sides of the street were in fact developed at different times. As early as the 17th century the London Spa opened here to capitalise on a natural spring. It developed as a place of recreation in the early 18th century. At this time the buildings that now form the southern side of Exmouth Market marked the northern extent of London, beyond which were fields leading to the village of Islington. They looked out onto a recreational area, known for tea gardens and ducking ponds that became known as Spa Fields. One of its buildings at the time was a vast domed neoclassical Pantheon, which had been built as a 'pleasure dome' but which after the bankruptcy of its operator, became one of many Methodist chapels funded by Selina, Countess of Huntingdon.

The northern side of the street was not completed until the early 19th century and was lined with shops from the outset, built to serve the growing residential population. It was at this time that the rotunda chapel was replaced by the dramatic church that stands in the street today, John Dando Sedding's Italianate basilica complete with campanile, dedicated to Our Most Holy Redeemer. The surrounding neighbourhood of Clerkenwell is still known for its strong Italian community, centred on the nearby Catholic Church of St Peter. Italian traders became active in the food and drink businesses that began to dominate the street to such an extent that it officially became a market in the 1890s.

By the 1970s the area was in sharp decline, run-down and dangerous. As businesses left, crime increased and the street, together with neighbouring

EXMOUTH MARKET

SO NAMED AFTER THE DRINKING ESTABLISHMENT, THE EXMOUTH ARMS, WHICH IN TURN WAS CHRISTENED FROM SIR EDWARD PELLEW, A NAVAL COMMANDER CHAP, THE VISCOUNT OF EXMOUTH. THE HOME OF THE FAMOUS LONDON SPA, AND LONDON TOWNS ONLY BASILICA STYLE CHURCH NO LESS. IN THE HEART OF CLERKENWELL, OR FONS CLERICORUM AS FITZ-STEPHEN NAMED IT AFTER THE ENTHUSIASTIC CLERKS THAT ACTED SACRED DRAMAS BY THE WELL IN RAY STREET DURING THE REIGN OF THE BIG MAN, HENRY 11. THAT BECAME THE STOMPING GROUND OF CLOCKERS, JEWELLERS, ENAMELLERS AND ARTISANS. NOW HOME TO FANCY FOOTED CREATIVES, DELIGHTFUL TASTERS OF FINERIES, LATE SUPPERS AND PORTLY BELLIES. WHERE GLASSES ARE TOPPED WITH RAINBOW LIQUEURS AND AROMAS TEMPT THE WEARIEST OF OFFICITES. THIS GEM OF A STREET, WHOSE HEART BEATS TRUE AND PROUD IN THE ROTATION OF BLACK AND RED CARRIAGES.

Spa Fields Park, became unsafe and unattractive. While Islington Council had invested in new paving in the 1980s, it was not until the 1990s that a successful strategy to revive the street was devised. This involved working with the principal freeholder, Debenham Property Trust, to encourage residents and businesses to occupy the upper floors of properties while removing planning restrictions on the ground floors. These had been designed to protect the street's retail function but were in fact preventing diversification. Further public-realm works followed, including wider pavements, new street lighting and bollards, creating an early example of shared space and encouraging businesses to animate the street outside their premises.

Then in 1997 a business arrived that would transform the street. Husband and wife team Sam and Sam Clark had been travelling in the southern Mediterranean and wanted to open a restaurant to showcase what was then a revolutionary style of cooking in the UK. Not only did they bring new ingredients, they even managed to reposition sherry as a fashionable drink. Their restaurant Moro (and now its little sister Morito) did the same for Exmouth Market.

Opposite below: Vic Lee's illustration of Exmouth Market, one of his series on London streets available from www.viclee.co.uk

The combination of the renewal strategy and the Moro effect changed the fortunes of Exmouth Market. It has since attracted new shops while retaining older businesses like the Farringdon Locksmiths & Hardware Store (established in 1908), and more recent but still long-standing businesses like the Singular Tattoo Parlour and, of course, the market itself. The council has developed an effective strategy to protect its markets, including Exmouth Market, Chapel Street and Whitecross Street. This recognises their vital role in the cultural, social and economic wellbeing of the borough and uses a light-touch approach to management, based on a three-way partnership between businesses, the council and landlords who value independent businesses. This seems to be working and sustains a delicate balance of keeping the streets successful without squeezing out local businesses.

Outcomes are not always perfect, of course, there is a design strategy for the street, but the resurfacing works to upgrade the patchwork of surfaces into unifying black tarmac is not to everyone's taste, and the metal shutters that come down when many retail businesses close for the

day – a legacy of the days when crime was a greater problem than it is now – still give the street an edgy feel at night. On warm evenings, though, when Cafe Kick and Brill Records spill onto the street, its reputation as one of London's cool hang-outs still feels intact. Exmouth Market is even exporting its talent to London's creative pretenders, with Bar Kick opening in Shoreditch and Caravan coffee bar now animating Granary Square at King's Cross.

This successful mix includes other neighbourhood uses. The Church Hall, at 24 Exmouth Market, is now a busy independent venue for local and citywide events, such as Spark London's storytelling nights. Investment in Spa Fields Park has created a space valued by the community again and, around the corner to the south, is Tecton/Berthold Lubetkin's revolutionary 1930s public building the Finsbury Health Centre. Festivals are important too, from the Italian community's annual procession for Our Lady of Mount Carmel each July to London Design Week.

A snapshot of the way that the street has changed over recent years can be seen in a framed print on the wall of the Exmouth Arms. The pub itself is part of this change, having been reborn in its current reincarnation only recently. The drawing by artist Vic Lee is part of his series of London streets and engagingly maps out the shops that lined the street at the time the print was made. Many of the names are still in the street outside, but some, including Strada, William Hill and Jessops, are no longer there. It is a fascinating snapshot of a very particular street. The caption above the map tells that the street was named for Admiral Edward Pellew, Viscount Exmouth, and was 'the stomping ground of clockers, jewellers, enamellers and artisans. Now home to fancy footed creatives, delightful tasters of fineries, late suppers and portly bellies.' This 'gem of a street' certainly has a unique and distinctive sense of place, it may only be a short stroll, but it remains a great, and rewarding, pleasure.

Grey Street, Newcastle

Winner 2010

Sweeps through a city like a street can,
Reflects the light from the sky like a street should;
You can see it on a map or a street plan
But Grey Street should be lived in to be understood
Or at least walked up, or danced in, or stood for a time
Just to take it all in, the feel of the place
Somewhere between picturesque and sublime
A true Geordie version of Grace.
And it's good that this street has the Theatre Royal
Because the whole of Grey Street is dramatic
After all drama's as deep as Newcastle's soil
And the voices on this street are almost operatic:
It's a place for the heart and a place for the feet.
Come and experience the glory of Grey Street!

When BBC Radio 4 organised a vote to find the best street in Britain in 2010, the winner was Grey Street in Newcastle. Nikolaus Pevsner agreed, describing it as 'one of the finest streets in England', while John Betjeman wrote: 'As for the curve of Grey Street, I shall never forget seeing it to perfection, traffic-less on a misty Sunday morning. Not even Regent Street, even old Regent Street London, can compare with that descending subtle curve'.

It is easy to see why Grey Street attracts such praise; it is a very beautiful street, curving and descending from Grey's Monument down the hill, lined with buildings of a similar age, built of stone, subtly different but with a unified rhythm and scale. Lying at the heart of Newcastle's Grainger Town – also a recipient of an Academy of Urbanism award – Grey Street, like Cockburn Street in Edinburgh (page 166), is deceptive. It may look like the sweep of a medieval street, the result of the organic growth of the city, but in fact, was very carefully designed. This is a very British type of civic design, laid out a few decades after the commissioners took their set square to Manhattan and a few years before Cerdà did the same to Barcelona; Grey Street and the wider Grainger Town is a piece of contextual planning that works with the topography of the site and melds itself into the surrounding city. It does this so effortlessly that you would think that its views and vistas were the result of happy accidents rather than careful compositions.

It was in 1831 that the merchant George Anderson died. He was the owner of a large house sitting within extensive grounds within the city walls of Newcastle. The estate was bought from his executors by a young builder, the 34-year-old Richard Grainger. He had been born into a modest family and had been apprenticed as a carpenter before going into business with his brother as building contractors and developers. By the 1830s the Grainger brothers had already successfully developed Eldon Square just to the north of Grainger Town. It therefore seemed to make sense to spend the huge sum of £50,000 on the Anderson estate. This did, however, leave Grainger with insufficient funds to actually undertake the development, so he presented a scheme to the town council suggesting a joint venture. The architect John Dobson had presented a similar proposal the year previous that had been rejected. Grainger, however, managed to overcome objections by moving his legal business to the solicitors firm of John Clayton in the city – who also happened to be Town Clerk.

Grainger's masterplan for the area was drawn up by his in-house architects John Wardle and

You would think that its views and vistas were the result of happy accidents rather than careful compositions

Above: A map from the early 1800s showing the house and grounds before the development of Grainger Town.

Below: Views of Grey Street including the glass panels for the benches installed as part of the public realm scheme in the early 2000s.

George Walker, although it is likely that John Dobson was also involved. It was an ambitious plan for the comprehensive redevelopment of 12 acres, covering not just the estate but much of the surrounding area and necessitating the demolition of the Theatre Royal and the recently completed market. The plan was based around three streets: Grainger Street, Clayton Street (named in grateful recognition for the help of John Clayton) and Upper Dean Street (later renamed Grey Street). The change of name commemorated Lord Grey and the passing of the Great Reform Act in 1832, which was marked by the erection of Grey's Monument at the top of the street in 1838.

The scheme was built across the valley of the Lort Burn, which ran to the rear of the city's medieval Bigg Market and may not have been as attractive as it sounds given that 'lort' is a Saxon word meaning 'filth' or 'excrement'. The burn was culverted and paved, its shallow descending curve giving form to the street. The curve, however, left very little room for development to the west of the street in the lower part of the valley. The buildings fronting this part of Grey Street may look substantial from the front but are incredibly shallow. This is an example of the amount of work required below the surface (or in this case behind the facades) to make the plan look so effortless.

The development took place over a relatively short period, starting in 1834 and being completed by the end of the decade. The final scheme included 325 shops, new meat and fish markets, a replacement for the Theatre Royal given pride of place at the top of Grey Street, apartments, 40 townhouses and professional offices. In total, the development cost £646,000 and gave Newcastle a new urban quarter the match of anything in the country. The buildings were executed by a small group of architects, including John Dobson, Grainger's in-house architects and John and Benjamin Green, who designed the Theatre Royal and Grey's Monument. They are all built of stone and classical inspiration (in truth an architectural style that was already a little out of date in the 1830s).

Today only about three quarters of the original Grainger Town remains. The balance was gnawed away, along with Eldon Square, by the 1960s planners. Newcastle in the 1960s under its legendary (and subsequently disgraced) council leader T. Dan Smith was to have become the 'Brasilia of the North'. The area to the east of Grainger Town gives a sense of what the redevelopment plans would have meant for the city as a whole, with its flyovers and underpasses and that particular Newcastle innovation, the tower block built on stilts over the street. In this climate Grainger Town was seen as an anachronism and there were many who argued that it should be included in the slum clearance programme. Fortunately, most of it survived and 244 of its buildings were subsequently listed.

However, it wasn't out of the woods yet and in the early 1990s 47% of its listed buildings were designated as being at risk and a further 29% were considered vulnerable. It was in this context that the Grainger Town Project was established in 1996 as a partnership between the city council, English Heritage and English Partnerships. The project ran until 2003, by which time £174 million had been spent on the area, seeing most of its buildings restored and brought back into use and extensive public-realm works. Like all regeneration success stories, walking through Grainger Town today you would never know that it was once so run-down that demolition was considered an option. It has once more become a place for offices and shops and has an increasing residential population.

The public-realm scheme means that like John Betjeman, you can once more experience Grey Street traffic-less, and not just on a Sunday. The upper part of the street is pedestrianised, while the lower section is closed to through traffic but with chevron parking for local businesses. The street has been restored to its original restrained and rather dignified beauty. Its shops were always of the upmarket variety and while some bars have been inserted into the heavy bases of its classical buildings, it is never going to be lively. Not that this was ever what it was intended to be. Grey Street, in contrast to the raucous Bigg Market, was always planned as a civilising influence on the city – and long may this continue.

Above: A view up Grey Street in the late 1800s which has changed very little in the intervening years.

High Street, Skipton

Shortlisted 2007

Above: The 'setts' in Skipton, used for parking when the market is not there.

Remember, this is Skipton: embrace the urge to skip
Down this High Street like no other High Street
Allow a Yorkshire-ish grin to play round your lip
And a dance of delight to grow from your two feet
And buy a pint, buy a pie, say hello to a feller
You've known since you were but a lad
Then buy something sweet from a market stall seller
Then nod to the feller from the previous line's dad
And smile to the family who've come for the day
(They call 'em comforts round here but they like 'em really)
Because this High Street's a place to work, rest and play
(Shame that line's been used already: it's the sort of touchy-feely
Line that fits this High Street to a T!).
Skipton High Street: I'm impressed;
As High Streets go, this one has to be the best!

Best place to live in Britain! That at least was the verdict of the *Sunday Times* in 2014 when it announced that Skipton had come top of its quality of life survey of English towns. So if you were expecting a northern mill town, you might want to think again. It was once a mill town, of course; its name means 'sheep town' and it was a hub for the 19th-century textile industry weaving cotton and silk from the west with wool from Yorkshire along the thread of the Leeds & Liverpool Canal. But today, according to the *Sunday Times*, it is the gateway to the Yorkshire Dales, a lovely place to live for commuters heading into the great cities of the north, it returns a safe Conservative MP and apparently has some 'very good schools'.

For centuries Skipton High Street was pretty much all there was to the town. Skipton hardly existed before the Normans built a castle on a defensible bluff in a meander of the River Aire in 1090. The castle was a frontline defence against the marauding Scots but also provided protection and sanctuary for the surrounding rural community in times of war. This was the impetus for the town to grow along the street leading from

the castle gates: the hourglass-shaped space that is Skipton High Street. A market charter was granted outside the castle gates in 1203 and the wide expanse of the street is more marketplace than thoroughfare. It is likely that the buildings that originally enclosed the space were built at the same time as the first market. Halfway along the street a narrow row of buildings stands within the space splitting the High Street from Sheep Street. These buildings are likely to have been market stalls that evolved into permanent buildings, as happened in other market towns like Ludlow and Chesterfield.

With just over 14,000 people, Skipton sits between the great belt of industrial towns that straddles northern England to the south and the hills of the Yorkshire Dales to the north. As a town it sits between these two worlds, alternating in its history between aristocratic pretensions and working-class graft. In the early 1600s it was the last Royalist stronghold in the north, fiefdom of the powerful Clifford family. They made the castle, which dominates the town, their family seat. It had originally been built by Robert de Romille following the Norman Conquest. Many towns in this book have Norman castles, most of which were built to keep an eye on the residents and ensure their loyalty. Skipton, however, like Richmond (page 94) is a Norman town and its form and structure is dominated by the castle.

The Royalist stronghold was besieged by Cromwell's troops in the 1600s. After a three-year siege an honourable surrender was negotiated and while Cromwell ordered that the castle be rendered uninhabitable, the town was spared. The castle was repaired in the years that followed by the formidable Lady Anne Clifford, who planted a yew tree to mark its reopening in 1659, a tree that still dominates the castle courtyard. Because of these repairs, Skipton Castle is one of the few intact medieval castles that survive today. It is still in private hands and acts as a family home as well as being a major tourist attraction.

By the following century Skipton was entering its period as an industrial town. It had become a major market for sheep and wool and its limestone quarry was supplying the early industrial cities to the south. The problem was transport and as early as 1744 an act was put forward to make the River Aire navigable as far as Bingley. Following opposition from the local gentry, this didn't happen for 30 years; however, it was eventually to be incorporated into the Leeds & Liverpool Canal that opened in 1816 after 46 years of construction (although some sections were operating long before that). Skipton's first industrial mill, High Mill, was opened in 1785 to spin cotton. This started as a water-powered mill but converted to coal with the opening of the canal and soon there were nine major mills in the town working with

cotton, worsted and silk. As in many industrial towns, this prosperity was channelled into building societies. The Skipton Building Society that opened in 1853 has grown to become the fourth largest in the UK and is still headquartered in the town.

The co-evolution of street and market may be the reason for some of the unique features that make both so successful. Most market towns have one or two market days a week, attracting stallholders who spend the rest of their week at other markets. Market days are really busy while the rest of the week is quiet and the regular shops, while welcoming the trade that market days bring, often struggle to come to terms with market stalls pitched outside their premises, hiding them from their customers. In Skipton the street is divided into three: the road, the footpath and the 'setts' where the market stalls are pitched (which provide parking when the market isn't there). The stalls face away from the road trading towards the shops so that the wide street becomes two shopping streets on market days, creating a circuit that would be recognisable to any shopping centre developer. In a final innovation passed down from history, the rent paid by each stall goes to the adjacent shop owner rather than the market authority, creating a symbiotic relationship between retailer and stallholder.

Originally the market would have been a livestock market for the sale of sheep as well as being a retail market for goods and services. The former moved out to an 'Auction Mart' on the edge of the town in the 1970s but the main market has remained in the same space where it was established almost 1,000 years ago. As Kevin Reid-Griffiths, Skipton's town crier

told the *Daily Telegraph* when the Academy award was announced, 'we have a market here most days where you can buy everything from cheese, meat and vegetables to car parts and telephones'. The market has no fixed stalls and operates on a first-come-first-served basis and so is not particularly pretty. There are none of the striped awnings and picturesque market furniture that you find elsewhere; the attraction of Skipton's market comes from its vitality and variety and the activity that it generates.

The market rights are held by the castle, not the council. Until 2011 they contracted the running of the market to Craven District Council. However, when the contract came up for renewal, this was transferred to the town council. This was indicative of the progress made in the governance of the town, which has seen the three levels of government – county, district and town councils – working closely together. Back in 2003 plans were announced for a Business Improvement District (BID) in the town, an initiative by which businesses vote to add a penny to their local rates in order to raise a budget to spend on the town. The Skipton BID raised £500,000 over five years and has funded a town centre manager as well as physical improvements and local events. In this way the business community has worked closely with the wider community, as symbolised by the Skipton Gala that has been held in the town every June for 100 years.

In its 2010 report *Clone Town Britain*, the New Economics Foundation highlighted Skipton as a case study of a high street that has resisted the march of the chain stores. The High Street is not entirely free of these; it has a small House of Fraser store and a range of retailers from Laura Ashley and Fat Face, to Poundland and Bargain World. Indeed, around half of the shops are part of national chains, but at least the independent shops are holding their own. The New Economics Foundation put this down to good town centre management and the fact that the market rents go to the shops. However, it also helps that the town has just one supermarket, Morrisons, which does not have an extensive non-food offer. Other large retailers have had to content themselves with small units within the town and therefore must compete on equal terms with the independent shops.

Today Skipton has moved away from its industrial past and has avoided the struggles of many northern mill towns. Its main employers are now the building society and recruitment firms (of which there are five in the town), while its major export is commuters. It would seem that Skipton and its High Street have survived the retail revolution and, now that the wave has passed, can look forward to a prosperous future as a proper Yorkshire market town.

Opposite above: The view of the High Street from the castle, showing the market stalls facing towards the shops.

Opposite below right: The street when the market is not there.

Opposite left and below: High quality stalls can be found within the town, while the livestock market has moved out of the centre. You do, however, still occasionally get sheep on the High Street.

Hope Street, Liverpool

Winner 2013

Imagine an axis; imagine a washing line
Hung across a city. Cathedrals, a theatre
And a hotel hang from the line
And flap in the century's breeze...

This is Hope Street; imagine an artery
Pumping life through a city, imagine
A walk from one end of Hope to the other end
Of Hope on a moonlit evening...

Yes, that's right. You're walking through Hope.
Imagine a street where the soul is brightened
And the coffee is the best you can get in a city
That loves to keep itself awake.

Hope Street. Aptly named. See you there.

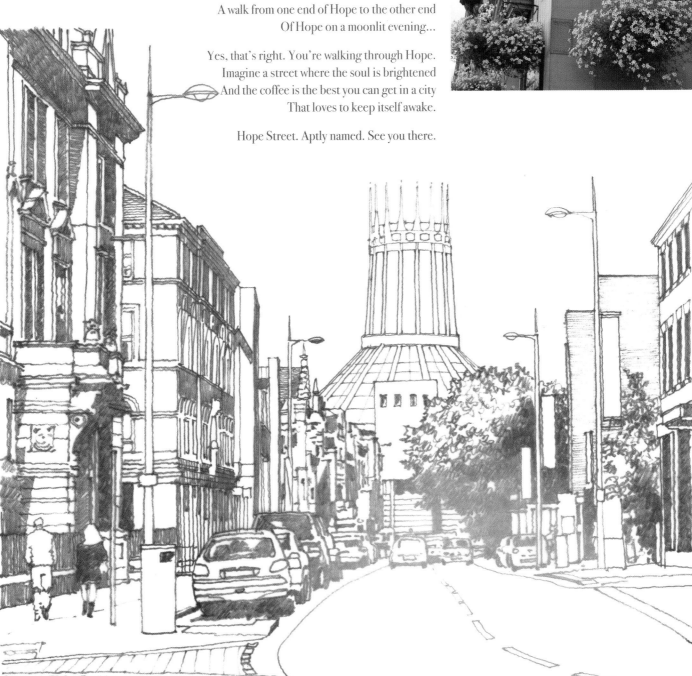

a partnership was formed between the city council, Liverpool 2020 and Liverpool Vision. Their vision saw Hope Street as the centre of a wider knowledge quarter and they worked with stakeholders including the University of Liverpool, Liverpool John Moores University and a series of major cultural institutions based in the area, to agree a strategy. This focused on the public realm and Hope Street was one of the first areas to be treated. The pavement was widened at the expense of the carriageway, although traffic was retained. New street furniture and public art was commissioned and grants were provided to renovate facades and install lighting. This face lift has been a catalyst, allowing Hope Street to rediscover its mojo, once again becoming a key part of the fabric of the city.

Hope Street has been around since the late 18th century, when Liverpool's trade with the Americas really took off, bringing with it rapid economic growth. The growing middle class demanded more genteel residential neighbourhoods and Hope Street, when it was first laid out, was on the edge of the countryside built at the top of a ridge above the teeming city centre. Its fresh air and views made it an attractive address for merchants, benefactors and philanthropists. It didn't remain on the edge for long as the land to the east was covered with more fine streets and squares, now largely

Tere are few streets with better bookends: to the south the sandstone form of Liverpool's Anglican cathedral and to the north the cone of its Catholic cathedral. Between the two runs Hope Street, which has reinstated itself in recent years as one of Liverpool's finest streets (in a city where there is a lot of competition for that title). It is not just the drama of its setting but the unique combination of cultural and entertainment venues and educational and social institutions alongside housing, hotels and offices that has grown up along the street that now forms the heart of a newly emerged cultural quarter.

Hard to imagine now, but barely ten years ago Hope Street was a very different place. Instead of being dominated by people enjoying its theatres and nightlife, it had spent a large part of the 20th century in something of a no man's land between the city centre and the university. An area that was neither one nor the other, a little run-down and dishevelled, car dominated and congested, it was little wonder that the street was overlooked; its rich history, impressive architecture and range of attractions largely unappreciated by all but the most devoted heritage connoisseurs.

Change may have seemed inevitable but would not have come without strong leadership. In recognition of the fact that the profound issues faced by the street had a broader impact on the city as a whole,

Plans were put in place to outdo not just the Anglican cathedral but to create a Catholic cathedral that would rival St Peter's in Rome

occupied by the university. By the Victorian era the city needed sites for a range of new institutions and the Hope Street area became the obvious place to locate them, much as happened in Kensington in London.

This has left Hope Street with a riotous concoction of major medical, educational and cultural institutions. The Mechanics' Institute opened in 1832 to provide educational opportunities for young men (it is now the Institute for Performing Arts), which was closely followed by the city's first girls' school in 1844 in a grand house on the opposite side of the street. The Liverpool Medical Institution opened in 1837, while Hahnemann Hospital was the first homeopathic hospital in the country when it opened in 1887. The Liverpool School for the Blind opened in 1791, but extended onto Hope Street in the 1930's. The original Philharmonic Hall was built in 1849, but destroyed by fire and rebuilt in the 1930's, with its namesake pub opposite.

But the biggest institutions of all were the two cathedrals at either end of Hope Street. Both now firm fixtures, they were epic projects in their own right, and their construction spanned most of the 20th century. By the time Liverpool's Anglicans had managed to

Above: Public-realm improvements on Hope Street, including public art, have provided an impetus for the wider regeneration of the area, including schemes such as the Hope Street Hotel.

Opposite: The view down Hope Street from the steps of the Catholic cathedral.

get agreement to build a cathedral at the end of the 19th century, there was no room in the city centre (the original site had been planned to be next to St George's Hall), so like the Victorian institutions it was pushed out to the St James Mount site at the southern end of Hope Street. Built to a design by the 22-year-old architecture student (and Catholic to boot) Giles Gilbert Scott following a competition in 1903, it took a further three quarters of a century and many refinements before it was finally completed in the late 1970s.

At the other end of the street a similarly drawn-out saga was unfolding. In the 1930s plans were put in place to outdo not just the Anglican cathedral but to create a Catholic cathedral that would rival St Peter's in Rome. Drawn up by Sir Edward Lutyens, it would have dwarfed the city if it had been realised, not that this was likely given an estimated cost of £27 million (near £700 million in today's terms). In an interesting familial twist, Giles' younger brother Adrian Gilbert Scott took over the project on Lutyen's death in 1944 and given a budget of just £4 million (still nearly £100 million today). By 1953 Scott had completed the crypt that Lutyens had designed but budget difficulties and concerns about the design having been compromised saw the project abandoned. An architecture competition was held in 1959, won by Frederick Gibberd for the building we see today. Construction started in 1962 with the first mass held five years later. The smaller conical structure was placed on the southern end of the crypt with a ceremonial flight of steps descending to Hope Street.

The recent public-realm improvements to Hope Street have sought to reconnect its different elements to make a coherent whole, while celebrating its history and culture. Two aspects in particular have been central to the proposals: that the design would place pedestrians ahead of cars, and that an emphasis would be placed on workmanship and detailing. Both have been a success. Footpaths have been widened and realigned to allow the free movement of pedestrians up, down and across the street. Now, when walking, the route feels quite natural – just as it should. Where possible, the existing Yorkstone paving has been retained, matched with new stone and granite kerbs, combining to instil a historic feel and character that is at once appropriate to the surrounding buildings. Corners have had particular attention. Restored to their original Georgian radii, they allow pedestrians to cross the street more freely, but have also been set to fall to carriageway grade, both easing wheelchair access and at the same time anticipating the roll-over of lorries. A further success has been the removal of unnecessary highway clutter, the new street furniture and lighting helping to create a strong relationship between the street, its spaces and buildings. The ceremonial steps to the Catholic cathedral have been refurbished and reconfigured by the landscape designers Landscape Projects to provide a grander setting at the end of the street.

Another consequence of the range of development along the street is its variety in street enclosure: at some points tight, the Georgian townhouses in particular creating a formal relationship with the street; at others much looser, where natural breathing spaces have been created where the larger institutions have stepped back from the street. New stone bollards in front of the Philharmonic Hall encourage casual sitting, providing a functioning space for the many outdoor events that occur throughout the year. The space outside the Institute for Performing Arts has been turned into a pleasant place to sit and absorb the happenings of the street. A piece of pubic art – a collection of suitcases by John King – has become a popular photo-op for weddings and tourists, sometimes simultaneously. The grant scheme has also been a success, particularly the lighting, which has helped to bring the different ages of architecture along the street alive at the same time as articulating the public realm.

These initiatives have had a galvanising impact on the street, acting as a precursor to other planned initiatives. The Everyman Theatre, built in the 1960s, has had a £28 million makeover that won the 2014 Stirling Prize, while the Philharmonic Hall has also undergone refurbishment. The former London Carriage Works, now a swanky restaurant and hotel, complete with urban bees on the roof, has plans to extend, as does the Hope Street Hotel, which is to take on the listed former Blind School. This is a really good example of public-realm works having a galvanising effect on a whole area. Hope Street once more provides a worthy setting for the rich array of jewels that it strings together.

Kensington High Street, London

Shortlisted 2009

If you stroll down High Street Kensington
From the underground station of the very same name
You'll see that the prospect is a pleasing one;
Because while many high streets look the same
This isn't the case with Kensington
This street looks like no other one!

If you stroll down High Street Kensington
You'll be amazed by the architecture
And how the morning sunshine shines upon
The Art Deco walls whose fine trajector
-y is something subtle, not full-on
Down the valley of High Street Kensington!

If you stroll down High Street Kensington
You understand shopping as theatre.
It's buy and sell with dazzling jewels on,
Somehow commerce getting fairly near ter
A fine cloak that your soul can don
A state of grace is High Street Kensington!

Running from the gates of Kensington Palace through the affluent surrounding neighbourhoods, Kensington High Street is, or at least was, the archetypal shopping street. It was once home to three of London's largest department stores as well as the iconic 1970s fashion retailer Biba. As with many of London's shopping streets, it is also an important traffic artery so that, unlike its pedestrianised cousins across the UK, it needs to wrestle with cars and buses as well as shoppers and residents. It is because of this that it became the first street to experiment with the idea of 'shared space'.

Kensington High Street began to take shape in the late 17th century, when the presence of the court at nearby Kensington Palace led to sporadic development along the route into London. At first this was mostly hostelries serving thirsty travellers but in the second half of the 18th century, as the surrounding areas were built up as well-to-do residential neighbourhoods, Kensington High Street emerged as a shopping street. London's expansion in the late 19th century caused the street to suffer from that very modern problem, congestion, prompting a series of municipal improvements to widen the street and remove traffic bottlenecks. Soon after, the arrival the railway turned Kensington High Street from a local high street into a fashionable, prosperous shopping street serving a much wider catchment area.

In the first half of the 20th century Kensington High Street became the archetypal shopping street in the era of the department store. Kensington had three of these grand institutions: Barkers of Kensington, Derry & Toms and Pontings. In the years leading up to 1960 the first two of these were turned into Art Deco palaces, each with seven retail floors. Derry & Toms even had a roof garden, covering one and a half acres with streams and a pond stocked with flamingos. Such was the popularity of the street that special trains were laid on to cope with the volume of shoppers drawn during the sales.

end of the street. The American retailer Whole Foods Market took over Barkers to open the UK's first organic superstore in 2007 and the street continues to be an important retail destination as well as the centre of the UK's music industry with the offices of Universal, Sony, EMI and Warner. In the mid 2000s it did, however, need to reinvent itself and to do that it needed to address once more its perennial struggle with traffic.

As the traffic on the street had grown over the years, the traffic engineers had responded in kind with more traffic engineering. Pedestrians were penned behind fences for fear they might step out into the grizzled traffic or, perish the thought, cross to the shops on the other side of the road. Today all of this clutter, fencing and crossing pens has been swept away and the street consists of two simple traffic lanes, no bus or cycle lanes, wider pavements and a central strip with trees and bike parking. It has been called shared space, but strictly it isn't; it has just been turned back into a normal street. It is still full of traffic but the relative status of the pedestrian and the vehicle has been equalised and the street, as a result, is much more civilised.

This solution is so obvious that it is hard to see why it would be controversial, but it most certainly was. It was promoted by the deputy leader of the council, the Conservative politician Daniel Moylan. He was told by his highway engineers that what he proposed was dangerous and would leave officers vulnerable to being sued by accident victims for not following highways guidance. Moylan's response was to tell his officers to write their committee report recommending that the work should *not* go ahead. He would then ignore their advice, absolving them of their legal responsibility. On this basis the work proceeded and seven years later the accident rate on the street has fallen while its retailing has been revived. Kensington High Street has become the model for high streets across London, reversing decades of highway engineering orthodoxy and perhaps also decades of decline as the pedestrian experience on these streets once more becomes a pleasure rather than a chore.

Unfortunately the street couldn't sustain three department stores. Barkers had bought the other two stores in the early 20th century but had continued to operate the three sites. They in turn were bought by House of Fraser in 1957 and by the 1970s Pontings and Derry & Toms had closed their doors. The latter was taken on by Biba, the smart Kensington boutique started by Barbara Hulanicki. Barkers struggled on until 2006 when it too closed after 135 years, by which time the retail world had moved on as the giant Westfield Centre opened nearby at White City.

This may have been the end of the era of the department store but it was far from being the

New Road, Brighton

Shortlisted 2010

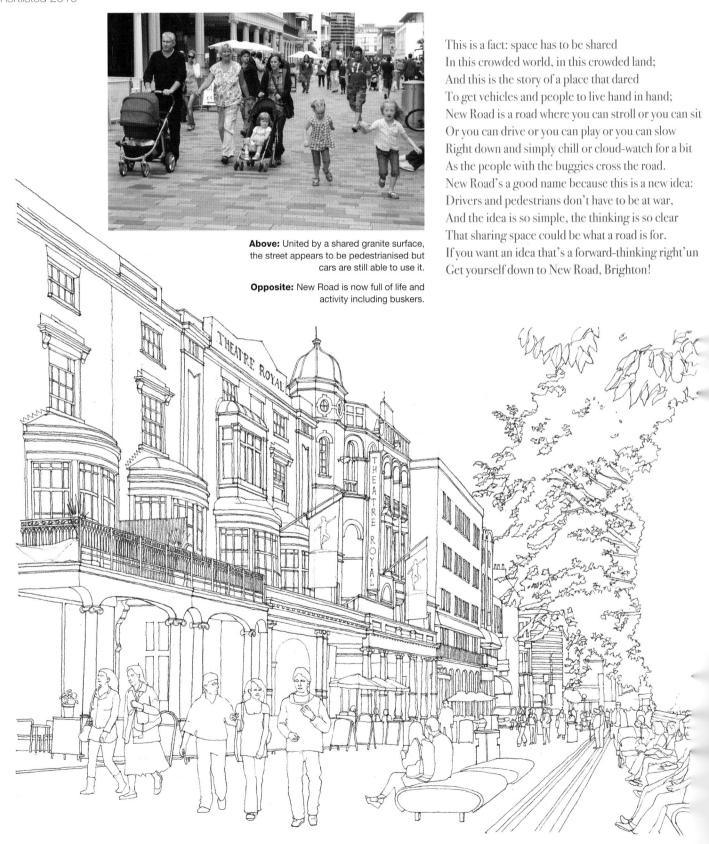

Above: United by a shared granite surface, the street appears to be pedestrianised but cars are still able to use it.

Opposite: New Road is now full of life and activity including buskers.

This is a fact: space has to be shared
In this crowded world, in this crowded land;
And this is the story of a place that dared
To get vehicles and people to live hand in hand;
New Road is a road where you can stroll or you can sit
Or you can drive or you can play or you can slow
Right down and simply chill or cloud-watch for a bit
As the people with the buggies cross the road.
New Road's a good name because this is a new idea:
Drivers and pedestrians don't have to be at war,
And the idea is so simple, the thinking is so clear
That sharing space could be what a road is for.
If you want an idea that's a forward-thinking right'un
Get yourself down to New Road, Brighton!

However, when traffic reverted back to the more direct route out of the city, New Road, despite its grandeur, became a bit of a backwater.

In the 2000s work was commissioned to revive the fortunes of the street. Gehl Architects were appointed together with the Manchester practices Landscape Projects and Martin Stockley Associates. They mapped pedestrian and traffic movement across the city to understand the hierarchy of routes and the role of New Road. Their conclusion was that New Road could become a lively public space. However, rather than exclude traffic, the decision was taken to create a shared space for both vehicles and pedestrians.

The street reopened in 2007 with a granite surface and no delineation between the pavements and carriageway. Street furniture includes a long bench along the Pavilion railings incorporating a lighting scheme by the artist Esther Rolinson. Trees have been cut back, allowing views of the Pavilion. At the same time many of the local businesses, the Theatre Royal and the Unitarian church included, have invested in their premises so that the western side of the street is now lined with cafes.

Much of Gehl's work is based on survey and observation. Their initial survey registered virtually no activity on the street, whereas in 2008 they registered more that 500 'staying activities' (people spending time in the street rather than passing through). Pedestrian activity had risen by 162% and cycling by 22%, while traffic had fallen by 93%. The safety audit stated that 'motorists appear to behave as though they are intruders in the street; give almost total priority to pedestrians; and most drive at the lowest possible speeds'. The reality is that the street has effectively been pedestrianised, so this is not a typical shared space as understood in the European context.

However, it is undoubtedly a huge success. In contrast to many new public spaces that fail to attract activity, in New Road careful analysis of the life of the city has allowed pedestrian activity to coalesce in a space that was previously largely deserted. One local businessperson on the Academy assessment team's visit wondered aloud where the thousands of people had come from. It may seem as if they have appeared by magic, but it is an alchemy borne out of a deep understanding of the workings of public space.

Visiting New Road in Brighton in the early 2000s was a confusing experience. Very grand and wide, it was lined on one side by magnificent Regency buildings and on the other by the brooding presence of the Pavilion gardens – although the Pavilion itself wasn't visible. It felt like a lost fragment of a great boulevard, cut off from the surrounding street network and relegated to the role of a back street, with all the attendant menace and seediness that implies.

Today it is apparently the fourth most visited place in Brighton, although it is probably some way behind the beach and the pier. Nevertheless, when the Academy assessment team visited in 2008, it was thronged with different people: buskers, diners at cafes, pedestrians, tourists, cyclists and (inevitably) tramps. Strangest of all, given all this activity, was that there were also cars, because New Street today is not a pedestrianised street but a shared space street. Indeed, Brighton Council claims it to be the first 'truly shared-surface, multi-modal, non-residential street in the UK'.

New Road is so called because it was built at the behest of the Prince of Wales at the start of the 19th century to divert traffic around his Royal Pavilion. For a while it was therefore the main street out of Brighton towards London, which explains its boulevard-like appearance. Befitting its importance, it was developed with fine houses and the prince gave royal consent for the Theatre Royal to be built in 1807.

'Motorists appear to behave as though they are intruders in the street; give almost total priority to pedestrians; and most drive at the lowest possible speeds'

Portobello Road, London

Shortlisted 2009

Right: Stalls and shops selling bric-a-brac and fashion line a street that can attract as many as 80,000 people a day.

O PORTOBELLO O!
You get row after row after row after row:
Shops putting on a show down Portobello
Go slow through the snow, get a wrap or a throw
Go hot in the sun, get a spending glow
Please don't say 'No,' just go with the flow
Down row after row after row after row
Of cafes and shops and stalls and you know
You're gonna get a bargain down Portobello!
So, for hats for above, for shoes for below
The odd stuffed crow, head of a buffalo
Photo of Lee Brilleaux, aromatic pillow
Hat in the shape of an armadillo
Row after row after row after row
After row after row after row after row
O it's bursting with life
down Portobello!

At the heart of the elegant white stucco neighbourhood of Notting Hill a colourful, defiantly lively road threads its way north. There's a difference in scale, of course, but on Saturdays with the antiques market in full flow, this west London street can feel more like the West End, filled with strolling people who are quite likely to have travelled a very long way to be here. If being a great street was judged by fame, then Portobello Road would give Oxford Street a good run for its money.

This almost mythical status has been helped by a healthy career in films, so even first-time visitors feel they have been here before, whether it was in *Bedknobs and Broomsticks* in 1971 or more recently in *Paddington* in 2014. However, the intimate streetscape of painted houses reached its widest audience in 1999 and, even after all that time, there are tourists who come looking for the landmarks where Hugh Grant and Julia Roberts played out their

romance in *Notting Hill*. The infamous blue door went to auction long ago, but the real-life film set is still clearly recognisable today.

Indeed, Portobello Road is like a film script written to reveal the backstory of the communities that have made it their home. Its winding route follows the path of a country lane where farmers set up market stalls in the 1860s to sell fresh produce to the growing residential districts nearby. Then in June 1864 a new era began, when the Metropolitan Railway opened a station, originally called Notting Hill, now Ladbroke Grove. As different immigrant communities followed, the variety of market stalls expanded. The antiques trade for which the market is best known took off after the Second World War as rag and bone businesses expanded and hundreds of stalls, shops and indoor arcades began selling bric-a-brac and antiques at the top of the hill between Chepstow Villas and Elgin Crescent. This Saturday market is what makes the road famous, but there are markets six days a week, and a strong local community of customers alongside the tourists. This is especially true for the fruit and vegetable stalls that dominate the central section of the road. When West African immigrants arrived in the 1950s they didn't want to travel to Brixton to buy their vegetables, so soon yams, okra and plantains began appearing alongside the cabbages and carrots. Further north towards the Westway flyover, stalls sell more practical, everyday things, and then towards Golborne Road things get edgier as the fashion

Portobello Road is like a film script written to reveal the backstory of the communities that have made it their home

market takes over. This is a popular location for young designers and fashion students selling new designs alongside vintage clothing.

It was from the Porto Bello Farm that once stood here, named after the town in Panama captured from the Spanish in the War of Jenkins' Ear in 1739, that the street takes its name. The gentrification that started in the 1980s has seen the area evolve from a shabby working-class district to one of the most desirable areas to live in the capital. This has been reflected in the market, which is both a focal point for local communities and an international tourist attraction. If success is measured in footfall, then Portobello Road is undoubtedly doing well. The recent '150 Years' celebration has seen weekly peaks of around 80,000 people. But success, and the area's rising property values, mean that commercial rents are squeezing out some of the longer-established businesses to be replaced with high-street names and new residential development. However, while the cast list may be changing, the power of the narratives that interweave along the street sustain the film, for the moment at least. The passion for the street is still strong; the future, perhaps, is less certain.

St Patrick's Street, Cork

Shortlisted for 2011

Walk down here in any kind of weather
And you'll feel the pulse of Cork beneath your feet;
Throbbing through your soles and your soul and whatever
Clothes you're wearing, to the beat of St Patrick's Street.
More than a row of shops, more than a place to spend,
It's like an ancient route that ancient people strode
Or a meeting place to turn a stranger to a friend
Or one of those thoroughfares that's more lifestyle than road,
One of those streets that never ever seems to end
Because the shops keep coming, and the laughter, and the talk
In a mixture that you have to call the St Patrick's Street blend
So come and feel that pulse, come and take that walk
On the street that defines just how life should be.
Come and dance down St Patrick's Street with me!

In 1999 a design competition was organised to look at ways to revitalise St Patrick's Street in Cork. The competition was won by the Catalan artist Beth Gali, who was appointed with a brief to bring a bit of 'Barcelona socialism to Cork'. Known locally as 'Pana', St Patrick's Street is the commercial heart of the city and it has been transformed from a place where pedestrians looked 'bullied and harassed' to a street where they are now 'kings and queens of their own domain' in the words of the director of Cork's Crawford Gallery, Peter Murray.

Cork is an international city. It may be on the far western fringe of Europe but this fringe, running from Lisbon and Falmouth to Galway and beyond (all places featured in this book), was once a superhighway of trade and migration. Cork became an important port exporting food to America and the West Indies and importing wine from Italy. At one time Cork Butter Market was the largest in the world, and today the English Market (so named to differentiate it from the nearby St Peter's or Irish Market) has an enviable reputation beyond Cork itself. French Protestants joined this cultural melting pot in the 17th and 18th centuries, fleeing religious persecution, and a Huguenot quarter remains an important part of the town. Linking these parts of the city is the wide sweep of St Patrick's Street. Cork is built on a large island at

To be 'doing Pana', strolling St. Patrick's Street in other words, has once more become a favourite pastime

the mouth of the River Lee and St Patrick's Street was once another of the river's channels. It was first turned into a canal, lined with shops and warehouses, and then infilled to create a wide street in 1783. The river channel dictated the street's shape and width, a grand foil to the tight network of streets to either side. Its gentle curve produces an ever-changing vista which, like Cockburn Street (page 166), produces a singular experience as the street's ends become disconnected from one another. Activity along the street also reacts to this variety like a river: enclosure producing areas of tightness and fast movement, and broader 'eddies' where people can stop and congregate. The city's figurative and spiritual heart, it is the place to be and be seen. Yet by the end of the 20th century St Patrick's Street was struggling. It had succumbed to the usual pressures; it was choked with congestion, polluted and cluttered and its shops were struggling to compete with out-of-town development. The question was not whether something should be done, but what?

The €13 million renovation project set out to create a new public realm for everyone. Like Kensington High Street (page 186), the approach was to tame rather than exclude traffic, reducing the road from four lanes to two and removing clutter and pedestrian barriers. Beth Gali's approach is asymmetrical, treating each pavement differently in terms of their width and design. The footpaths have been widened, so much so in some places that they form their own plazas where people can congregate. The eastern and western footpaths each have a different palette of materials – a mix of granite and limestone in a complex pattern that, to put it mildly, meant the stonemasons earned their corn. The galvanised steel lighting standards are the main feature. Reminiscent of ships' masts, those on the eastern side of the street are fixed, while those on the west are pivoted so that they can be moved into different positions. They create a sense of performance and drama and have become the unofficial motif for Cork.

The results speak for themselves. Initial scepticism that the proposals would lead to loss of trade or diminish the importance of the street have proven unfounded. The egalitarian ambitions for the project – to make the street somewhere that everyone can enjoy, have been realised. Events such as the St Patrick's Day Festival help to animate the space and commercial activity has thrived since the improvements. There is, in fact, now talk of pedestrianising St Patrick's Street entirely. To be 'doing Pana', strolling St Patrick's Street in other words, has once more become a favourite pastime even if the weather might not quite match that of Barcelona.

Steep Hill, Lincoln
Winner 2012

Halfway up or halfway down your breath begins to pull,
Your legs start to feel like you've been dancing for a month
Non stop.

Hold onto the handrail as you negotiate Steep Hill
And pause, take your time, gaze in the window of a cafe
Or a shop,

And picture people from the past or the years yet to come
Who took their time up this slope, paused and stood and looked
Or who will.

And celebrate the fact that some places simply aren't the same
As each other. They've got a handrail for instance.
They're unique, like Steep Hill.

incoln is a small city of two halves: the 'uphill', which has always been relatively wealthy, and the 'downhill', which is where the mucky business of commerce and industry has taken place. The sinuous strand providing a direct link between the two is Steep Hill. As its name suggests this is a winding, precipitously steep road, little more than a lane really, running from the Guildhall Arch in the centre of the city up to the cathedral that was described by John Ruskin as 'out and out the most precious piece of architecture in the British Isles'. The two parts of the town reflect its topography, standing as it does at the point where the River Witham cuts through a 50 metre high escarpment running north-south through Lincolnshire.

Lincoln's history has alternated between the 'uphill' and the 'downhill'. The original settlement sat around Brayford Pool at the base of the hill; the name Lincoln is thought to be derived from the Celtic word for 'pool'. Then in AD 48 soon after their invasion, the Romans built a castle on the top of the hill. As the invasion swept northwards and the surrounding lands fell under Roman rule the castle wasn't much needed for defence and became a settlement for retired Roman soldiers. The Romans deepened the River Witham, allowing them to make Brayford Pool a busy inland port. The map of Roman Britain shows the strategic importance of Lincoln on the main road, Ermine Street, running north to York and beyond. At the base of the hill, this was joined by Fosse Way from the Midlands. Both channelled their traffic into the only route up to the fortified settlement: Steep Hill. While it may look like a winding lane, it was once the Roman equivalent of the M1 motorway.

After the Roman withdrawal, Lincoln appears to have been largely abandoned for a couple of centuries, before growing once more to become an important Viking town. Then came the Normans and, as with many other towns in this book, they built a castle to pacify the town and, having done this, established the cathedral. These two institutions sit at the top of Steep Hill with their gates at either end of Castle Hill, creating one of the finest medieval set-pieces of any British city, made all the more dramatic when experienced after slogging up the cobbles of Steep Hill. The castle was used as a prison for 500 years and Castle Hill was a place of public execution. However, it is now open as a major tourist attraction displaying its

While it may look like a winding lane, it was once the Roman equivalent of the M1 motorway

Below: An engraving looking over Brayford Pool, showing the downhill town and the thread of Steep Hill leading up to the castle and cathedral.

history both as a medieval fortress and a Victorian prison. It also holds one of the four remaining copies of the *Magna Carta*.

The Steep Hill approach to the castle and cathedral is a classic piece of serial vision, in which the two towers of the cathedral appear as landmarks before being obscured by the wind of the street and the gradient of the hill only to be revealed again with a dramatic flourish as you reach the square at the top of the hill. One can only imagine the impact on medieval travellers who trod the same path. Indeed, up until 1550 the cathedral was topped with a spire that made it the tallest building in the world.

Today the name Steep Hill refers only to the central part of the street. However, it starts in the heart of the downhill city at the arch formed by the Guildhall. The first part of the street is called High Street and is lined with shops before the street bends to the right as it passes into the Straight and starts to work its way up the gradient, which is when you start to get your first good views of the cathedral. The Straight arrives in a beautiful small triangular space, marred only slightly by some poor recent pastiche buildings on its southern side, and then you are onto Steep Hill proper. However, before going further, it is worth turning right to visit the Collection, a gallery and museum of archaeology with an extension designed by the architects Panter Hudspith, which opened in 2005.

Back on Steep Hill, the gradient means that vehicles are excluded from the central part of the street where the shops thin out and housing predominates. Then the final push takes you into Bailgate, once more lined with shops and cafes, and onward to Castle Hill, where you may find a market in operation. Today the people who throng the street are tourists rather than travellers or old centurions, but Steep Hill continues to perform its historic function of connecting 'uphill' and 'downhill' Lincoln.

For those who find the slope a bit much, there is a 'walk and ride' bus shuttling passengers to the top of the hill. This was threatened with closure a few years ago following the withdrawal of funding. It was saved by the Lincoln BIG (Business Improvement Group), which was set up in 2003 and became a Business Improvement District in 2005 when more than half of the city centre retailers agreed to contribute a penny on their local rates to fund the scheme. The scheme employs city centre wardens providing security and helping to manage the public realm. It also organises activities like Lincoln in Bloom and the Christmas Markets as well as managing parking and bus operation, like the Steep Hill service. On the Academy assessment team's visit it was the work of the BIG that was credited for the immaculate condition of Steep Hill despite its heavy usage. It is a street whose modest appearance belies its historic importance, and which has managed to retain the feel of a real street rather than becoming a museum piece.

Union Street, Aberdeen

Shortlisted 2011

A city needs a striking thoroughfare
That's an artery and a river of stone
That leads you in and holds you there;
It's the city's sinew, the city's bone;
Aberdeen has the street called Union Street
Built as a gateway to reflect the pride
Of a city, and make the city complete
With a street as deep as it is wide;
To wander down this street is to wander through
A theatre of shopping, a ballet of buying
A street that fits Aberdeen like a shoe
A street that's moving and singing and flying!
I know you can't fly without wings, dance without feet,
But anything can happen on Union Street!

Who said ye cannae build a street of granite in the sky? Union Street, vaulting across the rooftops of medieval Aberdeen, did just that 200 years ago. A thing of wonder, Union Street was a grand statement of the civil and commercial power of the emerging city in the 19th century (although it would eventually bankrupt its council). Now Aberdeen's main thoroughfare, Union Street is the place where the people of the city come to celebrate when Aberdeen Football Club parade trophies in an open-topped bus – not that this has happened recently, admittedly. However, it does host many other parades, political rallies, markets and festivals throughout the year and was packed with more than 200,000 people in 2004 for the street's bicentennial celebrations.

At the end of the 18th century Aberdeen was a hopelessly cramped medieval city. Its main public space, Castle Street, may have had a certain grandeur, but reaching it from the outskirts of the town meant negotiating a maze of confusing, narrow, steep streets. At the time the surveyor Charles Abercrombie had been engaged by the county landowners to devise a turnpike system for the surrounding countryside. It seemed only sensible for the magistrates of Aberdeen to get him to have a look at how the turnpikes would arrive in the city while he was at it. As the medieval plan of the city (below) shows, to the west of Castle Street stood St Catherine's Hill beyond which the land dipped dramatically into the Denburn Ravine. Abercrombie suggested an audacious solution: cutting through the medieval fabric of the city and slicing 15 feet from the top of St Catherine's Hill before creating an elevated street

Below: Taylor's plan of Aberdeen from 1771, with the red line showing the route cut by Union Street.

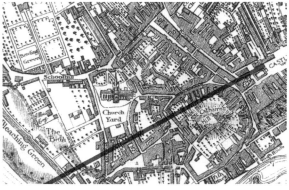

raised on brick arches and then constructing the graceful Union Bridge over the valley. The magistrates were slightly taken aback (and no doubt daunted) by the scale of the enterprise and sat on the report for more than a year. However, the idea was out, and gradually pressure built up from the worthies in the town. Committees were formed, estimates requested (woefully inadequate, it would transpire), an act of parliament raised, funding procured and architects engaged (then sacked after getting the levels wrong), new architects engaged, contractors appointed (also sacked after getting their figures wrong) and new contractors appointed so that work could finally start on 1 January 1801 with completion set for June 1805.

But even this was only half the story. The plan had been to fund the road from the feus along its length. These were building plots to be sold to developers, with restrictions as to what they could build (what we would now call a design code). The Union Street feurs were required to build four-storey buildings dressed in granite set eight feet back from the pavement, allowing light into basements. However, the economics didn't work and 12 years after the road opened, only one row of buildings had been completed. The city, struggling under £225,000 of debts, was forced into bankruptcy.

'It is time that it was run by ladies in hats provided of course that they are as formidable as they are charming'

The trustees responsible for the street, however, refused to relax the restrictions on the feus and it is precisely this stubbornness that has given us the grand street we have today. By the mid 1820s the economy had recovered and building finally started in earnest.

The original idea was that Union Street would be residential, a civilised extension of the crowded old city where its merchants could set up home. However so successful was the street in linking four of the city's five turnpike roads that it was thronged with traffic and people as soon as it opened. The city's aspirant retailers soon saw the potential and abandoned their cramped premises in the old shopping streets of Gallowgate and Broad Street for the grander premises that eventually started going up along Union Street. The city's professional classes, solicitors, architects and insurance companies populated the *piano nobile*, the grand first floors, of the classical buildings while artists and music teachers, hotels and even schools were to be found on the upper floors. But this wasn't all; Union Street was built on a viaduct so that there were floors below the ground floor fronting onto the lower-level streets of the old town. These were full of small manufacturers and tailors completing the mix and creating an entire multi-level city in the cross-section of the street.

In the 2008 update of her book *The Granite Mile*, Diane Morgan is scathing about the recent history of Union Street. She is saddened by the loss of the trams and the cinemas, the relocation of the universities to out-of-town sites and the undermining of the retailing by the St Nicholas and Bon Accord shopping centres. She worries about its 'clone town' shops and the concentration of late-night drunkards at its western end. She concludes rather enigmatically that: 'It is time that it was run by ladies in hats provided of course that they are as formidable as they are charming... have a love of real shopping, are au fait with the inner workings of the rag trade and are not inclined to be overwhelmed by aspiring developers.'

Ms. Morgan clearly has a particular view of how the street should be run and I'm sure we would all agree with her wish to ban window dressings consisting of nothing but posters about mortgages and interest rates on loans. She also disagrees with the recent pedestrianisation undertaken by the council at the eastern end of the street. However this, together with better policing of the evening economy, improved management and wider pavements in the sections where traffic remains, is having an impact. The trials and tribulations of the city fathers 200 years ago have bequeathed us a street that is as grand an urban set-piece as anywhere in Europe. Over time it will and must evolve but its granite stones will endure.

Places

Great places make up the fifth category of the Academy of Urbanism's awards. This is something of a wild-card and tends to be a portmanteau category for all of the entries that don't fit easily into the other categories: quaysides and squares, markets, castles and beaches (well, one castle and one beach). It is difficult consequently to define a thread that runs through this diverse group. However, they do all have something in common. They all lift the heart, quicken the pulse or make your day a bit better than it would otherwise have been. They are all good 'places', a concept that lies at the heart of the Academy's rallying cry: 'Space, *Place*, Life'.

Urban designers spend a lot of time banging on about the first of this trinity: *Space*. As urbanists we are urged to focus on shaping the spaces in between buildings rather than just the design of the buildings themselves. Good space depends upon scale and proportion, the width of streets and squares as a relation to the heights of the buildings that enclose them, the integrity of building lines, the hierarchy of streets and spaces and the composition of landmarks and vistas. Space is about the grand gestures of Paris' boulevards or the intimate web of London's back streets. This is the stuff of masterplans, design codes and manuals. We know, or think we know, all about space.

The last of the three, *Life* refers to the activity that animates these streets and squares. This is generated by the density with which an area is developed and the intensity of occupation of its buildings by people and businesses. It relates to the shops, cafes, bars and restaurants that spill their life onto its pavements as well as the squares and parks that encourage people to linger. Life is also prescribed in rule books and codes that stipulate minimum densities, a mix of uses, plot ratios and proportions of active frontage. We also know, or think we know, about life.

Place is more difficult. Place is what you are left with – or more often deprived of – once all the rules have been applied and all the masterplans built. Place is the 'there' in Gertrude Stein's often quoted comment about Oakland in California – that when she arrived there, 'there was no there there'. It is unfortunately often the case that new urban areas, once they are completed, don't quite measure up to the aspirations of the people who designed and built them. In terms of the rule book they are 'correct' in every respect, their spaces are well designed and they may even be well used, but they still lack a certain something. That certain something is a 'sense of place'.

Place is the quality of a space that makes it special. It is the intangible aura that makes a city, town, neighbourhood or street more than the sum of its parts, more than the product of its design code, more even than just the collective activity of its people. The quality of place is what makes urban areas lodge in the memory, what causes people to linger and to return. It is the quality that drives artists to paint them and poets to immortalise them in verse.

This sense of place is there in spades in the historic Grassmarket in Edinburgh, the Victoria Quarter in Leeds, Queen Square in Bristol or Tobermory Harbour on the Isle of Mull, all places described in this section. A sense of place is something that we are used to finding in historic towns and cities. These are places that lift the spirit and make you feel good, although it is not always easy to analyse why they do so. It could be something to do with the layers of history, the patina of age and sense of continuity, the conviviality of the life of the place or the beauty of its physical form. These qualities may be hard to describe, but they are even more difficult to bottle and almost impossible to create from scratch when designing a new place. It is therefore surprising that many of the 15 places in this chapter are not really old at all. Even those that have existed for a long time have done little more than to provide the materials and setting for a new great place.

Oxford Castle is a good example. It is a place with tremendous history and character but it was lost for centuries behind high walls and completely unknown to most of the people of Oxford. The site includes a Saxon tower, a Norman castle and a Victorian prison with some fine buildings and a dramatic setting. However, it had never been a 'place', at least not one where you would want to spend any time. Since the closure of the prison it has been skilfully transformed into one of the 'places' on the Oxford map, appealing to both locals and visitors and capable of competing with the city's other great attractions. Other great rediscovered places include Meeting House Square in Dublin's Temple Bar and the Wharf in Sowerby Bridge. Only 20 years ago the former was slated for demolition to build a bus station and the latter was to be filled in to create a car park. Both places were saved following campaigns by local people and have since been refurbished to the extent that it is now almost inconceivable that their destruction could ever have been contemplated.

Then there are great places that have been created from very modest ingredients. Perhaps the most dramatic example is a bleak and rather industrial stretch of sand at Crosby in the suburbs of Liverpool that now features on the cover of the north-west tourist brochure because of the sculpture *Another Place* by Antony Gormley. We might also include the modest neighbourhood of Victorian terraced housing in Brighton's North Laine, once threatened by a road scheme and now one of the UK's most extraordinary specialist shopping areas.

Then there is the transformation of run-down, unattractive city centre spaces into places that people now cherish. Sheffield has been nominated twice for the Peace & Winter Gardens and Sheaf Square. It is a testament to the success of these places that locals can no longer remember how awful they were, how the Peace & Winter Gardens was dominated by council offices known locally as the 'Egg Box' and how Sheaf Square was a roundabout on the ring road. Bradford's City Park has pulled off a similar trick, transforming a traffic-dominated area at the back of the police station into somewhere that will henceforth be the postcard image of the city and a symbol that it has turned a corner in its regeneration.

Creating entirely new great places is an even more difficult trick to perform. Only three newly built schemes have been nominated as great places. Brindleyplace was nominated in 2007 and is written up in the Academy's first book, *Place Space Life*. This section includes two more: Princesshay in Exeter and Kings Place in London. It is probably fair to say that neither quite match the sense of place of somewhere really old, although their nomination recognises the achievement in creating any sense of place in a freshly minted development. It is nevertheless difficult when building on a cleared site to generate the diversity and layers of interest found in a place that has developed over many years. There may, however, be lessons that developers and masterplanners can learn from the great places in this section:

One such lesson is to allow room in plans for diversity to develop. Bundling up retail space into large units to attract national retailers might make sense commercially, but it will not make a great place. What is necessary is to allow space for small units, suitable for independent retailers, where new business ideas can be tested. The older places find this easier to achieve: old buildings come in a variety of shapes and sizes and are often cheaper to occupy than new space that needs to be fitted out and produce a commercial return.

Linked to this is the idea that developers and their designers should resist the temptation to plan everything. Great places cannot be created on a drawing board; rather they grow over time, and it is this incremental (and often accidental) growth that creates their character, often in ways that their original designers couldn't have anticipated. Masterplans therefore need to create loose-fit frameworks that can evolve over time, leaving space for the unplanned and the serendipitous.

Another lesson is that great places are spaces where people wish to linger and where urban life takes on a life of its own. There is a tendency, as Anna Minton has documented in her book *Ground Control,* for commercial developers to want to control the use and image of their spaces with security guards, CCTV and even a ban on photography. This may be done in the hope of making the places more civilised and attractive but the effect is often the opposite. Kings Place is interesting in the way that it seems to present an alternative approach by making its foyer into part of the public realm of the city where people with no other connection to the building come to meet and hang out without feeling pressured to move on or even buy a coffee. It's not without control, of course, as you would no doubt find if you were homeless and tried to use the space, but there is a lower level of paranoia and this has the effect of a huge increase in activity.

What these places teach us is that the creation of great places is really hard, but that it is also what everyone involved in shaping our urban environment should be striving to achieve. It is important that we follow the rules of good urban design. Certainly, if we ignore these basic principles, it will be impossible to create great places. However, once all of the rules have been applied and the plans drawn, there is a need to sprinkle that little bit of magic that lifts an area and makes it special. Like good wine, this is something that becomes easier with time but it is not impossible in new development. Defining the magic of great places is not easy; it cannot be codified and is not easily replicated. It is something created by people who really understand cities. Dare I say it is something better understood by people who use and manage urban areas than it is by the architects and planners who design them? It is an art rather than a science and it requires an understanding of human behaviour and economics and a sense of theatre. In short, it is the emerging profession of urbanism.

City Park, Bradford
Winner 2013

Light here, please. Light here. Water and light
And a pool that's a mirror so look, just look
In the summer's glare or autumn's night
And you can read this place like a book,

So take your slow time with Bradford's story
Turn your page like the light seems to turn
On this water/glass setting that reflects the glory
Of the architecture and the light that helps you learn

That all cities need a place as lovely as this
To stroll or sit down in and take the air.
Come here now, Bradford, give us a kiss!
And don't tell me you haven't got a thing to wear

'Cos these reflections in water and light say it clear;
The future is Bradford's, the future is here.

embers of the Academy who arrived for the assessment visit to Bradford City Park did so with no great expectations. Many places have, after all, installed water features in recent years and the technology is such that they are all very impressive. But Bradford City Park – or 'Bradpool', as local people have started to call it – is different. It is urban theatre on a grand scale and, like the neighbouring Alhambra Theatre, the attraction is not so much the stage set, impressive as it is, but the actors and the drama.

So successful has the park been, in fact, that Primark regularly sells out of socks and towels at the weekend. On the overcast Monday morning of the Academy assessment team visit, it gradually filled with people as the pool filled with water over a five-hour cycle. And these were all the people of Bradford: youths on bikes, elderly people, women in burkas, students and families – a happy, relaxed mix of people rarely seen in British cities (other perhaps than on a beach) and certainly not in Bradford. This is where 'Bradpool' comes from; City Park is Blackpool in Yorkshire, Bradford's own urban beach. It's a place that makes you think that Bradford is going to be OK and makes you believe that the physical environment of a place really can be transformative.

Bradford is Britain's great lost provincial city. Similar in terms of population to Sheffield, Newcastle

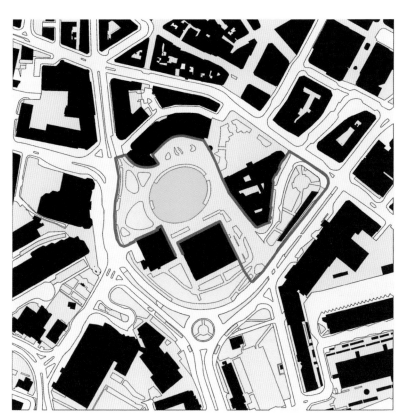

If Bradford could do this one thing, then anything would become possible

and Bristol, and once richer than all of its peers, it has fallen on hard times in recent years. This is partly the result of bad luck, partly bad timing and, it must be admitted, partly self-inflicted. Despite all of the money and effort expended on the city, most recently by the Urban Regeneration Company, precious little was achieved, even through the years of economic boom. With the worst possible timing, Westfield demolished part of the retail core, dug a big hole in the ground and were then forced to stop work on the new shopping centre as the credit crunch decimated the retail sector. Elsewhere, flagship projects like the Channel Urban Village were shelved while the redevelopment of the former Odeon was embroiled in a protracted campaign by heritage groups. So bad-tempered was this that a few years later the Odeon's supporters would mount a protest at the opening ceremony for City Park even as the rest of the city celebrated. It was an opening that looked like it too would never happen when the Mirror Pool – as City Park was originally called – failed to secure funding from the Lottery. To have built City Park in the face of all of this adversity is an act of sheer bloody-minded willpower. It became an all or nothing issue; if Bradford could do this one thing, then anything would become possible!

The story starts in 2003 when the Urban Regeneration Company commissioned Will Alsop to produce a masterplan for the city centre. The plan's main premise was that Bradford no longer had

Middle left: The original Alsop Associates masterplan and some of the other policy documents prepared for City Park.

Opposite: The Academy assessment team.

sufficient demand to build on all of its vacant sites and so should turn them over to create a linear park through the city centre. At the heart of this new park stood City Hall in a natural bowl, which the Alsop team suggested be flooded to create a pool. The impact of this masterplan was the subject of some debate, summed up by Daniel Cunningham writing for *Estates Gazette* in 2005: 'When Bradford's urban regeneration company put Will Alsop's masterplan on display at New York's Museum of Modern Art... some back in Yorkshire thought a building full of whimsical works of imagination was the best place for it. Alsop's vision for the former wool town, complete with a "business forest", man-made lake and plenty of space to "think and meet", left many local agents scratching their heads, even if it did grab the attention of Manhattan's art lovers'.

However, the ambition and imagination of the plan, unconstrained as it was by practicality and economic viability, gave birth to an idea that, even in a much reduced state, has an originality and power. The pool in the original plan would have required the demolition of the city's main police station and magistrates court. As luck would have it, the police were planning to move, but there was no way that the court could be relocated. The eventual design for the park therefore covered less than half of the area envisaged by Alsop.

The process of transforming the vision into today's reality included a Neighbourhood Development Framework developed by Arup and eventually a design competition that was won by Gillespies. It was the subject of an application to the National Lottery. However, conflict and debate continued to dog the proposals and when the planning application was submitted to committee, it was very nearly refused (requiring the casting vote of the chair). Subsequent to this came the news that the Lottery funds had not been secured.

It was that evening, in one of the function rooms of the Victoria Hotel that had been booked to celebrate the announcement of Lottery funding, that the council and Yorkshire Forward committed themselves come-what-may to delivering the pool. It was about this time that a new broom started sweeping through the city, instigated through the appointment of Tony Reeves as the new Chief Executive and Barra MacRuairi as Director of Culture and Regeneration. As Barra told us during the Academy assessment team's visit, at his job interview he said that his aim would be to allow Bradford people to become tourists in their own city. To this end he committed himself to delivering City Park, setting aside two hours every Thursday evening to meet with the project manager Shelagh O'Neill.

The result might be expected to be a slightly compromised version of the original vision – but it isn't, it is brilliant! As Shelagh told us, when the sun comes out, as it occasionally does in Bradford, something magical happens. And right on cue, just as the presentations to the assessment team finished, the sun appeared and the atmosphere changed as the space filled with happy, relaxed people. These Bradford people were still learning how to use the space, exploring its possibilities and (there is no other word for it) playing. This is helped greatly by a hands-off style of management. Before it opened, there was a great deal of debate about issues like alcohol, skateboards and bikes and anti-social behaviour. The brave decision was to say that the management would only intervene to prevent behaviour that risked damaging the space or harming its users. We watched kids circling in the water on BMX bikes and at lunchtime people in the surrounding bars were drinking alcohol. The mix of people, however, means that no one group dominates and, so far at least, a happy balance is being maintained.

The next step was to programme the space. This started in spectacular fashion with the opening event, which was reminiscent of the best days of the Bradford Festival. Soon after, it hosted the World Curry Festival. At the time of the assessment visit there were plans for the space to be programmed throughout the year although budget and management capacity was limited and the council was aware that it would need to build activity up slowly. However it is a resource for Bradford that the city will learn how to use.

The opening of City Park heralded a new confidence in the city. The completion of new offices for Provident Insurance, overlooking the park, secured 1,000 jobs, Bradford was named the first UNESCO City of Film and in 2015 the Westfield shopping centre finally opened, while new plans were agreed for the Odeon. City Park is more than just another fancy water feature. When the history of Bradford's regeneration is written, it may be seen as the moment when the city's fortunes at last started to change.

Crosby Beach, Sefton

Shortlisted 2009

Sand sifts, sand shifts, sand changes,
Sand slides and solidifies, sand alters in the light
Sand dances, sand crumbles, sand rearranges
Morning sand is different to how sand was in the night!

And now the crowds are walking in the stiff and bracing breeze
Bending from the whirling wind like scarved and hatted trees
Gazing at the metal people staring out to sea
The ones who could be human, who could be you or me.

Sand shifts, sand sifts, sand rearranges,
Morning sand is different to how sand was in the night
Sand crumbles, sand dances, sand changes
Sand solidifies and slides, sand alters in the light;

Crosby Beach can say something on how we learn from place
On how the sand's impermanence can be a kind of grace
How art and life can come together, beneath a moving sky
Watched by whirling seagulls and statues's frozen eye.

Sand changes, sand crumbles, sand dances
Sand rearranges, sand sifts, sand shifts
Evening sand is different to how sand was in the day
Sand alters in the light, sand solidifies and slides...

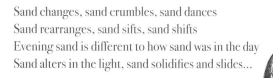

Another Place is not a project that could have come out of a consultation exercise or the workings of a partnership. Art doesn't work like that. No regeneration strategy would ever have come up with the idea of installing 100 cast-iron figures along a stretch of industrial beach. If it had, the powers that be, the planning authority, the bird lobby, the ecologists, the coastguards, the wind surfers and indeed the local community would have said no – indeed, did say no.

The work is the result of two pieces of inspiration: that of the artist Antony Gormley (of course), but also that of the South Sefton Development Trust that secured *Another Place* for Crosby. The piece, which consists of 100 life-size figures cast from Gormley himself, had been created as a touring work. Before coming to Sefton, the work had been displayed in Scandinavia, Germany and Belgium and was scheduled to go on to New York.

However, the work came to life in the harsh light of Sefton where the industrial silhouettes of the dockyard cranes and offshore wind turbines meet the austere presence of the windswept Sefton coastline. The figures are placed along a half-mile stretch of beach from the high to the low water mark; some are so far out to sea that they are submerged for much of the time and are already encrusted with barnacles. The rising tide covers most of the figures to be revealed again once it goes out. One unanticipated consequence has been the way the figures illustrate the shifting sands, being exposed one day and up to their waist, in sand a few days later.

trying to reach figures in the water as well as worries about navigational safety for boats or wind surfers colliding with submerged figures. At a stormy council meeting, where all of these concerns were aired, the initial planning application to extend the life of the piece was refused.

The magic of the piece lies in its ability to be both serious art – hauntingly beautiful when the beach is empty or the weather is bad – and yet at the same time to be accessible to local people on a busy summer afternoon when the beach is rammed with sunburnt families. In a survey 83% of visitors to the beach described the work as 'fun' and the figures have been adopted by people who dress them up, climb and draw on them and have themselves photographed with them. In doing so, of course, they become part of the work, yet within a few days the tide and wind have scrubbed the figures clean.

Another Place so clearly worked in Sefton that from the moment of its installation it seemed inconceivable to many people that it should ever go anywhere else. However, the battle to keep it was hard-fought and the battleground was the planning system. Many of the groups who had been uneasy about the temporary installation (but thought at least it was only temporary) became outright hostile to the idea of making it permanent.

The beach is an internationally recognised nature reserve, designated as a Ramsar site and a Site of Special Scientific Interest. Natural England and the RSPB were opposed to the installation because of worries about people being attracted onto bird breeding grounds at low tide. Indeed, there were concerns about the ecological impact of all these extra people being attracted to the beach. There were also safety concerns about people getting into difficulties

It was the outrage prompted by this refusal that brought home to people just how popular the piece had become. The South Sefton Development Trust together with the Liverpool Biennial started work on a permanent planning application and a fundraising campaign to secure the £2 million required to buy the piece. This was a complex process and the consent that was eventually granted is wrapped up in conditions and safeguards. Sixteen figures were moved off bird feeding grounds, reducing the length of the piece and routes were marked for the inshore lifeboat to access the beach at high tide.

None of the conditions have lessened the power of the work and the result is an extraordinary 'place'. It is all the more extraordinary because, while the people of Crosby loved their beach, it was hardly somewhere that anyone else would have visited. *Another Place* has promoted it from nowhere onto the cover of north-west tourism brochures. It has turned a relatively nondescript piece of semi-industrial coastline into a place that people travel from all over the world to see. The amazing thing is that, while it is true that people come to see the work, what they experience is the place – which is why the name *Another Place* is so appropriate. The work allows people to look at the beach in another way: not as a poor cousin of the sandy beaches further up the coast at Formby or Southport, but as a hauntingly beautiful place in its own right.

Above and below: The figures have a presence on the beach, whether as serious sculptures or as a companions to a family picnic.

Gillett Square, Hackney
Shortlisted 2012

All roads lead here. All thoughts lead here
To this vortex, this hub, this shifting perception
Of what a square can be. Stand here. Sit here.
Listen here: this square is here, makes here

A place to be. A definition of Gillett Square
Would have to take in this thriving collection
Of shopfronts and cafes. Tea square. Hair square.
And a saxophone solo drifting over the square.

All sounds lead to square. All talking is here
In the visceral here they call Gillett Square;
Here present, here future; renaissance is here:
Just listen, just take part, just complete the square.

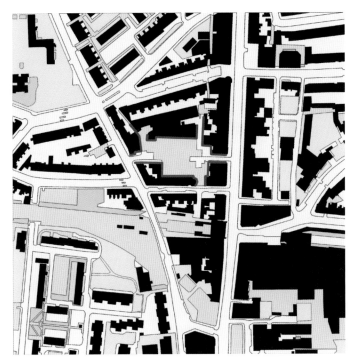

Dalston town centre. Their recommendations were accepted by the council and the square became part of local planning policy in 1998.

A partnership was formed in 2001 including Hackney Co-operative Developments, the local Groundwork Trust, Hackney Council, the Greater London Council, Vortex Jazz Foundation, a local developer MacDonald Egan (who had purchased the adjacent Stamford Works) and Hawkins\Brown Architects. The first step was the development of ten kiosks on part of the car park, designed by Hawkins\Brown. These were to win a Design Week award as well as an RIBA Small Buildings prize. Meanwhile, Hackney Co-operative Developments were working on the Dalston Culture House, which was to form the western end of the new square. This building includes a cafe and bar on the ground floor, the Vortex Jazz Club on the first floor and studio workspaces on the upper floors. Across the square MacDonald

Londonn in the 1980s was a hotbed of practical activism. The protest movements and squats of the 1960s and 1970s had evolved into projects to build housing co-operatives, develop community workspaces and indeed regenerate whole communities. One of the best-known groups, the North Kensington Amenity Trust, served as inspiration for Hackney Co-operative Developments, founded in 1982 in Dalston. This not-for-profit, community benefit company, targeted specifically at promoting black and ethnic minority, women-run and ethical businesses, has spearheaded the regeneration of the neighbourhood that has developed around a former car park since reborn as Gillett Square.

Dalston is one of the most diverse parts of London. In the 1980s (and still to an extent today) it was scruffy and run-down and had an edge of danger. It is the UK home of reggae and hip Hop, with more nightclubs than the West End and more artists than Hoxton. Its Ridley Road market is the epicentre of this vitality, with almost 200 stalls from every part of the world. Across Kingsland High Street from the market sits Bradbury Street. In the 1980s it was an area of vacant and derelict buildings and surface car parks that became the focus of Hackney Co-operative Developments' work to create a black and ethnic minority cultural quarter. Early work in 1993 by the design co-operative Collective Building Design suggested that the focus for this quarter should be a new square. A few years later this idea was picked up by consultants developing a regeneration strategy for

The community-owned ethos of the practical radicals of the 1980s offers a degree of protection against the invading armies of hipsters

Egan proceeded with the refurbishment of Stamford Works and a mixed-use workspace scheme including a library.

The square was designated as one of the Mayor's 100 Public Spaces and a cocktail of funding was assembled, allowing Whitelaw Turkington to be appointed to draw up plans for the space. Work was completed in 2006 to coincide with the opening of the Culture House. Since that time the square has become a cultural hub for Dalston. In an area of London without any public spaces, it is a focus for community activities and events and is surrounded by cultural workspace along with shops, cafes and bars.

The once scruffy Dalston has become fashionable, which is a good thing, isn't it? Dave Hill writing on his *London Blog* in 2013, reported a piece of graffiti on a wall in Dalston that read 'Hipsters, fuck off back to mummy', which gives a flavour of some of the tensions that success can bring. However, the community-owned ethos of the practical radicals of the 1980s offers a degree of protection against the invading armies looking for the next bohemian quarter to hang out. For how long this will preserve the unique character of Gillett Square remains to be seen. Until then we can enjoy one of London's great new public spaces.

Grassmarket, Edinburgh

Shortlisted 2010

You can eat you can drink you can sleep you can gaze
Up into the beautiful Edinburgh sky
And spot the sun coming through the morning's haze
And you almost feel you can fly
Because the Grassmarket lifts your spirits
Puts a grin on a serious face
Gives each waking hour a fillip
And you live life at Grassmarket pace!
It used to be a market, hence the name
Now they just sell life and excitement;
No two days here are ever the same
But they're just linked by enjoyment!
It's a song it's a dance it's a flying rocket
Come and take a ride in Edinburgh's Grassmarket!

'Colourful' is a double-edged adjective when it comes to describing urban places. Edinburgh's Grassmarket, much like Newcastle's Bigg Market or Dublin's Temple Bar, has been a trading, meeting and socialising place since medieval times. The modern equivalent however, as these places have found to their cost, can be cheap lager, late-night violence and early-morning vomit on the pavement. Such was the fate of the Grassmarket by the late 1990s. While its history and character still attracted tourists, its streets had become congested, its spaces little more than a car park and its evenings an occasional war zone.

The impetus for change came in 2004 when the Grassmarket was identified for improvement as part of the Capital Streets Programme. A partnership between the City of Edinburgh, the City Centre Management Company, Edinburgh World Heritage and Scottish Enterprise, the programme was set up with a remit to undertake public-realm works to help improve economic activity across the city. The Grassmarket with its vivid, layered history was an obvious priority. Agreeing that something needed to be done may have been easy, but agreeing what this should be was a more complicated affair. Local residents, bar owners, businesses and heritage groups all felt strongly about the problems but had very different ideas about the solution. A stakeholder group was set up and at an early meeting it was agreed that the project would 'be successful if it pleased most of the people, most of the time'. This became the test against which the project was continuously measured and guided a series of weekend Community Planning Workshops that eventually produced a collective vision. This sought to broaden the appeal of the Grassmarket, make it a safer, more pedestrian-friendly place and reconnect with its long history.

Bottom and opposite left: The environmental improvements have created a flexible, uncluttered space.

Below: They have also created a stage for public performance.

Agreeing that something needed to be done may have been easy, but agreeing what this should be was a more complicated affair

There are few more evocative neighbourhoods in Edinburgh than the Grassmarket. It was once a market in the valley outside the town gates where livestock could be traded without having to negotiate the steep slopes to the Old Town. After defeat at the Battle of Flodden in 1527, fears of an English invasion led to the city's defences being extended with the construction of what became known as the Flodden Wall, which looped around the Grassmarket. The motives were as much economic as they were defensive, since this meant that traders coming to market could be taxed. The downside, however, was that the wall would constrain the growth of the city for the next 250 years.

The Grassmarket was also the site of public executions, most famously the martyrs of the Covenanting cause. The public houses lining the Grassmarket memorialise this dark history, including the Last Drop Tavern, where the condemned had a last drink, and Maggie Dickson's, which celebrates the fortunate woman who survived the ordeal and was freed, deemed to have served her sentence.

With the demolition of the Flodden Wall in the 18th century, the focus of the city shifted. In Victorian times the Grassmarket became a poor quarter of lodging houses and missions. The relocation of the cattle market in the early 20th century led to a long period of neglect. Despite this, and that fact that few of the surviving buildings predate the late 19th century, the Grassmarket was included in the Old Town Conservation Area, and forms part of Edinburgh's UNESCO World Heritage Site.

A key objective of the Capital Streets Programme was to provide a greater range of activities that would attract families. The designs created a flexible, uncluttered space, using the gentle slope as a rake for performances. A series of pilot events were run over the course of a year to explore the use of the space, including markets, film shows, dance events and concerts. This was successful in helping to rebrand the area in the minds of both locals and visitors.

An area of darker paving was laid in the shape of the shadow of the gibbet along and improvements have also been made to the Covenanter Memorial. Parking was removed and pedestrian crossings improved in an approach to design that was simple yet effective, emphasising the historic enclosed form of the medieval marketplace.

These careful interventions have had the desired effect. Cafes and restaurants now spill into the space, creating a continental pavement cafe ambience. The bars are still active in the evening but are not allowed to dominate. The space has rediscovered its historic role as a place for the people of Edinburgh to linger, meet and spend time – still a place of entertainment, even if the attraction is no longer public execution.

Kings Place, London

Shortlisted 2013

Left out of King's Cross station's comings and goings,
And up York Way to Kings Place. Those architect's drawings
With their images of all those people going and coming
Never did this place justice; real people have made it breathe

In, out, like this: the news and the music coming and going;
Three orchestras. Count them: three. Listen to the music surging
Up those stairs, swirling round your head in the cafe, coming
Unexpectedly round a corner as you read your newspaper.

Round here is changing; Kings Place got it all going
And the Guardian's here, you can feel the Place thinking
And jazz sends you notes that never stop coming
In canal light and sky light and art light and glass light.

The remaking of a city turns on places like this;
A Place built on music, truth-telling and bliss.

Can a building be a great place, at least a place in the way urbanists would understand it? Urban places are generally found in between rather than within buildings. They are places where people can linger, that are animated by the life of the surrounding buildings and where the theatre of public life is acted out. In short, they are part of the public realm. Yet by all of these tests Kings Place is, as its name suggests, a 'place'. Its atrium is open to everyone to come in, sit and meet without needing an appointment or having to buy a coffee. It is a space animated by the 3,000 people who work in the building and the many thousands more who come to a concert, visit a gallery, drink in its bars or eat in its restaurants. Like Nolli's map of Rome, which showed the inside of public buildings as public spaces, Kings Place has created a great indoor urban place.

Kings Place was conceived by the Leeds-based property developer Peter Millican. He reasoned that, as office users demanded larger floor plates, more of the city was being privatised. He therefore imagined Kings Place as an office scheme that was also a public space. It includes 500,000 square feet of space of which 300,000 square feet is lettable (a terrible gross-to-net ratio, as many agents and developers have remarked). Yet the common areas are anything but common. The entrance gives onto a huge atrium the height of the building that links the street to the canal basin at the

rear. At the entrance is a sculpture gallery and the atrium includes a coffee shop, a conference space and a bar and restaurant with a terrace on the canal. Above this, the main tenant of the offices is Guardian Newspapers, who occupy three floors and have their own entrance.

However, it is what lies beneath that is the real marvel. The building is sunk deep into the ground with three basement levels. The atrium opens up into a wide staircase descending to the two levels of gallery space and a range of cultural facilities. These include three halls: a studio space capable of seating 220, a traditional concert hall with 420 fixed seats and the St Pancras Room, an auditorium for speech that seats 100. There are also three rehearsal spaces, recording and broadcasting facilities, dressing rooms, a teaching room and office space for the London Sinfonietta and the Orchestra of the Age of Enlightenment plus a range of smaller music organisations. This has all been bequeathed to a charitable music foundation that programmes the space.

All this in a building that opened in 2008, as the world was consumed by the credit crunch. As we were told, Peter Millican was either really clever or incredibly stupid. Indeed, during their visit the Academicians spent a long time trying to understand whether Kings Place really had discovered an alternative reality for property development or, as some

commentators have argued, whether this is in fact an extraordinary piece of philanthropy.

The story starts in 2000 when Peter began looking for a site to build his office of the future. The site he selected on York Way was very off-pitch at a time before the decision to locate the Eurostar Terminal at St Pancras and prior to the Kings Cross masterplan being agreed. This did, however, mean that the site, a former depot employing 30 people, was cheap, even if it did come with some baggage: prostitutes on the street, a reluctant planning authority and a general difficulty in envisioning it as an office location. However, the scheme proceeded, Dixon Jones were appointed as architects following a competition and the concept took shape. The key

> It is what
> lies beneath that is
> the real marvel

moment was securing Guardian Newspapers as an anchor tenant. They had been looking for an alternative to their cramped premises near Kings Cross and were attracted by the concept for the building and the fact that since it was still on the drawing board, they could design their offices.

Other prelets followed, including Network Rail and Logica, with the result that the building was fully let on the day it opened. Other property developers may regard the building as being hopelessly uneconomic, but it is impossible to separate the generosity of its concept from the fact that it has been fully let and profitable since it opened.

On the visit we came to the conclusion that cities would be much better places if all offices were built this way, but that this was probably unrealistic. We were not, however, clear whether this made Kings Place less important as a replicable model or more impressive for the achievement of it being built.

Meeting House Square, Dublin

Shortlisted 2010

If you need a place that's the essence of simply Being There
Then raise a glass and drink a toast to Meeting House Square;
Meet a friend and see a film or simply walk around
But you'll find your shoes are floating three feet off the ground;
And you're singing or you're dancing or you're quiet or you're loud
And the gentle evening silence is a taste of things to come
Or it's fooling you and soon the music grabs your senses
The blood is pounding in your veins because this square is a drum
That beats the rhythm of the city and it lowers your defences
Till you accept the focus, the Meeting House Square hum
That's a hum of life, a buzz of joy, a feeling in your soul:
Somehow right here in this square you're human and you're whole
And you breathe in the atmosphere, you feast on Dublin air
A banquet for senses that we call Meeting House Square!

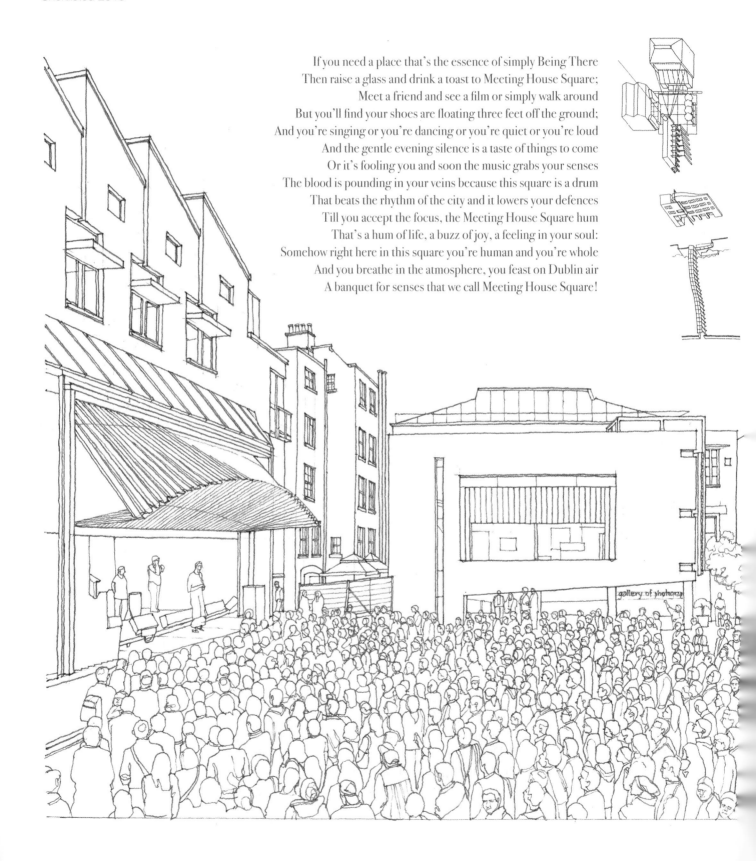

Theirs was an anti-architecture plan; rather than grand gestures, it worked with the grain of the area

The year of Temple Bar's salvation was 1991. That was the year when the Irish government took the decision to cancel the bus station project that would have seen the clearance of much of this historic part of Dublin. The state-owned bus company CIE had been buying buildings in the area for a number of years and, rather than demolish them, had been letting properties on short leases. The inevitable result was that the area was colonised by small-scale cultural and creative artists and business, who inevitably had started a campaign to save the area. On cancelling the bus station, the government transferred the buildings that had been acquired to Temple Bar Properties, an agency established to regenerate the area.

One of this agency's first tasks was to organise an international architectural competition. This was won by a consortium of young local architecture practices calling themselves Group 91, including Paul Keogh, Rachael Chidlow, Sheila O'Donnell and John Tuomey. Theirs was an anti-architecture plan; rather than grand gestures, it worked with the grain of the area by proposing a series of public-realm interventions and infill buildings. The plan led to a programme of public investment that saw new and refurbished buildings being created for 12 cultural institutions including institutes of film, photography and music, a school of acting and two arts centres, one for children. These, together with new residential and commercial space, were housed in uncompromisingly modern buildings, sensitively inserted into the historic fabric of the area. The Group 91 plan was to create a new wandering axis, running parallel to the main east-west street, through a series

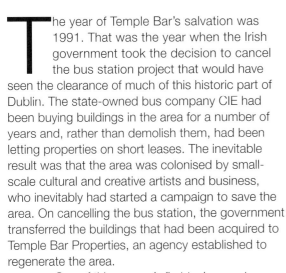

of alleyways and squares. At the heart of this was Meeting House Square, a space hollowed out from the centre of an urban block behind a former 18th-century Presbyterian meeting house. This was refurbished to house the Irish Film Institute while new buildings were commissioned on the other sides of the square to house the Gallery of Photography, the National Photographic Archive and the Ark children's cultural centre with its outdoor stage.

The public space was designed with outdoor performance in mind. The Film Institute uses it as a cinema while the Calatrava-designed stage opens up in the other direction to create a theatre. Recently a retractable roof has been added in the form of four huge umbrellas, extending the usability of the space. The square has come to symbolise the regeneration of Temple Bar with a year-round programme of events and activities. However, even when not in use, the sequence of spaces around Meeting House Square forms a particularly satisfying urban experience. You can wander from lively streets through tight alleyways, which in turn open into unexpected spaces leading to other alleyways and spaces. These spaces make Temple Bar feel much bigger than it actually is and create an urban sequence that would grace many Italian cities.

North Laine, Brighton

Shortlisted 2009

COUNTRY SONG AND OPERA

Why country song? Why opera?
Well they can both hold huge emotions
And they don't go through the motions
And I've got a growing notion
That North Laine's just like that!

Its setting's operatic; over the top, dramatic
You can eat and drink and stroll and shop,
Lounge with purpose or wander erratic.
Dress like a hipster! Go over the top!
Buy something that's been chucked from an attic!
Browse and buy, squeeze each last drop
From a place that sends you quite ecstatic
Get clothes for a punk or a goth or a fop
Or a nylon shirt that throbs with static!
Get your boots into action, move those flip flops
Get a cappuccino that tastes authentic
To anybody with a heart or a soul or a brain
The place to be seen is YEEHA! North Laine!

Above and opposite:
The narrow streets
are visually cluttered
(in a good way) and
crowded with people.

A tight grid of Victorian streets in an unpromising location next to Brighton Station has become one of the liveliest neighbourhoods in the UK. Full of independent shops selling bric-a-brac, clothes, records and other alternative items, the neighbourhood also includes a tightly packed residential community, workshops, creative business, restaurants, traditional pubs and trendy cafes as well as Brighton's new library.

Often misspelt, the name of the neighbourhood is North Laine – in the singular and with an 'i' and not to be confused with the 'Lanes' of Brighton, the old Saxon town with its tight narrow streets that lies between North Laine and the sea. 'Laine' was the name for the medieval shared fields that once surrounded Saxon Brighthelmstone. These were laid out as a grid and were accessed by paths called 'leakways', which became streets as the town expanded.

The early expansion of Brighton in the Regency period spread along the coast. The later Victorian development was more prosaic, spreading inland and following the pattern of the medieval fields. North Laine was built as a series of terraced streets to house the workers in the nearby locomotive works. Its structure and architecture are identical to thousands of similar neighbourhoods across the country. What makes it an amazing 'place' is the way that the people and businesses of the area have turned such ordinary material into a unique urban environment.

Brighton has an L-shaped shopping centre. The two main shopping streets are North Street, which runs parallel to the sea towards Hove, and London Road, which, as its name suggests, is the road to

London and is therefore at right angles to the sea. The two streets join around the Royal Pavilion, which is not a shopping area. So North Laine, lying in the crook of the L, became the link between them.

The footfall created by this retail geography caused a secondary shopping spine to develop through North Laine including New Street, Regent Street and Kensington Gardens. For many years this was populated with electricians, hardware shops and cafes as well as a shop selling nurses' uniforms (there are still shops selling nurses' uniforms but the customers are no longer nurses). Some of these shops still exist, including a fantastic woodworking business. They have, however, been joined by hundreds of independent shops selling clothes, books, second-hand records, antiques and bric-a-brac. One local shop selling hand-made cosmetics grew to become the Body Shop. Today the central spine is lined with independent businesses, each with a distinctive shopfront and many decorated with murals. This street is packed with people and the activity has spread onto the east-west streets.

As with many such areas, this transformation grew out of adversity. In the 1970s the area was threatened by a road scheme that would have demolished roughly a third of the neighbourhood. This gave birth to a campaign, and people in Brighton are very good at campaigning. When the road scheme was shelved, this opposition turned to activism to promote the area as an alternative shopping and businesses quarter. However, as it became successful, the focus shifted from promotion to protection of its diversity as independent businesses started to be squeezed out by national chains. The shop units in the area are small and under a variety of ownerships, something that has provided a degree of protection from the encroachment of national retain chains. The North Laine Traders Association

The people and businesses of the area have turned such ordinary material into a unique urban environment

maintains a database of property and rents. They can't prevent landlords charging higher rents, but they can advise businesses what level of rent a particular unit will support and in doing so they are able to control rents to an extent. Their efforts mean that a balance has been maintained and the area has not been gentrified as has happened in places with a similar history such as Covent Garden. Customers would in any case probably not welcome national chains. One local retailer, who has grown a chain of six shops, feels the need to conceal this by giving each outlet a different name and changing the identity of each every few years.

The buildings of North Laine are decorated with murals, distinctive shop signs, graffiti and public art – a bohemian look that can be found in other places now. However North Laine was one of the first such boho quarters and is aware that the look can be overdone. The planning authority was originally resistant to the signage and murals, having made it a Conservation Area. However, they now work with the traders to promote the image of the area. Today North Laine remains lively, independent and local. The people shopping and walking in its streets feel like a cross-section of Brighton people, even if many of them are probably tourists. Such areas feel so well established that it is easy to forget how fragile they can be – teetering between the twin threats of decline and gentrification. North Laine has survived because it has recognised the threat and because there are local structures in place to look after its interests. The hope is that the fragile balance that has created its special character can be maintained.

Oxford Castle
Winner 2009

WHAT I DID AT OXFORD CASTLE

I woke up inside the prison walls for a full English breakfast.
I peered inside the cells and felt the weight of guilt.
I shouldn't have had that second sausage
But it was staring me in the face. So I did.

I wandered round the castle and looked in an apartment.
I had a vision of living within easy reach of pasta.
I shouldn't have had a vision of wandering down for spaghetti
In my pyjamas and my slippers. But I did.

I thought about how these days anything is possible;
How history doesn't just have to be there, crumbling,
It can be part of the present and part of the future
A simple idea, of course. With burgers.

I went back to my room and I ordered room service.
I looked at some art, I listened to jazz and I shifted
My definition of what a castle can be: it can be a model
Of how to live your life. With ice cream.

xford is a city full of great places, many of them associated with the university. However, for centuries there has been a place in the city where you wouldn't have been so keen to spend time. Hidden behind high walls and unknown to most of the people of the city lay a Norman Castle. Long before the foundation of the university, Oxford was a thriving Saxon town. Heavily damaged following the Norman invasion of 1066, the city and its surrounding lands were granted to Robert D'Oyly, who built a castle to subdue the locals. A stream was diverted to create a moat along the line of what is now New Street and Castle Street and walls were built that were to close off the site for almost 1,000 years. As with many castles, the site served as a prison from its very early days. However, after the Civil War (when Oxford had briefly served as the Royalist capital), this became its predominant use. Conditions in the early years were so notoriously bad that in 1785 the Oxford County Justices bought the site and commissioned the building of the prison that still stands today.

Above: A view from the new visitor attraction in St George's Tower towards the section of prison wall removed as part of the scheme.

This is what happens when a developer takes the time and falls in love with a place

In 1996 the Home Office closed the prison and the county council obtained an option to buy the site. Commercial advice at the time was that a redevelopment scheme was unlikely to be viable. The historic sensitivity of the site and the unwillingness of the conservation lobby to see the removal of the walls combined with the problems of reusing an old prison building made it difficult to see a solution. Despite this, the county council wrote a development brief and put it to the market. Most of the 34 developers who expressed an interest suggested that the prison could be used as student housing – a sinister take on a 'nature versus nurture' experiment perhaps – that just felt wrong. Eventually, a developer was selected and the county council together with the city council and other stakeholders started working with them. However, nine months later a viable scheme was far from being realised and perhaps more importantly the developer was simply not right for the site, not having the right feel for the buildings. The county council therefore turned to the developer who had come second in the bidding process and the Trevor Osborne Property Group was appointed in 2000.

In the six years that followed the site was brought back to life through a process of careful urban renewal. Rather than develop a grand masterplan or resort to iconic architecture, Trevor Osborne – who ran the project personally – immersed himself in the history and architectural heritage of the site. He and his design teams got

to know and understand every inch of the building and were able to develop a scheme to open it up in a way that won the trust of the planning authorities and conservation groups. The main prison has been converted to a Malmaison hotel, while new blocks along Castle Street provide residential accommodation and much of the ground floor is a sequence of good-quality restaurants and cafes. The scheme also includes a new tourist attraction run by the Oxford Preservation Trust, who have refurbished St George's Tower and interpreted the history of the prison. The public realm is made up of a series of courtyards, each of which has a different character. The prison reception yard has become the main cafe and restaurant area, while the exercise yard is a quiet garden used for occasional performances. Part of the wall has been taken down to open the site up to the conical motte in an area also used for performances. Walking around the scheme, it all seems so logical and comfortable that it's hard to imagine that anything else could have been done. This is the mark of a successful scheme, of course, but it also disguises the struggle and toil required to get it built.

The first set of problems were commercial. The prison is a traditional panopticon design with cells accessed from metal balconies off a central atrium. The cells are small and the walls are thick. Who on earth would want to stay in a place with such dark associations? A deal was, however, done with Malmaison by offering a lease in which the rent paid was based on the level of room occupancy. Cells were knocked together so that each room is created out of two cells with the original doors and window bars retained. They are still a little cramped but guests are disappointed if they don't get a cell room. Once the hotel was secured, the ground-floor spaces were offered to a carefully selected range of cafe bar operators, like Carluccio's, to create the right ambience. While it would have been nice to have more independents, the viability of the scheme was so finely balanced that quality chains with good covenants were important to raise finance. However, public subsidy and Lottery funding did allow public uses to be included like the museum in St George's Tower and a public gallery.

The second problem was the need to win over the heritage lobby, who initially viewed the scheme with deep suspicion. While there was clearly a desire to bring the site back into use, there was a fundamental contradiction between the historic form of a castle/prison and the desire to open up the site to the public. The scheme couldn't work without the removal of the prison's wall that separated the prison building from the castle mound and there was also a need to open up a route from Castle Street. To address these issues, a consultative forum was established. This met regularly to discuss concerns and while it is probably not the case that everyone was happy, the developer made significant efforts to respond to the concerns expressed.

Ironically, one of the concerns that local groups expressed was the prospect of the space being privatised. As Trevor Osborne says, the completion of the building works is only the start of the process of creating a great space. A management company was therefore established to manage the estate and the commercial space and to organise a programme of events throughout the year. This does mean that the 'public' realm is private – the management company closes it once a year to prevent rights of way from being established. This feeds into the debate about the privatisation of public space. Wandering through Oxford Castle, it does not feel like you are in an overly controlled environment but it would probably be best not to try and busk, unless, that is, you have been booked by the management company. Nevertheless, Oxford Castle is a fantastic scheme. This is what happens when a developer takes the time to fall in love with a place. It is full of small details that would never have survived a scheme designed in an architect's office and tendered to a contractor.

Opposite: The view from St George's Tower over the rooftops of the scheme towards the university.

Below left: The central gallery of the former prison, now frequented by hotel guests.

Below right: Part of the intimate sequence of spaces created around the site.

Princesshay, Exeter

Shortlisted 2011

Next time you're down the south-west way
Get yourselves to Princesshay!
A place to work and rest and play
And dress yourself in fine array
To twirl, parade, pose and sashay
'Cos no day's Early Closing Day*
And once you're there you'll want to stay
You'll never need to go away
With no desire to go astray
So let's present a fine bouquet
Let's whoop and yell and shout Olé!
Or if we're staid, Hip hip hooray.
As everybody stands to say:
Three cheers for the mighty Princesshay!

*except of course on Christmas Day

Can a shopping centre really be a great urban place? Surely the retail mall is the anathema of urbanism? Well Princesshay in Exeter, along with a small number of other retail schemes built in the 2000s, show that this may not always be the case. This was a period that saw the evolution of the shopping centre. The previous generation of enclosed, artificially lit malls evolved into naturally lit arcades knitted into the street network of their host cities. Then some brave soul decided to do away with the roof altogether and reinvented the pedestrianised shopping street. This evolution can be seen through the Bullring in Birmingham, Liverpool ONE and Princesshay in Exeter, the latter completed in 2007. Had the recession not happened, the evolution may have continued through the Retail Quarter in Sheffield or the Meadows in Nottingham. However, Princesshay is beached at the high water mark of retail planning and it is only right that we should ask whether it is a great urban space.

Princesshay is beached at the high water mark of retail planning and it is only right that we should ask whether it is a great urban space

Below: Princesshay as it was in the 1960s.

Bottom: The redeveloped Princesshay today.

The princess in question was our present Queen, who unveiled a plaque on the site in 1949 to mark the start of rebuilding work after the war. In 1942 the RAF had bombed the historic German city of Lübeck and Hitler, in retaliation, launched the Baedecker Blitz. Named after a German touring guide of England, the raids targeted historic cities across the UK. Exeter was hit on 23 and 25 April and 37 acres of its centre was damaged and destroyed.

Tragic as this was, there were those within the town who also saw an opportunity to sort out the woefully dated fabric of the city. C.J. Newman, the town clerk at the time, was accused of demolishing far more buildings than was strictly necessary in the aftermath of the Blitz. The city fathers wasted little time in appointing a proper town planner to draw up plans for reconstruction. Thomas Sharp was a past President of the RTPI and author of the best-selling nine-penny book *Town Planning* published in 1940 (which had sold 250,000 copies!). He set about creating a modern town plan of bypasses and shopping precincts, much of which was never realised. However his great contribution was to propose a new street, to be called Princesshay running parallel to the high street and focusing on the axis of the cathedral tower. The result was the country's first pedestrianised shopping street and was widely publicised at the time. Indeed, Sharp published his plans in his book *Exeter Phoenix* by the Architectural Press. There is a debate in the cities that were redeveloped after the war about the environments created. Increasing, the quality of the architecture is recognised and there are those, for example in Coventry, who argue for preservation. However, much of the architecture and all of the urban planning has not aged well and in Exeter redevelopment was seen as the only option.

A retail redevelopment was promoted by Land Securities, who owned the site together with the Crown Estate. The plan by Chapman Taylor retains Princesshay partly as an arcade (left) and partly open to the elements (main drawing). The scheme includes 530,000 square feet of retail space with 60 stores and attracts 9.5 million people annually. A second phase includes a John Lewis store, and the overall effect has been to transform Exeter's retail ranking. But is it a real place? There was controversy soon after it opened when it was revealed that the centre was employing mobile device tracking technology, plotting the movements of customers via their mobile phones. The 'streets' are private spaces, patrolled by security guards and CCTV and occupied exclusively by national retail chains. This is certainly a very good shopping centre – whether it is a very good piece of urbanism is a moot point.

Queen Square, Bristol

Shortlisted 2012

On a bench in Queen Square in the Bristol sun
I open my sarnies, reflect on the scene:
The walking, the sitting, the talking, the ones
Who just stand for a moment and grin.
Funny how words sometimes get it all wrong:
Square says 'enclosure', 'restriction',
A geometric tightness of angle and form,
So this square's a fine contradiction
As it lets people out, lets them breathe and delight
In the life-force a city can bring;
As I sit on this bench all my dreams can take flight
And I can't sing, but I wish I could sing.
Because just for a moment the world's a fine place;
In Queen Square with the public in a fine public space.

Queen Square's timeless elegance is not quite as timeless as it seems. To walk through the square today, with its mannered Georgian buildings and mature plane trees, you would think that it had always been a calm oasis within the historical heart of Bristol. It is hard to imagine that for much of the 20th century it played startled host to a dual carriageway that cut diagonally across its lawns, dividing around the statue of William III and carrying roaring traffic onwards around the city's inner relief road.

Conceived in 1936, the road sliced across the square, squeezing improbably between the buildings at opposite corners. By the 1990s it had become so integral to the city that as many as 200,000 vehicles were using it every day. This of course took its toll on its host: the green space was lost to a combination of traffic, noise and pollution; parking around the edge of the square resulted in the loss of traditional boundary walls, not to mention crowded and broken pavements. As a result a third of the square's buildings had fallen vacant, contributing to a neglected, down-at-heel air. Something had to be done.

Bristol City Council, together with the Queen Square Association and with support and funding from English Heritage, embarked on a multi-phase plan to arrest this decline. The first step was the most difficult: closing the dual carriageway. This was initially done as a temporary measure to win over those who couldn't see how the city could survive without such a well-used traffic route. Gridlock didn't ensue and a couple of years later Phase 2 could proceed, when the closure was made permanent as part of changes to the wider street network. Buses were relocated to the perimeter, enabling the road to be grubbed up and the centre of the square to be reclaimed for public use. Phase 3 turned its attention to the

Opposite: Queen Square today.

Below: The same scene prior to the work beginning.

buildings around the square. The reintroduction of boundaries and the enhancement of the paving and landscaping sought to restore this once grand square to its former glory.

The queen in question was Queen Ann, who came to the throne in 1707. Work had started on the square in 1699 and by 1720 it was largely completed. It was built on marshy land just outside the old town and was designed to make an impression, claimed to be one of the largest residential squares in Europe and the first landscaped square outside London. Crucially for the city's merchants who made it their home, it provided the right amount of manners and sophistication while also being in a handy position near the docks, allowing swift access to their business on the adjacent quaysides.

It is hard to imagine that for much of the 20th century it played startled host to a dual carriageway

As well as recreation, the square provided a forum for protest, sometimes with disastrous consequences. In 1831 the Bristol Riots were triggered when Bristol's recorder, Sir Charles Wetherell, spoke against the widening of voting rights in the Reform Bill. When the riots were over, three days later, large parts of the north and west side of the square lay in ruins. As a result the merchants decided to move out, leaving their houses to be converted to offices or subdivided into lodging houses. This led to a long period of decline.

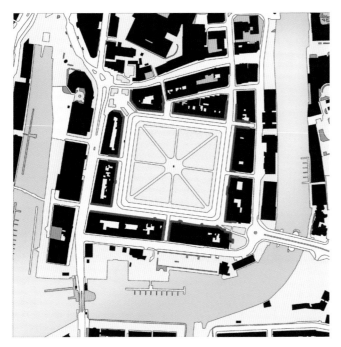

Today, with the improvements completed, the square has been given a new lease of life. Businesses have returned to take advantage of this 'new old' address. Boundary features and railings demarcate the perimeter of the square as if they'd never been removed, while the plane trees provide a foil to the buildings, allowing glimpses out to the surrounding streets. The public realm creates a unifying, connecting surface where everyone (and no one) has priority. The Queen Square Association organises events throughout the year animating the space and improvements have been extended to include the creation of Thunderbolt Square and the pedestrian link to Pero's Bridge.

This is a story of urban repair and acupuncture that has given back to the city one of its great spaces. It still acts as a vital artery, but of a different, more sustainable sort: a 21st-century highway of cyclists and pedestrians making their way to the waterfront, the railway station or the city centre. Perhaps best of all, it is now possible to simply spend time enjoying the peace and tranquillity of what is once more one of our greatest Georgian squares.

Sheaf Square, Sheffield
Winner 2010

The passenger now leaving Platform Five
Arrives in a place of shining steel
And it makes that passenger glad to be alive
Because where you are dictates how you feel
And even on a day when it's chucking it down
Sheaf Square puts a spring in the tiredest step
This vista makes a smile from the deepest frown
And fills you full of vim and verve and pep!
And people are standing by the sculpture
That curves with light and runs with water
And they take photographs of each other
Here's a boy and a girl and a mother and daughter...
This place makes you participate; you feel you are a player
Utopia, Nirvana, or if you like: Sheaf Square!

W alking out of Sheffield Station on a sunny day is one of the most uplifting arrival experiences of any British city. Emerging from the station, the sun bouncing off the cascading fountains, you are guided up the hill by the 80-metre-long *Cutting Edge* sculpture representing the forging of a stainless steel blade and itself glinting beneath a veil of water. You cross Sheaf Street and head up the tree-lined, granite-paved Howard Street to the amphitheatre of Hallam Square, across Arundel Gate, through the Millennium Galleries and via the vast glass-covered Winter Garden and arrive at the Peace Gardens in front of the town hall. It is one of the most dramatic urban sequences in the UK and none of it existed 15 years ago.

Back then you would have emerged from the station to be confronted with a large roundabout on the ring road and forced along narrow pavements up the forgotten Howard Street to be confronted with a second major traffic route on Arundel Gate. Beyond that lay a tortuous route up the hill around the council offices, affectionately called the 'Egg Box' (because that is what they resembled), to a rather sad set of municipal gardens. It's a wonder that anyone bothered. This is one of the most radical transformations of any British city, led by public-realm

This is one of the most radical transformations of any British city, led by public-realm works and pushed through by sheer force of will by the council

works and pushed through by sheer force of will by the council.

The sequence of spaces is part of what Sheffield calls the Gold Route, first proposed in 1996 as part of a masterplan by Allies and Morrison. They suggested that a new route be created from the station via Hallam University to Devonshire Square and Sheffield University. Following this, a bid was made to the Millennium Commission, which contributed £20.5 million of Lottery funds towards the £41 million required for what became known as the Heart of the City project (which was shortlisted for the Academy of Urbanism's 2008 Great Place Award). The scheme saw the demolition of the Egg Box and the conversion of the municipal Peace Gardens into a fine public square, opened in time for the Millennium celebrations. In the two years that followed, the Millennium Galleries and the Winter Garden, both by Pringle Richards Sharratt Architects, were opened adding new sections to the Gold Route.

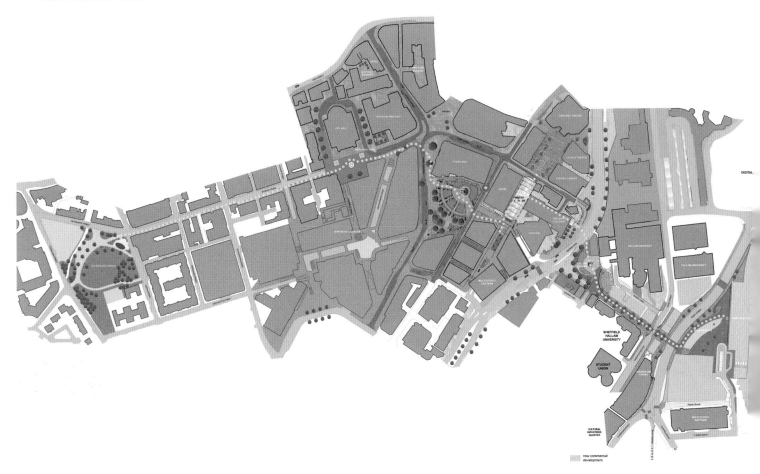

new commercial development

At the same time the city was looking to the next stage of the works. The Urban Task Force chaired by Richard Rogers reported at the end of 1999 and recommended that urban regeneration companies be established to drive forward the renaissance of UK cities. Sheffield and Manchester were first off the mark and in February 2000 Sheffield One was established to spearhead six key projects in the city centre. It commissioned an updated masterplan from the US urban designers Koetter Kim and appointed Alison Nimo, fresh from the Manchester Millennium Company, which had spearheaded the reconstruction of the city centre after the IRA bomb.

The first project on their to-do-list was Sheaf Square which, at the time, was a high-capacity traffic island severing the station from the city centre. When Network Rail announced that it was to spend £13 million to upgrade the station, Sheffield One commissioned a masterplan from EDAW to redesign the space outside the station. The highways engineers were persuaded that they could do without the roundabout, and furthermore that a 'super crossing' could be created over the ring road. This is a wide, high-capacity pedestrian crossing paved in granite that allows pedestrians to navigate the ring road without being cowed by traffic. It looks so obvious now it is completed, but try suggesting this across any other city's ring road and you will start to appreciate the scale of the achievement in Sheffield.

Working with the city council's internal Regeneration Projects Design Team, EDAW designed the square as a sloping space with a cascading set of pools and the stainless steel *Cutting Edge* sculpture. Designed by Si Applied and Keiko Mukaide, the sculpture weighs 80 tons, making it one of the largest stainless steel artworks in the world. The city council also worked with Jeremy Asquith to redesign the bespoke street furniture that had been created for the Heart of the City scheme so that it could be fabricated in stainless steel rather than the original cast bronze. The whole area is brought to life at night by a striking lighting design by Sutton Vane Associates, while the natural stone of the fountains has been hand-finished by Johnsons Wellfield Quarries of Huddersfield.

This attention to detail and careful design and use of quality materials is what marks Sheffield out. It developed in-house expertise in the creation of high-quality public-realm spaces and also invested in ongoing management. All of the spaces in the city centre continue to look immaculate, unlike some public-realm schemes in other cities completed at the same time.

The original masterplan included sites for a number of new buildings that will frame the space. Proposals were put forward in 2008 but the recession caused them to be put on hold. They will, however, come forward as the city's economy picks up and when they do, Sheaf Square will become even better. However, the fact that it works so well today, even before its enclosing buildings have been built, is testament to its design and the quality of its execution.

St Andrew Square, Edinburgh

Shortlisted 2011

This place is a festival all on its own;
And a fringe, and a late-night cabaret.
A geometrical statement in light and stone:
Changing exhibition, permanent display.
This place is a picture on a crisp new note;
The sound of money and the noise of living,
It's lovers walking in winter coats
Or summer evenings spent believing
That the world is better for St. Andrew Square
The world is brighter for a place like this
With a kind of indefinable Edinburgh flair
Stronger than a handshake, lovely as a kiss.
And if all this poetry makes you sick
Then go and have a coffee at Harvey Nick's!

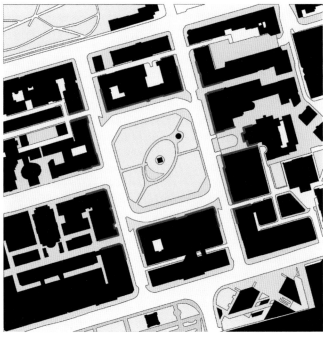

St Andrew Square was reborn in 2014. The city's first trams in almost half a century once again began to glide through the space, a Spiegeltent was set up during the Edinburgh Festival and the year was rounded off with a helter skelter, fairground and ice rink in the square to celebrate Christmas and Hogmanay. All of this was overlooked by the city's Harvey Nichols department store and, no doubt, also the ghosts of the city's bankers and merchants for whom the square was built in the late 18th century. Nothing like this happened in the first 250 years of the square's history. It was created as a private space for the exclusive use of the surrounding residents. However, as the residents moved out, it became a marginal space, slightly neglected and prone to occasional anti-social behaviour.

The square is the earliest part of Edinburgh New Town. It was designed by James Craig, who won the competition of a lifetime to plan an extension to reduce the chronic overcrowding in the city in 1766. At the time he was a newly qualified stonemason with no architectural training and only 26 years old. He was rewarded with a gold medal and the freedom of the city, even if his proposals were considered unbuildable and the New Town was largely built without his involvement. His career never quite measured up to the promise of his early success and he didn't live to see his plans built.

Craig's plan was the simplest of the six shortlisted entries for the competition. He proposed a new street along the ridge that ran east-west across the site, linking two new squares: St Andrew Square to the east to represent Scotland and George Square to the west to represent England (later renamed Charlotte Square). George Street (named after George III) ran between the squares, creating a grand vista with a church at either end. The polluted Nor Loch, which separated the scheme from the city, was to be turned into formal gardens with a new bridge connecting the Old Town and the New Town.

The plans were approved by the king in 1767 but progress was initially slow. The city's merchants were reluctant to make the first move and a £20 premium was offered to the first builders. The completion of North Bridge over the loch in 1772 helped, making access easier and allowing the construction of St Andrew Square to commence. One of the earliest residents was the philosopher and economist David Hume. He had been persuaded to build a house on the square by his friend, the architect Robert Adam, in the hope that such a high-profile resident would attract others. It worked and soon Sir Lawrence Dundas was convinced that the square was a fit place to commission his new town residence, provided that he could have the central plot that had been reserved for the church. Fifty years later Dundas House would become the head office of the Royal Bank of Scotland. By that time St Andrew Square was already home to the head offices of the British Linen Bank and the National Bank of Scotland. Even before the New Town was completed – with the construction of Charlotte Square in the 1820s – St Andrew Square had been transformed from a genteel residential quarter into the city's main financial centre.

The square itself is a large green space, dominated by the Melville Monument. The gardens were collectively owned by the square's residents and reserved for their sole use. The residents of the wider city would have experienced the square only as a mysterious green backdrop to the surrounding streets, inaccessible behind high railings.

Brokering a deal to bring the space into public use meant getting the agreement of the owners of the surrounding properties, who were now scattered across the world. It also involved the agreement of the city council and UNESCO (since the New Town is a World Heritage Site). Finally, agreement was reached and the landscape architects Gillespie were commissioned to develop a £2.6 million scheme for the transformation of the square funded by the City of Edinburgh Council and Scottish Enterprise. The scheme included new paths and a water feature along with a cafe that generates sufficient income to cover the maintenance of the space, the ownership of which remains in private hands. The use and character of the space has been transformed since it was reopened in 2008. Essential Edinburgh has been working to promote a program of events throughout the year, culminating in the 2014 festivities, by which time St Andrew Square really had become one of the key public spaces in Edinburgh. A space that had been hidden for two and a half centuries had finally been given to the people of Edinburgh.

The city's residents would have experienced the square only as a mysterious green backdrop to the surrounding streets, inaccessible behind high railings

Tobermory Harbour, Isle of Mull
Winner 2011

This poem is in praise of sunlight on water,
Ferry timetables, and showers for all;
Buildings much more than mere bricks and mortar,
Weather that plunges from sunshine to squall.
This poem is in praise of a gem of a harbour,
A link to the mainland, the future, the past,
To leisure and sitting and back-breaking labour
To skies that seem endless and seas that are vast.
This poem is in praise of a place that's essential
To Mull, to prosperity, to a region, a nation
And a realisation of endless potential:
This poem is a sonnet of sheer celebration!
The harbour's a song and a play and a story
A painting, a sculpture: pure Tobermory…

It was in the summer of 1983 that a CalMac Ferry by the name of *Columbia* arrived in Tobermory to be greeted by what the local press described as 'a few floating mines, a shark's fin and a periscope that kept going round and round'. This, together with a 'blast like a depth charge going off', caused the ship's captain to think that berthing at the pier, which was packed with protesters, was perhaps not the best idea and launches were summoned to take the 30 passengers ashore. 'It was all peaceful stuff' the Reverend Alan Taylor was quoted as sating at the time. 'We certainly do not want to break the law, but we can promise more picturesque action in the future'.

Tobermory until that time had been a relaxed sort of place from which the outside world seemed very remote. It is not a particularly ancient town, having only been established at the start of the 19th century. It was in 1786 that John Knox, an agent for the British Fisheries Society, had been sent to survey the west coast of Scotland for a harbour that could be used to exploit the area's fish stock. The natural harbour known as St Mary's Well (or, in Gaelic, Tobermory) was ideal. Over the years that followed, the town prospered, becoming the largest settlement on the Isle of Mull.

The life of the town revolved around the Mishnish Pier, where the ferry from Oban docked and where 'coasters' and 'puffers' plied their trade, bringing coal and other essentials to the island. The protest in 1983 was the result of a decision by the state-owned Caledonian MacBrayne ferry company to suspend services because the pier had become unsafe. It so happened that it was also in 1983 that the Crown Estate, owners of the seabed and foreshore around the whole of the coast, decided that it would no longer allow free unregulated moorings. The two events galvanised the community into forming the Tobermory Harbour Association, which has grown over the intervening years to become the most important organisation in the town.

The campaign against the pier closure was partially successful; the pier was rebuilt, although this didn't include roll-on, roll-off facilities, which were now 25 miles away at Craignure, and historic family links from Tobermory to other islands were lost. Meanwhile, the Harbour Association was granted the right

> 'We certainly do not want to break the law, but we can promise more picturesque action in the future'

Above: A grainy picture from the local paper of the 1983 protesters.

Below: An original concept drawing for the Ledaig scheme.

Above and left: The completed development, including the Taigh Solais visitor centre.

Bottom: An aerial view of the bay, showing the new area of land created and the boat moorings.

to manage moorings on the bay, bringing a degree of order to the slightly chaotic mix of fishermen and leisure boats as well as generating an income. The association soon realised that the best way to get things done was to do them itselve.

Early projects included a slipway and improvements to moorings. However, larger plans were afoot because the problems of congestion were now not so much on the sea as on the very limited space ashore. In the late 1980s the Harbour Association proposed to backfill an area in the south-west corner of the bay to create a new piece of land that could be used for parking and boat storage along with a promenade and landscaped area. The Ledaig scheme, as it was called, became possible a few years later when the building of a new road on the island generated a large volume of rubble that needed to be dumped somewhere.

It is rare that a car park becomes a catalyst for regeneration but the Harbour Association has used it as a focus for its activity. The culmination of this work was the opening in July 2008 of the Taigh Solais scheme (which is Gaelic for 'lighthouse'). This Lottery-funded project includes a visitor centre and workspace providing offices and income for the Harbour Association. It is now the centrepiece of a prosperous town that is a magnet for tourists. Many come because of its picture-postcard charm, its brightly coloured buildings and, of course, because it was used as the setting for the children's TV series *Balamory*. However, the town is more than just a tourist honeypot; it sustains a strong local community and a local fishing industry.

Looking to the future, the Harbour Association is planning to make Tobermory a hub for sea traffic on the west coast of Scotland, opening up more remote islands and expanding trade. The town's unique character and atmosphere owes much the beauty of its natural setting but what makes it special is the community action channelled through the Harbour Association that has taken responsibility for its future. Rather than waiting for distant governments in London and Edinburgh to act, local people have got on and done it for themselves. As Brian Swinbanks, Chair of the Harbour Association, wrote in 2013, 'Huge thanks are due to the wonderful people of Tobermory who love this perfect bay and who live and work by the rhythms of the sea'.

Victoria Quarter, Leeds

Winner 2012

Step in here and feel suddenly alive,
Suddenly beautiful, somehow available
For experience, somehow more aware
Of who you are and who you can be,
Somehow strolling down the cusp
Of history and the future, somehow

Caught up in a great enhancement, a great
Surge of anticipation, a great grin spreading
All over your face as you gaze and walk
And sip a coffee that's as sharp as the light in here;
You're somehow suddenly great,
like this place.

of streets, arcades and buildings now known collectively as the Victoria Quarter had seen better days. Located on Briggate, Leeds' main shopping street, the Grade II* Listed arcades had fallen into disrepair and the area had become a shadow of its former self. It was an area ripe for redevelopment and, had it not been for the listed buildings, would probably have been cleared to build a more 'conventional' mall. Instead, a new owner, in partnership with the city council, set about a large-scale refurbishment programme. The work saw the restoration of the County and Cross Arcades and the creation of a new 'Grand' Arcade by constructing a contemporary stained glass roof over Queen Victoria Street. The area is now the prime shopping location for the Leeds demi-monde, anchored by a Harvey Nichols department store.

During the early part of the 19th century, the area was a mass of slaughterhouses, butchers and fruit and vegetable stalls. At its heart was a bazaar selling meat on its lower floor and fancy goods and haberdashery above. However, as Briggate started to develop as a shopping street, the developer Charles Thornton saw an opportunity to create something a little more refined. The mid 19th century had seen the first retail revolution with the mass production of consumer goods and the development of new types of shops and retail environment. As with the arcades in Cardiff (Page 160), the middle classes wanted to shop in clean, safe environments where they weren't going to muddy their boots or encounter the lower classes. The arcade was the result of this process, the first in England being the Burlington Arcade in London.

Leeds embraced this retail revolution perhaps more than any other northern city and at one point it boasted eight arcades where the growing middle class could see and be seen. Thornton's was not the city's first arcade but it did aim to outdo the others in terms of its splendour and opulence. The masterstroke was not just to include a variety theatre within the scheme, designed by the renowned theatre architect Frank Matcham, but to ask him to design the arcades as well. Matcham was responsible for more

R
emind us again: what is the difference between an arcade and a shopping mall? Apart, that is, from the fact that as urbanists we value the former and dislike the latter. Both provide covered retail environments, protected from the weather, and are in private ownership. The Victoria Quarter in Leeds, owned and operated by the shopping centre developer Hammerson, is a case in point. It illustrates that, within city centres, arcades and malls are essentially the same animal. The malls that we hate are those on the periphery of towns, surrounded by parking and accessed from the motorway. City centre malls, arcades, shopping centres – whatever you want to call them – are a device to increase retail frontage, to open up the heart of urban blocks and to provide some respite from the weather. It's just that some are badly designed, with low ceilings, artificial lighting and muzak, while others like the Victoria Quarter are very beautiful.

Well, it is beautiful now. This was not the case in the late 1980s when the collection

This gaudy theatrical excess was applied not just to the theatre but to the new shopping arcades as well.

than 200 theatres and music halls, including the London Palladium and Coliseum, the Hackney Empire and Glasgow's King's Theatre. His proposals for the Empire Palace Theatre in Leeds were every bit as elaborate and decorative as his other work: a confection of faience, rich marbles, gilded mosaics and handsome cast and wrought iron, as well as carved and polished mahogany. In Leeds this gaudy theatrical excess was applied not just to the theatre but to the new shopping arcades as well.

When the theatre opened in 1898, it boasted all of the modern facilities of the time, including electric lighting and a sliding roof. On its opening night the audience was entertained by music hall singers, dancers and acrobats and, most intriguing of all, a certain Professor John Higgins, otherwise known as 'the Human Kangaroo'. Successful for a large part of the 20th century, the theatre fell victim to the limited space available on its tight site; acts chose to go elsewhere and it was forced to close in the 1960s. All that now survives is the rear stage door, visible from County Arcade. Without the theatre the surrounding streets and arcades started to struggle, lacking investment and falling out of fashion.

This was the situation in the early 1990s when plans were developed by the Prudential for the refurbishment of the arcades. By this time the arcades had become Grade II* listed buildings, ruling out demolition and

prompting a clever and imaginative scheme that mixed old and new, imbued with the spirit of Frank Matcham. Fortunately, one of the original shopfronts had survived, and this was used as a template to recreate the mahogany frames and gilded Art Nouveau window-frames that now adorn all of the shops. The site of the former theatre became the first Harvey Nichols department store to be built outside London, anchoring the development and ensuring its upmarket credentials. The centrepiece is Queen Victoria Street, which was fitted with a glazed roof to create the Grand Arcade. The artist Brian Clarke was commissioned to design the stained glass roof that runs the length of the street. The 750-square-meter roof is the largest stained glass window in Britain and acts as the perfect contemporary counterpoint to the Victorian exuberance below. The artist Joanne Veevers was also commissioned to design mosaic floor panels for County Arcade.

The result is a collection of richly decorated spaces and buildings creating what we might call a 'total shopping experience'. The Victoria Quarter attracts ten million visitors a year and is home to many upmarket retailers including Vivienne Westwood, Louis Vuitton and Paul Smith. Many of its retailers, like the Arrogant Cat Boutique, Firetrap and Agent Provocateur, were encouraged by the quarter to build their first stores outside London. This rarified, luxury retailing may not be to everyone's taste, but it is very much in the spirit of the original Victorian shopping arcades with their exclusive appeal to the affluent middle classes. It is both a very old model of retail development and something quite new: a shopping centre that feels lively, urban and connected to its surroundings. The developers of modern retail malls should take note.

The hope at the time of the Academy assessment visit was that Hammersons, who acquired the Victoria Quarter in 2012, had taken note as it developed plans for the area to the east of the Victoria Quarter to build the Victoria Gate scheme. This consists of two curving malls (arcades) from the end of Queen Victoria Street to the entrance of a new John Lewis anchor store. Whether the result feels like a mall or an arcade will tell us much about whether the Victoria Quarter really is the future of city centre retailing or just an interesting oddity from the 1990s.

The Wharf, Sowerby Bridge

Shortlisted 2013

This is the story of Sowerby Bridge
And the things you would find in't Rochdale Canal:
Floating car tyres or an old faded fridge,
A glove waving at you like it was your pal...

But now that glove's beckoning: see, over here
Look what's been realised down by the water;
A shaping, remaking, a real making clear
Of a future for Sowerby Bridge, one that ought to

Place it right in the centre of this region's map;
You can eat here or drink here or book B&B's
Or go on a cruise, be lulled into a nap
And dream of the future in places like these:

Where the old and the new co-exist side by side,
Turned the past to the present
with skill and with pride...

In 1996 a boat arrived in Sowerby Bridge that had travelled over from Manchester on the newly reopened Rochdale Canal. In the same year the Sowerby Bridge Wharf Partnership was formed, bringing together local businesses, leaseholders and public-sector bodies co-ordinated by the Prince's Regeneration Trust. Both events were the culmination of a campaign dating back to the mid 1970s to highlight the potential of Sowerby Bridge Wharf.

The reopening of the Rochdale Canal had been achieved by stealth. Sections of the canal had been restored through a series of what seemed be unconnected environmental improvements at a time when the reopening of the whole canal seemed unimaginable. Meanwhile, in Sowerby Bridge a battle had been fought and won to prevent the canal basin being filled in for a car park. While 1996 might have been the end of these campaigns, it was also the start of a process that would see the refurbishment of the wharf as a place for leisure and business.

The first canal boat arrived in Sowerby Bridge in 1759. What is so extraordinary about this date is that, as children across the UK are taught through the

national curriculum, the world's first industrial canal, built by the Duke of Bridgewater, wouldn't be opened for another three years. The 'canal' in Sowerby Bridge was not in fact a canal at all, but rather the western extent of the Calder and Hebble Navigation, a system of navigable waterways running from the Pennines down to the ports of the east coast. Then, in 1804, another canal arrived in Sowerby Bridge when the Rochdale Canal was cut across the Pennines, creating a link to the textile towns of Lancashire and the ports of the Mersey.

There was, however, a problem. The boats on the Rochdale Canal were too long to fit through the locks on the Calder and Hebble Navigation, while the smaller boats from the east were too inefficient to take through the bigger locks on the Rochdale Canal given the issues of water supply. So Sowerby Bridge – almost 300 feet above sea level – became an unlikely port to tranship goods between the two canal systems. It thus occupies a pivotal position in the history of UK canals. Its earliest warehouse – romantically if not altogether accurately called Warehouse 4 – dates from 1770 and is one of the first canal warehouses in the country. The adjacent Salt Warehouse was built in the 1790s and, on the slope above the basin, there is a complete set of canal buildings, including the weighing house, the overseer's house, stables and an extraordinary mixed-use building consisting of warehousing at the canal level, and a Methodist Sunday school above, accessed from the high street.

Sowerby Bridge, almost 300 feet above sea level, became an unlikely port

Such is the evident importance of the complex that it is no surprise to see the wharf cherished. However, as with so many regeneration stories, what seems obvious in hindsight was once anything but. The wharf had already fallen into a pretty poor state when the canals were nationalised in 1948 and it went downhill from there. In the 1970s British Waterways leased the whole site to a local person who gave undertakings that the complex would be refurbished, something that he was never able to do. He did, however, create three sub-lets to businesses using the canal, including Shire Cruisers. When in the 1990s pressure from British Waterways caused the head lease to be put on the market, it was the three tenants who called in the Prince's Regeneration Trust to help create the Sowerby Bridge Wharf Partnership to spearhead the area's regeneration.

The partnership wanted to buy the head lease, but British Waterways insisted that it was obliged to make a commercial return, which made a viable scheme impossible. Representations were made to the Commons Select Committee on

Environment and Transport, who made a site visit led by their formidable Chair Gwyneth Dunwoody MP. She made it clear, in no uncertain terms, that British Waterways was wrong, opening the way for the partnership to buy the head lease. By that time Warehouses 1 and 2 had already been refurbished by British Waterways but the Salt Warehouse and Warehouse 4 were in a very poor state. A cocktail of public and Lottery funding was put together, amounting to £2.7 million, which allowed the warehouses to be refurbished for business use. Road access to the wharf was improved and the gatehouse converted to a cafe with a new sculpture by Roger Burnett. The overseers house has been refurbished as a dental surgery, with the stables below providing creative workspace. The wharf itself is now busy with moorings and the comings and goings of Shire Cruisers, who operate the boatyard and a leisure fleet from the basin.

The wharf has become a lively part of Sowerby Bridge life, the destination for the town's Rushbearing Festival, which involves a maiden, a rush cart and a good deal of real ale. It is home to a number of pubs and restaurants but no housing, something that the partnership has resisted, seeing the wharf as a place of work. These achievements would be impressive in a large city, but to create a regeneration project of this scale in a town of fewer than 10,000 people is remarkable. The wharf is now home to 270 jobs and a range of start-up and relocated businesses. It is testament to the determination of a group of people over many years who have created a special place that has transformed the town.

David Harrison's drawing of London's South
Bank from the Academy's first book.

Conclusion
What we can learn from place

I n this book we have told the story of 75 very disparate places. These include 11 continental cities and 66 places within the UK and Ireland. These places include many of our largest provincial cities both as a whole and in terms of their neighbourhoods and streets. They include 15 mostly historic towns plus an assortment of special places that defy categorisation. The selection is not scientific, although there has been a filtering and evaluation process that has taken place through the voting by the Academicians. These places can be seen alongside the 30 that were shortlisted in the first two years of the awards and the 60 that have been shortlisted since. Together this amounts to 165 places that represent the Academy's judgement of what constitute the best urban places in the UK and Ireland, and the best cities in Europe. Some have called for greater rigour and research in the selection process for the awards, but we would question whether this is really possible in assessing the intangible cocktail of characteristics that make a great place. Sure, we could look at property values and crime statistics, business start-up rates and ratios of green space, and we would end up with a very middle-class set of places. For this we would suggest that you refer to the various rankings of the most liveable, coolest, funkiest, innovative cities and neighbourhoods undertaken by organisations like the Economist Intelligence Unit or publications like *Monocle* or the *Sunday Times*. The 165 places identified by the Academy of Urbanism are the result of the collective wisdom, knowledge and prejudices (perhaps) of 550 or so of the UK's leading urbanists. They include many of the leading urban designers, planners and architects in the UK along with surveyors, developers and other urban professionals spanning the public and private sectors. They don't have a monopoly on experience of what makes a good place but they should know what they are talking about. So what can we learn from their judgement?

The first conclusion from this book is that the best urban places in the UK and Ireland are a match for anywhere in the world. We have neighbourhoods and urban places that stand comparison with the best in Europe. We have streets and squares that are beautiful urban spaces, teeming with life and vitality. We have creative quarters that have been regenerated and brought life back to our towns and cities. We have extraordinary urban interventions that create a little bit of magic that lifts the spirit and lodges a town or city in your memory. However, at the scale of the settlement the picture is not quite as rosy. The Cities section of this book is the only one that allows us to make a comparison between the cities of the UK and those on the continent. London, Dublin and Edinburgh were shortlisted in the first year of the Academy's awards, which is not surprising because they are the three cities in the British Isles that really do stand comparison with the great cities of the world (although in very different ways). In this book we have the provincial cities of Bristol, Glasgow, Manchester and NewcastleGateshead set alongside 11 continental cities, only two of which are capitals. If we are honest, the British cities still don't come off tremendously well in the comparison. This is despite the huge improvements that have taken place in the last few decades. Manchester and Glasgow in particular had collapsed in the late 1970s and, while they did not quite plumb the depths of modern-day Detroit, they were not far off. All four British cities have undergone a tremendous renaissance but, while all include quarters that are as good as any of the European cities, they still have a long way to go. Walk a few hundred metres from Manchester's Northern Quarter, Glasgow's Merchant City, Newcastle's Grainger Town or Bristol's Harbourside and you will be confronted by intrusive roads clogged with traffic, vacant sites, modernist housing estates and dereliction. It is not that the regeneration of these cities is a facade, but that so far it is yet to reach large parts of the conurbation. Walk a little further in each of these cities and you will encounter truly terrible suburban housing estates, and a nowheresville of sprawl, retail parks, industrial estates and motorway junctions. There is still much to be done.

This might be a little unfair because in the visits to European cities we were only shown the best bits. The periphery of cities like Bordeaux is, if anything, worse than any British city in terms of sprawl and ugly out-of-town retailing. However, the cores of all of the continental cities in this book contain much larger areas of continuous urban vitality and form than the islands of urbanism in British provincial cities. This is even true in places like Hamburg and Freiburg that were largely destroyed in the war. Most of these European cities have extensive networks of urban streets containing a diversity of street life, enclosed by buildings of scale with active ground-floor uses. It is simple stuff, and once existed in British cities as well as those on the continent. But Britain had the misfortune to live through a period of planning in the 1960s when we thought that there was a better way of building cities based on the theories of the modernists and the traffic engineers. We destroyed our urban fabric and, having done such damage, the re-creation of good, simple urbanism is really difficult.

So while the UK and Ireland can produce really good pieces of urbanism, these flashes of brilliance are the exceptions in towns and cities that can still be quite poor. Too much of the urban fabric in the UK and Ireland is the result of commercial forces, suburban housebuilding and car-dependent development. The planning system is either too weak to change this, or in some places is part of the problem because its policies actually make mixed-use urbanism more difficult. It is an uncomfortable fact that most of the places in this book were built before the modern planning system – some without any plan, some with a masterplan and a simple set of rules that created a flexible framework that the area has grown into over many years. This may be how great places were created but it is questionable whether the same levels of flexibility would create great places today. We tried this with Enterprise Zones in the UK, where planning restrictions were lifted, and the results were Canary Wharf in London and the Meadowhall Shopping Centre in Sheffield. This leaves planners with a dilemma. If they do not control development, the results in the modern age tend to be dreadful. Yet planning restrictions, while very good at stopping really bad things from happening, are not great at promoting really good things. We might speculate that the UK could learn more from the continental cities in this book, which have been much more interventionist when it comes to masterplanning, but much less so when it comes to the detail of development.

However, we should not blame planners for all of the problems of British cities, that would be unfair. A force much more corrosive to good urbanism is urban decline. Where the market is weak or declining, urban areas left to their own devices can fall into vacancy and eventually dereliction and no plan, however well conceived, can help. By taking the long view of many of the places in this book, we can see that this process of growth and decline works in cycles. Many of the places, particularly the neighbourhoods, started as wealthy residential districts before being industrialised and later falling into decay when this industry declined or moved away. At this low point, the availability of cheap low-commitment space attracted artists and creative businesses and over time the area started to pick up, values started to rise and the area began to regenerate. This process is currently underway in Detroit which, far from dying, is becoming a seedbed for new ideas and creativity that could never exist in the high-rent areas of other American cities. If this regeneration is left to run for long enough, the rising values can start to push out these creative businesses as developers are attracted to convert or redevelop the buildings. Thus the cycle starts again.

In this book we have neighbourhoods and indeed whole towns and cities at various stages of this process. Manchester and Glasgow are on this journey, as are towns like Hebden Bridge and Stroud and neighbourhoods like Birmingham's Jewellery Quarter and Nottingham's Lace Market. We should not, however, fall into the trap of assuming that the process of decline and renewal is inevitable. We don't often lose whole cities but there are many streets and neighbourhoods that don't pull out of their death spiral and never recover. Which brings us to the process of urban regeneration. Most of the places in this book include stories of their renaissance at the hand of a regeneration agency, a visionary mayor or a community group. In some cases these city saviours may be claiming credit for something that would probably have happened anyway, but this is not to diminish the importance of leadership. Whether it be the visionary mayors who are so often part of the story in continental cities or the community activism of Hebden Bridge or Gillett Square, leadership makes a huge difference in harnessing these wider economic forces. Places with a strong vision and leadership will regenerate more quickly and can shape the renewal of their place to create somewhere special. The lesson from the places in this book are that sustained regeneration comes from strong leadership and vision translated into a range of small-scale interventions to encourage the process of renewal ('urban acupuncture' as Jaime Lerner, former mayor of Curitiba, calls it). Big capital projects can be important, but this book includes a number of examples of flagship schemes that have failed to replicate the Bilbao effect. Meanwhile, the steady process of promoting good urbanism is what brings about lasting change.

Having addressed the problems of decline, many of the places in this book have also faced the problems of success. What do you do when values rise to the point where the indigenous activity that you have worked so hard to promote starts to be squeezed out? Can you stop the cycle at the sweet spot where the area is full of lively independent businesses and thronged with street life and before the corporates and the chains move in and take over? North Laine in Brighton and Exmouth Market are the starkest examples of this process and the traders in these areas have had some success in stopping the regeneration clock so that the party can continue. Whether this can continue forever is uncertain and the tensions are perhaps at their most visible in Brixton where there have been riots against gentrification.

The rarest category in this book is the new-build urban area. Lots of the places have seen extensive new development, but perhaps only Accordia in Cambridge is a place created from scratch. Others like Coin Street in London, Oxford Castle and Princesshay in Exeter have involved redevelopment so extensive that a new place has been created. This is the first phase of the cycle when new neighbourhoods and places that didn't previously exist are created and is the most difficult form of urbanism. We are better at conserving and enhancing existing areas than creating new ones. The best advice this book can give is to build as best you can and leave to stand for a few decades. If after a century or so a new successful neighbourhood has not emerged, then you should probably start again.

There are many brilliant books on urbanism. Most focus on making the case for urbanism, for the sake of human society, for the environment and for the health of our economy. Most of these books are read by people already convinced of these things and are used to supplement and reinforce their arguments. Only a few authors such as Jane Jacobs and more recently Edward Glaeser have broken out of this self-reinforcing debate. This book doesn't try and add to the overwhelming case that already exists for the benefits of urban development. What it does instead is to 'Learn from Place', which is the core purpose of the Academy of Urbanism. This book has presented 75 places and told a little of their history. These are not 'good-practice' case studies. The regeneration industry has been obsessed with good practice for years and many regeneration projects have been written up as good practice even when they have not been particularly successful. Instead, this book has tried to uncover the backstory that has shaped each of these places. Sometimes the key events lie deep in their history; sometimes they are much more recent. Some of the places are the result of inspirational leadership and astute policy; others are the result of chance and good fortune or just the forces of urban growth and regeneration that operate despite the efforts of planners and policy-makers. There are no templates or simple best-practice lessons to be learnt here. However, cumulatively these urban stories hopefully convey a little of the paradox of urbanism: that it is at once very simple while also being fiendishly complicated. Leave it to its own devices and things generally sort themselves out (or go horribly wrong); try and plan and micro-manage and the complexity will overwhelm you.

Picture Credits

David Harrison's drawing of Las Ramblas in Barcelona.

Index

The Academy of Urbanism

The Academy of Urbanism is a self-funded, politically independent organisation led by over 500 leaders, thinkers and practitioners involved in the social, cultural, economic, political and physical development of our villages, towns and cities.

The Academy was formed in 2006 to recognise, learn from, and promote excellence in place-making. Since then the Academy has grown to work proactively with places to nurture and help them become more resilient.

The Academy's aims are to:

- Advance the understanding and practice of urbanism through evidence-based inquiry
- Provide an inclusive forum for dialogue across all disciplines
- Fulfil a proactive role in shaping places through sharing knowledge and partnering with communities
- Foster, validate and celebrate excellence in place-making.

It seeks to achieve these aims through:

- Acclaimed events and debates around the UK and Ireland
- A high-profile international awards scheme
- Industry-recognised publications
- Learning visits and masterclass workshops
- A diagnostic service offering Academicians' expertise to assist places.

If you would like any more information about the Academy, please contact Stephen Gallagher:

sg@academyofurbanism.org.uk
020 7251 8777
www.academyofurbanism.org.uk

David Harrison's drawing of Edinburgh.